MW00654059

The Hegemon's Tool Kit

A VOLUME IN THE SERIES

Cornell Studies in Security Affairs

Edited by Robert J. Art, Alexander B. Downes, Kelly M. Greenhill, Robert Jervis, Caitlin Talmadge, and Stephen M. Walt

Founding series editors: Robert J. Art and Robert Jervis

A list of titles in this series is available at cornellpress.cornell.edu.

The Hegemon's Tool Kit

US Leadership and the Politics of the Nuclear Nonproliferation Regime

Rebecca Davis Gibbons

Cornell University Press

Ithaca and London

First published 2022 by Cornell University Press

Library of Congress Cataloging-in-Publication Data

Names: Gibbons, Rebecca Davis, author.
Title: The hegemon's tool kit : US leadership and the politics of the nuclear nonproliferation regime / Rebecca Davis Gibbons.
Description: Ithaca [New York] : Cornell University Press, 2022. | Series: Cornell studies in security affairs | Includes bibliographical references and index.
Identifiers: LCCN 2021054750 (print) | LCCN 2021054751 (ebook) | ISBN 9781501764851 (hardcover) | ISBN 9781501764868 (pdf) | ISBN 9781501764875 (epub)
Subjects: LCSH: Treaty on the Non-proliferation of Nuclear Weapons (1968 June 12) | Nuclear nonproliferation—Political aspects. | Nuclear arms control—Political aspects. | Nuclear weapons—Political aspects. | Nuclear nonproliferation—Government policy—United States. | Nuclear arms control—Government policy—United States. | Nuclear weapons—Government policy—United States. | Nuclear nonproliferation—International cooperation. | Security, International.
Classification: LCC JZ5675 .G55 2022 (print) | LCC JZ5675 (ebook) | DDC 327.1/747—dc23/eng/20211123
LC record available at https://lccn.loc.gov/2021054750
LC ebook record available at https://lccn.loc.gov/2021054751

To my family

Contents

Acknowledgments

At the time of publication, this book will be ten years in the making. I am grateful to many individuals and organizations for supporting me over the past decade. The writing was solitary, but the process was not.

I was first inspired to examine the politics of nuclear weapons when I was living among the displaced Bikini community on Kili Island in the Republic of the Marshall Islands. In teaching elementary school, part of my job was teaching the history of nuclear weapons and the arms race that led their relatives to give up their homeland, their atoll, "temporarily" in 1946. Bikinians were told their move was for "the good of mankind and to end all world wars." The displacement was not temporary and today the Bikini community is spread over the Marshall Islands and the United States. Their sacrifice should not be overlooked.

Several mentors helped me develop my thinking about this book. I am grateful to Keir Lieber, Matt Kroenig, Dan Nexon, and Liz Stanley for savvy advice, thoughtful feedback, and much needed guidance when I was stuck. I also benefitted from the wisdom of Lise Howard, Elizabeth Arsenault, Erik Voeten, Michael Bailey, Daryl Press, Kelly Greenhill, Alexander Montgomery, Scott Sagan, and David Edelstein. Kai-Henrik Barth, in particular, played a significant role in helping me develop my interest in nuclear nonproliferation.

I am thankful for the financial support provided by Georgetown University's Government Department and the Frank Stanton Foundation. The year I spent at the RAND Corporation as a Stanton Nuclear Security Fellow, under the mentorship of Lynn Davis, was one of the most productive of my career. The other Stanton Fellows at RAND, Chris Clary and Edward Geist, provided valuable feedback for this book.

The past decade has been a beneficial time to study nuclear matters and my thinking has been shaped by participation in the Public Policy and Nuclear Threat's Nuclear Boot Camp at the University of California, San Diego; the Nuclear Studies Research Initiative; and the Center for Strategic and International Studies' Project on Nuclear Issues. Through these programs I have received helpful feedback from Linton Brooks, Frank Gavin, Rebecca Hersman, Jeff Kaplow, Jane Vaynman, Paul Avey, Christine Leah, Caroline Milne, Eliza Gheorghe, David Santoro, Matt Harries, Benoît Pélopidas, Rupal Mehta, Rachel Whitlark, Philipp Bleek, Tristan Volpe, and Robert Brown among many others.

I am fortunate to have so many inspiring and supportive colleagues. My international relations cohort, Raphael Cohen, Rafael Frankel, Andrew Imbrie, and Gabe Scheinmann provided constant support and though we had many disagreements, they were always friendly ones. In addition, Eric Brewer, Thane Clare, Anjali Dayal, Jeff Donnithorne, Jennifer Dresden, Devin Finn, Paula Ganga, Rob Karl, Jooeun Kim, Haillie Lee, Yu-Ming Liou, Rebecca Lissner, Meghan McConaughey, Beth Mercurio, Adam Mount, Paul Musgrave, Dani Nedal, Michal Onderčo, Fouad Pervez, Todd Robinson, Michael Weintraub, Maddie Schramm, and Heather Williams have been helpful and supportive colleagues. I am lucky to consider them friends. Megan Stewart, in particular, has been an invaluable source of moral support and astute feedback since we first met.

For much of the time I was working on this book, I was fortunate to be part of a contractor team supporting the US Air Force's Strategic Stability and Countering WMD office. My colleagues, both military and civilian, were a sounding board for ideas and a crucial source of feedback. I am especially grateful for advice and moral support from Justin Anderson, Darci McDonald, Tom Devine, Jeff Larsen, Sarah Gamberini, Christina Vaughan, Tim Miller, Dutch Miller, Joe Hogler, Josh Pollack, and Lew Dunn. In addition, I owe a great debt to over forty current and former officials who were willing to be interviewed for this book. Many were extremely generous with their time and expertise. In particular, I want to extend my gratitude to Thomas Graham Jr., Susan Burk, Dean Rust, John Carlson, and Norman Wulf.

From 2018 to 2021, I was associated with the Belfer Center's Project on Managing the Atom and the International Security Program, first as a fellow and then as an associate. I learned so much from my colleagues Nobuyasu Abe, William d'Ambruoso, Aaron Arnold, Hyun-Binn Cho, Tyler Jost, Mariya Grinberg, Reid Pauly, Nick Anderson, Nicholas Roth, Denia Djokić, Mariana Budjeryn, Najmedin Meshkati, Jayita Sarkar, Stephen Herzog, David Arceneaux, Ariel Petrovics, Christopher Lawrence, Sébastien Philippe, Cameron Tracy, Katlyn Turner, Benjamin Zala, and Aditi Verma. The leadership of MTA and ISP, including Matthew Bunn, Steven Miller, Stephen Walt, Will Tobey, John Holdren, and Francesca Giovannini are so very busy and yet make time to guide fellows in research and life. Jacob Carozza and Susan Lynch provided seemingly endless support. Marty Malin read and commented on parts of this book before his passing in the spring of 2020. Marty, thank you; I wish I had been able to know you better.

I was fortunate that Jennifer Erickson, Jane Vaynman, Målfrid Braut-Hegghammer, and Nick Miller participated in a book workshop with me in the summer of 2020. Their feedback was extremely helpful. The University of Southern Maine and MTA supported this workshop. I am forever thankful to Roger Haydon, Michael McGandy, Alex Downs, and Clare Jones for shepherding this book through the review and publication process at Cornell University Press.

Finally, I am most indebted to my family for their love and support. My parents have always placed a strong value on my education and have championed my goals without question. I will always be grateful to them for their love and their example. My mother waded through international relations theory and nuclear jargon to proofread my final drafts. My two brothers, Jeff and Chris, are always a source of humor and support. My in-laws have been cheerleaders throughout. Members of my large extended family were willing to listen to me talk about nuclear nonproliferation, and that is no small thing. My maternal grandfather, Joseph Klenk, has read most of my scholarly articles and has always provided thoughtful comments. He read and proofread early drafts of this manuscript and was the first person I called when I learned that it would be published. I hope I make him proud. And then there is Ryan and our two daughters, Sydney and Josephina. I brought Kenneth Waltz's *Theory of International Politics* to read by the pool on our honeymoon (in hindsight, this was probably not a good idea). We have "vacationed" to conference locations. Ryan has sat through many dinners that revolved around academic conversations and departmental goings-on. In short, Ryan has been there every step of the way as I completed this book. His patience for this process has been unwavering and for that I am deeply grateful. My children have had a tired, and often distracted, mother as I worked to complete this book. They provide me motivation and inspiration on a daily basis and I hope that they also seek out hard challenges and find the personal satisfaction in completing them. It is to Ryan, Sydney, and Josephina that I dedicate this effort.

Abbreviations

ACDA	Arms Control and Disarmament Agency
AEE	Atomic Energy Establishment (Egypt)
ANC	African National Congress (South Africa)
AP	Additional Protocol
APEC	Asia-Pacific Economic Cooperation
BAPETEN	Nuclear Energy Regulatory Agency of Indonesia
BATAN	National Nuclear Agency of Indonesia
CIA	Central Intelligence Agency
CTBT	Comprehensive Nuclear-Test-Ban Treaty
CWC	Chemical Weapons Convention
DPRK	Democratic People's Republic of Korea
ENDC	Eighteen Nation Disarmament Committee
EURATOM	European Atomic Energy Community
G7	Group of Seven
G8	Group of Eight
GATT	General Agreement on Tariffs and Trade
IAEA	International Atomic Energy Agency
ICBM	intercontinental ballistic missile
IMF	International Monetary Fund
INF	Intermediate Range Nuclear Forces
INFCE	International Fuel Cycle Evaluation
LDP	Liberal Democratic Party (Japan)
LTBT	Limited Test Ban Treaty
MLF	multilateral force
NAM	Non-Aligned Movement
NATO	North Atlantic Treaty Organization

NDU	National Defense University (United States)
NPT	Treaty on the Non-Proliferation of Nuclear Weapons
NSG	Nuclear Suppliers Group
NWFZ	Nuclear-Weapons-Free Zone
OSCE	Organization for Security and Co-operation in Europe
PNE	Peaceful Nuclear Explosion
PrepCom	Preparatory Committee Meeting (NPT)
PSI	Proliferation Security Initiative
RevCon	Review Conference Meeting (NPT)
SALT	Strategic Arms Limitations Talks
SLBM	submarine launched ballistic missile
SORT	Strategic Offensive Reductions Treaty
START	Strategic Arms Reduction Treaty
TPNW	Treaty on the Prohibition of Nuclear Weapons
UN	United Nations
UNSC	United Nations Security Council
WMD	weapons of mass destruction

The Hegemon's Tool Kit

Introduction

Understanding Adherence to the Nuclear Nonproliferation Regime

In the early nuclear age, the threat of nuclear war loomed large in the public imagination. These fears intensified in the 1950s with the development of hydrogen bombs, weapons whose destructive power dwarfed the atomic bombs dropped on Hiroshima and Nagasaki. US schoolchildren, some wearing dog tags so their bodies could be identified following a nuclear detonation, were trained to protect themselves from nuclear attack in classroom duck-and-cover drills. In 1957, the writer Nevil Shute published *On the Beach*, in which Australians await their demise as a radiation cloud drifts toward them from a nuclear exchange on the other side of the globe. Though not scientifically accurate in its depiction of nuclear effects, the *New York Times* best-selling novel captured the horror of invisible radiation. Nuclear terror reached palpable levels with the Cuban Missile Crisis in October 1962 as Americans and Soviets went to bed not knowing if they would wake up the next morning or be incinerated in their sleep. A few months later, President Kennedy—who knew luck was critical to the peaceful resolution of the Cuban crisis—told the press, "Personally I am haunted by the feeling that by 1970, unless we are successful, there may be 10 nuclear powers instead of four, and by 1975, 15 or 20."[1] This was a world in which political leaders feared that many more harrowing nuclear crises might well unfold. An often-overlooked part of Kennedy's famous prediction, however, is the president's phrase "unless we are successful." In fact, they were; efforts made by Kennedy, his contemporaries, and subsequent leaders have prevented his 1963 prognostication from coming true. To date, nine states possess nuclear weapons, and these weapons have not been detonated in war since 1945.

One reason for this outcome is that in the late 1960s many nations came to a consensus on a multilateral treaty by which the majority of states would publicly and legally renounce nuclear weapons.[2] In joining the 1970 Treaty on the Non-Proliferation of Nuclear Weapons (NPT), all member states except the five declared nuclear powers—the United States, the Soviet Union, the United Kingdom, France, and China—agreed not to develop nuclear weapons in exchange for access to peaceful nuclear technology and the promise of eventual disarmament.[3] By creating the NPT, the primary drafters—the United States and the Soviet Union—sought to prevent additional proliferation at a time when several technically capable states were expected to build nuclear weapons.[4]

An almost universal NPT and the existence of several other nonproliferation agreements were not foregone conclusions. In fact, in the 1970s, many thought the NPT was a failure. The scholar Hedley Bull wrote in 1975 of "the growing skepticism not only about the Treaty but also about the wider endeavor to control the spread of nuclear weapons."[5] In a 1975 Central Intelligence Agency (CIA) report about likely proliferators, one of the report's sections was titled "The NPT Is Questionable."[6] Two years later, the scholar Ashok Kapur wrote "So far, the NPT regime has barely survived."[7] In many ways, the regime's success is surprising. The NPT boasts all but five members of the international community.[8] Under the treaty, members have consented to make their nuclear activities transparent by inviting international inspectors onto their sovereign territory and allowing remote tracking of their nuclear sites. The regime has endured through changing global power dynamics and overcome significant challenges from states that have taken actions in violation of their NPT commitments. But the NPT was just the beginning. As new dangers have emerged or weaknesses in the treaty have become apparent, the international community has worked together to forge

new pacts that bolster the NPT's goals. Together these agreements make up the nuclear nonproliferation regime, defined as the set of institutions and activities aimed at curtailing the spread of nuclear weapons and dangerous nuclear material.

Many scholars and politicians have pointed to the nuclear nonproliferation regime as a significant achievement in international security. This success is especially astounding given that the regime asks the majority of states to renounce the most powerful weapons on the planet—weapons that many consider a means of providing existential security.

The Argument

Why do states adhere to the nuclear nonproliferation regime? The answer lies in decades of painstaking efforts undertaken by the US government. Since the development of the NPT in the late 1960s, most US administrations have cared deeply about preventing the emergence of additional nuclear weapon states. As the most powerful state in the system during the nuclear age, the United States has had many tools with which to persuade other states to join or otherwise support nonproliferation agreements. Some states, however, require more persuasion than others. States that are more embedded within the US-led order—states whose policy preferences and political values are largely shared with the United States—adhere relatively quickly. The United States must work harder to persuade states that are less embedded. At times, US allies employ these persuasive tools as well, helping the United States to build the order from which they all benefit.

This book demonstrates that when a nonproliferation agreement or activity is established, the US foreign affairs bureaucracy begins to employ several low-cost diplomatic tools. The United States will try to persuade all states to join the new initiative at bilateral and multilateral meetings. Often these efforts will succeed in convincing US allies and partners to commit. For those that remain unpersuaded—states that are less embedded within the US-led order—the United States will engage in high-cost diplomacy, such as appeals from high-level executive leadership. If necessary, the US government will move on to employ positive inducements to bring about participation in the regime. For the least embedded states, including states antagonistic toward the United States, the previous tools are unlikely to work, and occasionally US leaders will decide to pause their persuasive activities, awaiting a more fruitful time to engage. In many cases, the United States will coordinate with its closest allies in deploying all of these tools of persuasion. In sum, this book makes clear that the agreements that make up the nuclear nonproliferation regime were necessary for the United States to achieve its nonproliferation goals—the content and evolution of the treaties and agreements mattered—but the regime needed the United States to become widespread. The regime should thus be considered part of the post–World War II US-led order.

This argument complements and expands on scholarship that highlights the US role in promoting nuclear nonproliferation, but it differs from existing accounts that emphasize coercion or norms as the most important factor in regime adherence.[9] Most of the US persuasive activity related to the nuclear nonproliferation regime involves diplomatic outreach and inducements, while coercion is rare. Normative accounts overlook the level of effort required to persuade states to adhere to regime agreements. Even in a favorable normative environment, the United States often has had to employ persuasive tools to achieve regime adherence.

The Creation of the US-Led Order

In the aftermath of World War II, US material power was unmatched; its closest peers had been devastated by war. With this immense power, the United States sought to create an international order across several areas of global politics. The term *hegemon* to refer to the United States in the nuclear age is purposely chosen and is defined as a state that uses its unparalleled material power to create order within the international system.[10] To a much greater extent than previous orders led by dominant states, the US-led version was created around multilateral institutions.[11] US leaders opposed bilateral and exclusionary arrangements that could lead to conflict and allow strong states to dominate weak states.[12] As Miles Kahler writes, this US version of multilateralism "expressed an impulse to universality."[13] It was not the multilateralism of the Concert of Europe in which a handful of powerful European states came together to make rules and mediate conflict; this was a multilateralism in which all sovereign states—weak and strong, but juridical equals—could participate. It was also an order that uniquely benefited the United States as the hegemonic power.[14]

The United States engaged in a flurry of institution building in the 1940s and early 1950s, creating the International Monetary Fund (IMF), the United Nations (UN), and the General Agreements on Tariffs and Trade (GATT) system. It would also promote multilateralism in Europe, supporting the European Atomic Energy Community (EURATOM) and the European Coal and Steel Community, a forerunner to the European Union, and establishing a multilateral political and military alliance, the North Atlantic Treaty Organization (NATO). All of these organizations benefited the United States by fostering global security and prosperity and helping it maintain a dominant position in the system. Together these US-promoted institutions and the norms that undergird them have come to be known as the US-led global order. Although it is often called the liberal international order, not all elements of this order are liberal in nature.[15] The order has never been all-encompassing; some states have always resisted its rules. Nonetheless, it is useful to consider the rules, norms, and institutions created by the United States as forming a kind of order. This order is characterized by the desire to create universal rules and the commitment to the institutionalization of those rules, to reward followers and punish violators. The rules are often described as promoting free trade, democracy and the security of democracies, and seeking multilateral solutions to global problems.[16] The nuclear nonproliferation regime should be considered part of this order as well.

In its true universalism—the United States sought membership for all states in the international system—the nuclear nonproliferation regime is more akin to the United Nations than the elements of the US-led order that were shared mainly by liberal Western nations during the Cold War. The United States could prosper by trading with its European and Pacific allies, but its security interests required promoting nonproliferation globally. The motivation for seeking a global nuclear nonproliferation regime was strategic for both the United States and the Soviet Union, but it took years for the two superpowers to realize the need for a global regime.

The idea of controlling nuclear weapons has its origins in the early years of the nuclear age, but it would be two decades before the United States and the Soviet Union began negotiating the nonproliferation regime's foundational treaty. Soon after the advent of nuclear weapons, the two superpowers began sparring over ways to control the bomb.[17] They each rejected the other's early plans to eliminate nuclear weapons in the mid-1940s. And then in 1949, the Soviet Union surprised US leaders in becoming the second nuclear-weapon-possessing state, exploding a nuclear device only four years to the month after the Hiroshima and Nagasaki bombings. The two global competitors would go on to compete to supply other nations with civilian—but dual-use—nuclear technology in the 1950s.[18]

Starting in 1958, members of the international community, led by Ireland, called for stopping the spread of nuclear weapons in several UN General Assembly resolutions. Initially wary of the Irish resolutions,[19] US and Soviet leaders eventually saw the value of a global nonproliferation treaty. In the mid-1960s, they came together and cooperated to create a treaty aimed at stopping the spread of nuclear weapons.

The final version of the NPT text, adopted in 1968, established five official nuclear-weapon-possessing states—the United States, the Soviet Union, the United Kingdom, France, and China—selected because all five had exploded a nuclear device before January 1, 1967. The treaty obliged these nuclear weapon states not to assist "in any way" the wider proliferation of nuclear weapons. All other states would join the treaty as nonnuclear weapon states, required never to seek nuclear weapons or assist in developing them. The treaty required the nonnuclear weapon states to conclude nuclear safeguards agreements with the International Atomic Energy Association (IAEA) (article 3) and codified the "inalienable right" of all states to pursue nuclear technology for peaceful purposes (article 4). In the treaty's article 6, states agreed to "pursue negotiations in good faith on effective measures relating . . . to nuclear disarmament."[20] The NPT entered into force in 1970 once it was ratified by forty states as well as the three depository nations: the United States, the Soviet Union, and the United Kingdom.

Why did it take so long for the United States and the Soviet Union to cooperate to draft the NPT? As Andrew J. Coe and Jane Vaynman point out, US and Soviet leaders could have pursued an agreement like the NPT in the late 1940s or 1950s, but they did not. It took until the 1960s for the two superpowers to see a global nonproliferation treaty as aligned with their strategic interests.[21] There are several reasons why this realization did not come about until the mid-1960s.

First, in the early years of the nuclear age, some US and Soviet leaders were less concerned about their allies building nuclear weapons, as this development could bolster their respective sides in the tense East-West competition.[22] Thus, they did not see a need for a worldwide nonproliferation agreement. By the 1960s, however, this thinking had changed as nuclear-weapon-possessing allies of both superpowers, especially China and France, behaved more independently than their patrons would have liked.[23] For example, France wanted a nuclear posture independent from NATO, which culminated in Paris pulling out of NATO's integrated military structure in 1967. This concern was later expressed in a July 1974 classified US assessment of nonproliferation policy following India's May 1974 test. The report reads, "Acquisition of nuclear weapons would also give nations a sense of greater independence, thus complicating international diplomacy and diminishing American influence."[24]

Second, the terror of the 1962 Cuban Missile Crisis drove home the fact that many more terrifying nuclear crises could arise if additional states developed the bomb.[25] The superpowers also worried a smaller nuclear power could catalyze a nuclear war that could escalate to include their much larger arsenals.[26] According to Avner Cohen, the Cuban Missile Crisis "reinforced Kennedy's conviction that the spread of nuclear weapons was a global danger that must be stemmed."[27]

Third, China's nuclear test in 1964 compounded the superpowers' proliferation worries, as they believed China's explosion would lead other states, such as Japan and India, to seek nuclear weapons as well. Nicholas L. Miller argues that US leaders have promoted nonproliferation globally because of their belief in such a nuclear domino theory, whereby one state's proliferation causes several other states to consider developing nuclear weapons.[28]

Fourth, the superpowers realized they could be prevented from acting in areas of interest around the globe if smaller states could deter them with nuclear weapons. The July 1974 strategy paper explains this concern: "If nuclear weapons competition among third countries developed, and if various nations or even subnational groups could threaten the United States with nuclear violence, our defense posture might require extensive and costly restructuring."[29] This concern is consistent with Matthew Kroenig's finding that states seek to prevent proliferation in regions where they can project power because they do not want to be deterred from acting in a region of potential strategic interest.[30] With global power projection capabilities, superpowers want to prevent all proliferation.[31]

Finally, nuclear weapons proliferation could contribute to a change in power dynamics at the regional or systemic level, with a superpower losing its position of primacy.[32] As Shane J. Maddock puts it, US nonproliferation policies have served "to maintain a uniquely powerful position for Washington within the international system."[33]

While US leadership in developing the NPT has long been evident, more recent research has emphasized the singular role of the United States in promoting nuclear nonproliferation globally. According to Ariel Levite, one of the reasons "why the nightmare proliferation scenarios of the 1960s have not materialized" is in part because of the "unique role of the United States in combating global proliferation."[34] Francis Gavin argues that nuclear nonproliferation is "a core, long-standing, and driving goal of U.S. grand strategy" that the United States has pursued through a variety of means to include "treaties; norms; diplomacy; aid; conventional arms sales; alliances and security guarantees; export, information, and technology controls; intelligence;

preemptive counterforce nuclear postures; missile defense; sanctions; coercion; interdiction; sabotage; and even the threat of preventive military action."[35] Similarly, Jonathan Hunt argues, "The preponderant influence of the United States remained the key" to the survival of the NPT.[36]

Existing literature on nuclear nonproliferation also generally overlooks the efforts of the United States in relation to those of the Soviet Union. An exception is Hunt's history of the NPT, which notes the importance of the Soviet role but argues it was "nonetheless secondary" because nonproliferation efforts "relied upon Washington's global relationships and clout."[37] Not only did Washington have greater global influence than Moscow, but it also appears to have valued regime universalization more than the Soviet Union did, working diligently to gain the commitment of even the smallest states and those without any interest in nuclear technology. While both US and Soviet leaders used the rhetoric of a universal treaty and universal safeguards,[38] US leaders engaged in greater efforts to secure full universalization. As a 1980 US General Accounting Office (now the Government Accountability Office) report on the NPT explains, "Countries with little or no nuclear capability or potential are not ignored, as adherence by just one additional state increases by two the difference between the number of parties and nonparties and thereby serves to further isolate the nonparty states."[39] In contrast, the Soviet Union was more concerned with promoting the NPT among the Warsaw Pact states and within states of strategic interest, such as West Germany and South Africa. The US quest for universalization reflects its recognition of the benefits that come from a universal regime, including a strong global norm of nonproliferation.

Beyond the NPT, the United States, as hegemon, has led the international community in establishing and promoting adaptations to the nuclear nonproliferation regime when weaknesses have become apparent. One such weakness burst into view in May 1974, when India detonated a nuclear device in a test it referred to as a "peaceful nuclear explosion."[40] In a failure of imagination, US and Canadian leaders had not anticipated that poorer states like India could develop nuclear weapons when they provided New Delhi—and many others—with nuclear technology and material. With the Indian test, the importance of the NPT increased, but widespread membership in the NPT was not enough. India's test raised concerns about the potential negative ramifications of peaceful nuclear supply. Realizing the challenge of policing the nuclear market alone, the United States convened the six other major nuclear suppliers in 1975 to create a list of items that they agreed could be exported only if the purchasing state had safeguards in place. The US-convened Nuclear Suppliers Group (NSG) continues to set rules for nuclear trade and had expanded to forty-eight members as of 2021.

The discovery of Iraq's clandestine nuclear program in 1991 also highlighted a weakness of the existing regime and led the hegemon to seek an adaptation. This time it was a problem with the existing IAEA safeguards protocol, known as the comprehensive safeguards agreement. After the discovery, the United States led the international community in a five-year process of negotiating a more stringent agreement. The IAEA finalized the Model Additional Protocol in 1997. The NSG and the Additional Protocol (AP) are just two of the ways in which US leaders have led the international community in adapting the nuclear nonproliferation regime as flaws became apparent. These adaptations—though unpopular among some states—improved the institutional mechanisms for deterring proliferation and thus contributed to the regime's effectiveness by boosting confidence among its membership. Adaptations are especially important within this regime, as research indicates that past violations of the NPT may beget future violations as states lose confidence in regime institutions, whereas fewer recent violations means that states are less likely to violate the treaty.[41]

The impetus to adapt the nonproliferation regime and formulate new agreements when weaknesses have become evident is the same one that originally caused the United States to pursue the creation of the NPT. It is not that other states did not perceive these weaknesses, but they had less strategic interest in global nonproliferation than the United States and did not have the same ability to convene all of the necessary states to make the needed changes. Moreover, other states did not have the same resources to persuade other states to support regime adaptations.

In sum, the nuclear nonproliferation regime is best considered an element of the post–World War II, US-led order. It was a project created by the United States and the Soviet Union to meet their strategic interest in maintaining their positions of power. The United States took the lead in promoting the regime to all states. Thus, any theory that seeks to explain why states join the nuclear nonproliferation regime must therefore consider the global role of the United States and how other states respond to its leadership and, more specifically, its promotion of the agreements and activities that make up the regime.

Emphasizing the importance of a dominant power in explaining nuclear nonproliferation regime adherence is consistent with hegemonic stability theory (HST), or hegemonic-order theory. HST was developed originally to explain patterns in the global economy. Its proponents argued that for a liberal economic system to function well, a powerful or hegemonic state needed to promote and support it. Charles Kindleberger has argued Great Britain served in this role before World War I and the United States has since World War II. He attributes the economic crisis of the interwar period to the lack of a hegemonic power actively leading global order.[42] More generally, the theory expects that hegemonic powers will provide order in the international system by creating regimes and coercing or inducing compliance.[43] With the widespread belief in American decline in the early 1970s, HST scholars—including Kindleberger, Robert Gilpin, and Stephen Krasner—anticipated global challenges if the United States were unable to maintain its dominant role in international politics.[44]

While this theory has an intuitive draw, it has faced many detractors.[45] They argue that economic data do not support such a theory or that, contrary to theory's expectations, cooperation may increase after the hegemon's decline.[46] One of the most significant critiques comes from institutionalists who argue that the hegemon is not necessary for the sustainment of institutions and regimes and that these institutions can continue to facilitate cooperation after hegemonic decline.[47] Robert O. Keohane made this argument in 1984; a more recent iteration comes from G. John Ikenberry, who contends that the institutions created by the United States will be able to outlast its dominance.[48] An examination of the fifty years of the nuclear nonproliferation regime, however, indicates that it is unlikely to survive as an effective constraint on proliferation without a powerful state backer. The United States and the institutions it created have been the key factors in creating global confidence that states will not proliferate and that they will be punished if they do. Without a powerful state like the United States promoting the regime, it could begin to wither, and states could lose faith in its ability to detect and punish cheaters. If foreign leaders begin to question whether the regime is still working effectively to curtail proliferation, they may wonder if their neighbors are considering a nuclear weapons program, causing them to consider it too. In sum, if the regime no longer has the backing of a dominant power, the world may witness an increase in the number of nuclear weapon states.

Where the present project diverges from traditional HST is in the expectation that the hegemon benefits less than other states from the order it provides. In its traditional reading, a benevolent hegemon provides public goods for other states in the international system. More recently, Carla Norloff has argued that the United States has in fact benefited disproportionately from the economic and security orders it has promoted since 1945.[49] In creating and promoting the nuclear nonproliferation regime, the United States has also benefitted disproportionately. Persuading the majority of the states in the international system to refrain from building nuclear weapons allows the United States to maintain its freedom of action around the globe and sustain an alliance system that supports other areas of its ordering project.

The Nuclear Nonproliferation Regime Matters

Nuclear weapons are the most devastating weapons ever invented. Large nuclear weapons are capable of destroying entire cities, killing and sickening millions. With each additional state that possesses nuclear weapons, the chances of nuclear use, either intentional or accidental, increase. Moreover, each additional nuclear weapon state causes its neighbors and adversaries to consider whether they also should develop nuclear programs.[50]

The strategic implications of this immense destructive power led the United States to create and promote the nuclear nonproliferation regime. An international regime is defined as the "principles, norms, rules, and decision-making procedures around which actor expectations converge in a given issue-area."[51] The principles, norms, rules, and decision-making procedures within the nonproliferation regime directly address the threat of nuclear weapons by constraining the number of states that possess nuclear weapons and nuclear materials. Beyond the IAEA and the NPT, a number of treaties and agreements compose the formal architecture of the nonproliferation regime. Some of the most important include the 1971 Comprehensive Safeguards Agreement required for all NPT members, the 1997 Model Additional Protocol (a more stringent safeguards agreement), the 1980 Convention on the Physical Protection of Nuclear Material and its 2005 amendment, the 1996 Comprehensive Nuclear-Test-Ban Treaty (CTBT), and five regional Nuclear-Weapons-Free Zones (NWFZ). Since 2005, United Nation Security Council Resolution 1540 and follow-on resolutions have required improvements in states' export control laws. These resolutions were created in response to revelations of the Pakistani scientist A. Q. Khan's illicit nuclear supply ring. Informal elements of the regime include the NSG, an organization of nuclear technology supplier states that sets guidelines on sales of nuclear technology, and the Proliferation Security Initiative (PSI), an effort to promote global cooperation on the interdiction of illicit nuclear materials and technologies.

Iran's nuclear activities since the early 2000s are instructive for assessing the value of the nuclear nonproliferation regime for international security. Iran's membership in the NPT and the many resulting inspections of the country's facilities by the IAEA, as the monitoring entity for the NPT, eventually led to Tehran's referral to the UN Security Council, six rounds of economic sanctions, and negotiations with a group of countries comprising the United States, Russia, China, France, the United Kingdom, and Germany. Without the web of norms and institutions surrounding the NPT—and Iran's initial commitment to this regime—the international community as a whole would have known far less about Iran's nuclear program and would have had to approach its suspected nuclear weapons program with ad hoc measures. Without the regime in place, it would have been significantly more difficult to apply multilateral pressure on Tehran and achieve the near-global consensus on instituting sanctions. Indeed, there are a number of distinct mechanisms that explain why the nuclear nonproliferation regime reduces proliferation.[52]

First, the regime has helped create and promote global standards of appropriate state behavior related to nuclear weapons and materials. As Harald Müller and Andreas Schmitt illustrate, since the NPT established a nuclear nonproliferation norm in 1970, close to 70 percent of states conducting nuclear weapons activities have stopped doing so.[53] The norm has grown stronger with time as suspected cheaters have come to be considered irresponsible members of the international community.[54] Indeed, most new proliferators in recent decades are states that are norm breakers in several areas of global politics.

Second, commitment to the treaty creates nonproliferation stakeholders within states who could help counteract the influence of other factions within government who may wish to seek nuclear weapons.[55] Stakeholders may include foreign ministry staff and diplomats who attend the regular NPT Preparatory Committee and Review Conference meetings and become socialized into the institution.[56] Or they could be members of the civilian nuclear energy establishment who want to ensure that their state continues to have access to peaceful nuclear technology as specified by article 4 of the NPT.[57]

Third, if leaders in an NPT member state decide to cheat and build nuclear weapons, the program becomes more costly than it would be for a nonmember.[58] Factions within a state attempting to proliferate must either attempt to neutralize those NPT stakeholders who oppose proliferation or spend time and resources hiding the program from the public and other members of government. These efforts are likely to make the nuclear weapon program more challenging in terms of cost, time, and coordination.

Fourth, the regime deters proliferation by making cheating more apparent to the international community. Because of regular inspections, states under IAEA safeguards will have difficulty hiding a clandestine program. This is especially true if the state has the most stringent safeguards agreement, the Additional Protocol, which allows widespread inspector access within a state. If a state expels inspectors or refuses to respond to questions from the IAEA about its nuclear program, it is sending a strong message to the international community to pay more attention to what is transpiring in that state. IAEA safeguards provide a trip wire or a warning bell to the international community. In addition, since 1990, when the IAEA instituted reforms to keep member-provided intelligence information secret, members, and especially the United States, have provided helpful intelligence to the agency. Alison Carnegie and Austin Carson find that this increase in the provision of intelligence has improved the IAEA's detection capabilities.[59]

Finally, when states do cheat and seek a nuclear weapons program despite having signed the NPT, the regime infrastructure creates a means to develop a unified response to noncompliance, such as economic sanctions. The regime is especially useful for helping to create multilateral pressure on the cheating state. In other words, the regime lowers transaction costs of many states cooperating. This cooperation is exemplified by the international response to Iranian nuclear activities since 2002.

It is unlikely that many of these benefits—creating hurdles to proliferation, providing warning when it occurs, and establishing mechanisms to address proliferation—would be as successful absent the multitude of treaties and agreements that make up the regime. The "screen or constrain"[60] debate about whether treaties simply screen out states that would not comply anyway or constrain states discounts another important point: states are not static entities whose interests are frozen when they join a treaty. A state may ratify the NPT and then consider a nuclear program years later, but because that state has become embedded in the nonproliferation regime, taking action that contravenes the NPT becomes complicated.

Due to all of these mechanisms, it is unsurprising that a great deal of qualitative and quantitative research has found that the NPT has had a constraining effect on states' proliferation behavior.[61] As one example, recent statistical research examining the debate over whether treaties constrain state behavior or merely screen out states has found evidence for the NPT as a constraining mechanism. Joining the NPT reduces the likelihood that states will proliferate "even when accounting for the possibility that countries may be more likely to join the treaty when they have already decided to remain nonnuclear."[62]

Theoretical Contributions

In addition to explaining the inner workings of the nuclear nonproliferation regime, this research has implications for three interrelated topics important to contemporary international relations: the future of nuclear order, the process of global order making, and the declining ability of the United States to promote global order.

The findings of this book indicate the future of nuclear order may be in jeopardy. The United States is losing the means to exert global influence—tools in its tool kit—at a precarious time for the regime. Relations among great powers are becoming less predictable, and nuclear weapons are taking on renewed significance in most nuclear possessor states. Nuclear arms control appears on the wane, and many nonnuclear states argue the basic bargain underlying the NPT has fallen apart. To the consternation of the United States, the majority of NPT members back a treaty that bans nuclear weapons for all states, the Treaty on the Prohibition of Nuclear Weapons. What will it mean for international security if the United States is less able to continue in its role as the primary sustainer of the nuclear nonproliferation regime during these uncertain times? Whether China will take on this role is an open question. Theoretically, China would be expected to view global nuclear nonproliferation as a strategic goal as its economic and military interests expand across continents, just as the Soviet Union and the United States did before. But even if this does eventually occur, there could be a gap between periods of superpower leadership, weakening the regime.

The empirical portion of this project also offers novel insights into how hegemonic powers engage in global order making. While the fact that dominant states seek to create order within the international system is well established, there is far less understanding about *how* these powers create order.[63] The existence of an order after all, means that global rules are generally followed by many states, most of the time. This book delves into the practices of effective global order making. How does the United States persuade other states to follow its preferred rules? What are the most useful tools of influence, and when are they likely to succeed? From diplomatic and educational outreach by lower-level US bureaucrats to personal letters and calls by the president and other top leaders to positive inducements and coercion, the United States has traditionally maintained a vast array of persuasive tools and an extensive bureaucracy to support their use. While this book covers the ways in which tools of influence promote the nuclear nonproliferation regime, these tools also are widely used in other areas of US foreign policy. This book therefore fits into the body of scholarship that G. John Ikenberry and Daniel Nexon refer to as "Hegemony 3.0," which focuses on, among other topics, "processes at work in hegemonic politics and hegemonic ordering, such as the bargaining, contestation, and cooperation that operates within hegemonic systems."[64]

This project highlights the many means of influence available to a hegemonic power like the United States. It emphasizes the importance of having a US federal bureaucracy devoted to foreign policy to carry out these tools of influence. Historically, this bureaucracy has been unparalleled in size and scope compared to the bureaucracies of all other states. Its magnitude has provided the United States the ability to communicate constantly, via cable or in person, with officials from around the world. The United States has had more individuals covering the full spectrum of ongoing international affairs topics—from terrorism, humanitarian disasters, and civil wars to trade disputes, environmental efforts, and foreign elections—than any other state, in most cases by a significant degree. Whereas many states require their foreign ministry officials to cover a portfolio that includes several distinct topics, the United States usually has at least a handful of people per issue. That diplomatic depth has been a significant contributor to the US ability to create and shape global order.

In addition to the crucial contributions of its diplomatic corps, the United States has been able to employ military and economic aid and advanced technology to craft positive inducements for promoting cooperation within its order. It has used the appeal of its large domestic market as a form of leverage or has threatened to shut off aid or market access to compel foreign governments. The United States has also been able to use its sway within key global institutions, such as the World Bank and the International Monetary Fund, to shape the behavior of other states. In sum, the material power and global position of the United States has allowed it to maintain many levers of influence in the international arena, and these tools allow it to promote its desired form of international order.

Lastly, this book suggests that the ability of the United States to promote global order is declining. The empirical chapters detail the significant level of effort the United States has undertaken to craft, promote, sustain, and adapt one element of global order. The capacity of the United States to pursue and maintain its global ordering projects across several issue areas is weakening, due both to structural changes in international politics—the rise of other powers—and policy decisions by recent US administrations that could have long-lasting effects. As a hegemonic power in relative decline, the United States may begin to lose many of the means through which it is able to influence the decisions of other states. When competitors to the United States provide aid that is comparable to or more generous than that offered by the US government, US leaders are less able to achieve their policy goals; the cutoff of US aid becomes a less powerful threat. When competitors produce military equipment that is perceived to be on par with that supplied by the United States, the offer of advanced US military technology is a less useful tool of persuasion. When the United States loses its stature in international institutions, it is less able to use these institutions to pursue its global goals.

Beyond waning material capacity, the foreign affairs bureaucracy has experienced budget and staffing cuts and a loss of clout relative to the Defense Department, leading to reductions in the breadth and stature of the US diplomatic corps. This trend, which has been evident over the past three decades across administrations of both parties, serves to weaken the ability of the United States to influence other states. Another way in which US global influence is weakening is by the diminution of its alliance relationships. The following chapters demonstrate the importance of close allies in promoting US-backed nonproliferation policies. If these allies lose faith in US leadership and seek a more independent path due to the actions of the United States, they will be less likely to help promote US-preferred policies.[65] In terms of its ability to shape global order, the United States weakens its diplomatic corps and its relations with its allies at its own peril.

Preview of the Book

Chapter 1 provides a theory explaining adherence to the nuclear nonproliferation regime. It establishes several observable implications assessed in the empirical chapters that follow. Chapter 2 offers a detailed history of US nonproliferation policy by presidential administration. Chapter 3 illustrates how the United States influenced the decision-making processes in Japan, Indonesia, Egypt, and Cuba as they considered whether to join the NPT. Chapter 4 chronicles a key period in the history of the nuclear nonproliferation regime, the debate in 1995 over the extension of the NPT, and describes how the United States and its allies achieved their goal of indefinite extension. Chapter 5 portrays the way in which the United States led the international community in adapting the IAEA's safeguards system, once the weaknesses of the original agreement became apparent in the early 1990s. The conclusion considers the impact of the Treaty on the Prohibition of Nuclear Weapons on the nuclear nonproliferation regime and offers implications of this research for theory and policy.

CHAPTER 1

Explaining Adherence to the Nuclear Nonproliferation Regime

Why do states adhere to the nuclear nonproliferation regime? Why do some states take much longer to do so than others? When global nonproliferation agreements or activities are established, US officials use a series of tools to bring all states on board. They begin by employing low-cost diplomacy; then, if necessary, they move on to high-cost diplomatic actions, followed by positive inducements, and then occasionally coercive threats. In these efforts, the United States is often aided by its close allies. The level of effort required to persuade states to adhere reflects how embedded they are within the US-led global order.

The Dependent Variable

Existing literature points to the strategic importance of nuclear nonproliferation for the United States.[1] Why do the rest of the states in the international system adhere to agreements within the nuclear nonproliferation regime? Regime adherence, the dependent variable, is assessed in two different ways in this book. The first conceptualization is the most straightforward: At a given time, is a state committed to a particular nonproliferation treaty, agreement, or activity? A second way adherence is assessed is by the time it takes states to join a new nonproliferation treaty, agreement, or activity.

The concept of regime adherence examined here is distinct from compliance. In the institutional literature, compliance usually refers to whether a state is abiding by the requirements of the agreement to which it has already joined; it is "a state of conformity or identity between an actor's behavior and a specified rule."[2] In some cases, noncompliance with international treaties and agreements is egregious and obvious, such as torturing citizens while a signatory of the Convention against Torture or pursuing nuclear weapons while a nonnuclear weapon state within the NPT. This type of noncompliance with the NPT has been examined at length in the nonproliferation literature as it seeks to understand why states proliferate.[3] There are other minor examples of noncompliance within the nuclear nonproliferation regime, including submitting safeguards declarations to the IAEA late or not submitting them at all. Though it is preferable that states do not submit their safeguards declarations late, in most cases this delay has little substantive meaning.

Adherence, in contrast, is about whether and when states join agreements in the first place.[4] For most regime agreements, joining means ratifying or acceding to an agreement.[5] The widespread membership in nuclear nonproliferation agreements is substantively meaningful and contributes to the broader regime in several ways. First, as additional states join the NPT and conclude the required safeguards agreements—agreements that permit international inspections—the international community will learn more about states' nuclear activities. Safeguards agreements, especially the most stringent ones, allow international inspectors to scrutinize all aspects of states' nuclear activities, from mining uranium ore through disposing of nuclear waste. Inspections increase confidence of all member states in the ability of the regime to deter and detect proliferation. In other words, the existence of international inspections means that joining the NPT is not just "cheap talk"; states risk discovery and punishment if they take actions contrary to the treaty. Second, widespread membership in the regime strengthens global norms and standards related to appropriate and inappropriate nuclear activities. More specifically, the NPT has created a global norm of nonproliferation for the international community.[6] Additional regime norms relate to the secure handling of nuclear material, controlling sensitive technologies, and banning nuclear testing. In general, norms arising from agreements become stronger as more states sign on.[7] At the time of this writing, only five states remain outside of the NPT, making its nonproliferation standard almost universal. Finally, more member states means that there is more likely to be widespread support for punishing the minority of members that have undertaken activities that violate the NPT.

The Independent Variable

When a new US nonproliferation campaign begins, whether it aims to promote the extension of the NPT or secure membership in an agreement, the United States uses various diplomatic channels to reach out to all states in the international system to request their support and participation. The great effort put forth by the United States to promote nonproliferation agreements and activities means that all other states have come to associate the regime with the US-led, global ordering project. They know that the United States seeks a strong and widespread nonproliferation regime and will work to achieve these goals. States' responses to the request for adherence thus reflect their overall relationship with US global leadership. For some states, US leaders must try much harder and over a longer period to secure their support. Because the United States seeks universal participation to establish global rules and norms, its leaders have historically undertaken these painstaking endeavors. In addition to the work by the US government, often US allies will adhere to agreements and then join US leaders in their persuasive efforts. These efforts usually begin with employing low-cost diplomatic actions; then, if necessary, move on to high-cost diplomatic actions, followed by positive inducements, and occasionally, coercive actions.

LOW-COST DIPLOMACY

US leaders begin a new campaign for regime membership or support for a regime adaptation by engaging in low-cost diplomacy. Low-cost refers to the effort required by the US government: The diplomatic actions undertaken are routinely conducted by the US State Department as part of its normal activities. Specifically, the diplomatic corps sends out cables to its embassies around the world. In the cables, which include talking points about the initiative, the embassy is instructed to send a US representative to convey the points to the host country's leadership.[8] In this communication, the US government aims to educate the target state about the new initiative and request its commitment. The talking points make clear why the United States sees the new agreement as beneficial to the international system. Importantly, the diplomat makes clear that the initiative is a priority to the US government.

If an initial diplomatic request fails to achieve adherence, the United States will engage in additional low-cost diplomacy by sending requests via démarches to target governments. The US State Department defines a démarche as "a formal diplomatic representation of one government's official position, views, or wishes on a given subject to an appropriate official in another government or international organization. Démarches generally seek to persuade, inform, or gather information from a foreign government. Governments may also use a démarche to protest or object to actions by a foreign government."[9]

In démarches about nuclear nonproliferation regime adherence, the United States will ask foreign leaders to comply with a specific policy action, such as joining an agreement or supporting an effort to adapt the nonproliferation regime. Dean Rust, who served as staff assistant to the director of the Arms Control and Disarmament Agency (ACDA) in the 1970s, recounts that among his many responsibilities he "helped out on NPT work such as démarches to nonparties urging them to join the Treaty."[10] In the lead-up to the 1995 NPT extension decision, the US State Department sent hundreds of démarches around the world to provide information about extending the NPT indefinitely. The démarches made clear the importance of

NPT extension to the United States, and their volume underscored the point. In trying to persuade states to join the NPT in the 1970s or vote for its extension in 1995, the United States worked closely with allies, who joined in the effort to send démarches and make high-level appeals.

In addition to démarches, the United States often uses multilateral meetings, whether on the topic of nonproliferation or not, to insert language in support of regime initiatives in the meetings' final consensus documents. In many cases, the United States would be sending diplomatic representatives to these meetings anyway, but the forums provide additional venues to promote nuclear nonproliferation goals. The final document language becomes part of a declaration that is publicized by all of the participating states. Agreeing to permit the language to be included in a final document allows states to make a minor commitment in support of the particular nonproliferation activity or agreement. These kinds of final documents are not legally binding, but they can represent a small initial commitment that might lead to a bigger one, or what psychologists refer to as the "foot in the door" effect.[11] This tool also provides an avenue for future follow-up with states that have not yet committed, as US diplomats capitalize on the existence of the preexisting agreed on text to remind nonadhering states of their previous public commitment. For example, US officials have pushed for the inclusion of language on an Additional Protocol safeguards agreement in many multilateral meetings. The George W. Bush administration was successful in securing language on the importance of the Additional Protocol in the final declaration of the November 2004 Asia-Pacific Economic Cooperation (APEC) Ministerial meeting in Santiago, Chile. The statement reads, "Ministers also recognized that all APEC economies are implementing, have concluded, or aim to conclude an Additional Protocol with the International Atomic Energy Agency by the end of 2005, reflecting their determination not to allow illicit nuclear activities in our region through their collective commitment to expanded transparency on nuclear-related activities."[12] Setting a deadline in the text was especially useful because it allowed US officials to follow up with participant states that had not concluded the safeguards agreement by 2005, remind them of their former commitment, and ask when they could comply. This tool helps US leaders to take advantage of international peer pressure, as states may not want to be the lone outsider from such an agreement. In addition, the United States has often used G7/G8 and G20 meetings to promote nuclear nonproliferation agreements and activities.

For some states, repeatedly being the target of low-cost diplomacy from the United States and its allies may eventually lead to their adherence. If this additional diplomatic activity brings about commitment, it may mean the target state leaders were persuaded of the value of the agreement. Persuasion is a "process of convincing someone through argument and principled debate"[13] that "involves changing minds, opinion, and attitudes . . . in the absence of overtly material or mental coercion."[14] Through persuasive language, US officials highlight the benefits of a particular agreement for the security of the international system as a whole and to the state in particular. Officials will also often note how many other states have joined the initiative, especially in the state's region. For example, when trying to persuade Trinidad and Tobago to adhere to the NPT in 1979, the US government pointed out that it was just one of three states in its Nuclear Weapons Free Zone (NWFZ) that had not ratified the NPT.[15] The underlying assumption of this line of argument is that the target state does not want to be isolated and will be influenced by the behavior of its neighbors. All of these attempts at persuasive arguments are aimed at tipping the scales in states' cost-benefit assessment. The arguments do not work equally on all states, however. Persuasion is more likely to be effective when foreign diplomats are interacting with individuals whom they like and whom they see as authority figures.[16]

HIGH-COST DIPLOMACY

For states that do not respond to low-cost diplomacy, US officials must continue their campaign and engage in diplomatic activities that are costlier to the government. US leaders, including cabinet officials and the president, may decide to make a direct, personal appeal to the target state's leadership. The plea may be delivered in person, via phone, or in a letter sent through a diplomatic cable. This approach is most useful for emphasizing the importance of the initiative to the US government. US leaders face significant time constraints, as they must address numerous competing interests and concerns. Taking the time to call or write to another leader about an initiative is costlier than sending routine cables or taking advantage of multilateral meetings staffed by bureaucrats and, therefore, sends a stronger signal of US priorities. Foreign ministry personnel usually handle the diplomacy surrounding nuclear nonproliferation; the executive is not often involved in the issue on a day-to-day basis. But when a foreign leader receives direct communication from the president or vice president, the issue gains prominence and attention within that leader's state. After this outreach, there should be no doubt in the mind of the target state's leader that the United States prioritizes the initiative and wants a specific action to be taken. When this tool succeeds, it is possible that the target state's leader calculates that it would be wise to comply with a personal request from the US leader. While this plea will not include any positive inducements or threats, the communication may lead to calculations in the mind of the target leader along this vein. For example, the target leader may want to request something of the hegemonic power in the future, and abiding by its wishes now could be beneficial later. When the two leaders meet, the target state leader can remind his or her counterpart of the state's previous cooperation when making a request for US support. Or the target leader may recognize a bargaining opportunity and attempt to secure something in return for cooperation with the request. The target leader may also consider that displeasing the US leader could have negative consequences for the state in other issue areas.

During his presidency, Jimmy Carter sought to bring additional states into the NPT. To convince holdouts, he sent personal letters to the leaders of Indonesia and Sri Lanka requesting they join the treaty. Similarly, leading up to the vote over the extension of the NPT in 1995, President Bill Clinton personally called many foreign leaders asking for their support. In both cases, these personal requests appear to have succeeded in persuading foreign leaders to join the NPT. Occasionally, a high-level official from a close US ally will make an appeal to another state if that allied leader is thought to have special influence in the target state.

POSITIVE INDUCEMENTS

If diplomatic requests from high-level US officials fail, the US government may consider offering some benefit to secure the commitment of resistant states. Positive inducements, defined as a "transfer of benefits" in return for a specific concession, may include economic aid, trade agreements, military aid, security assurances, or even the promotion of policies of interest to the target state.[17] Because the appearance of bribing a state for its commitment has downsides for the United States, the target state, and the nonproliferation regime, these discussions are often held behind closed doors and without an explicit statement of the quid pro quo. An overt trade could lead other states to expect the same treatment in the future and resist committing until they receive it. In addition, the appearance of a trade could undermine the legitimacy of the regime and risks making the target state's leadership appear to be a pawn of the US government. Instead, in a meeting, US diplomats will typically mention the provision of new foreign aid, the supply of nuclear technology, or new military sales in the same conversation in which they request adherence to the initiative. The goal of this discussion is for the foreign leader to make the link between benefits the United States may provide and the US policy priority. The foreign leader will have to assess whether it is worth it to say no when benefits are on the table. The logic of commitment by inducement follows more traditional thinking about how hegemonic powers achieve their goals, through the manipulation of material resources. Because of its unique position of power, the United States often has many different ways in which it can provide positive inducements for states to comply. But even an implicit quid pro quo can be detrimental to US interests. Conditional aid undermines the legitimacy of the regime causing it to appear as though the agreement is not sufficiently valuable on its own merits. The regime is in part built on the idea that all members share the standards and values of the agreements they have signed on to, and while many states do, the need to induce some member states undermines that idea. Chapter 4, which explores the 1995 extension of the NPT, will illustrate this conundrum for the United States as some government officials offered positive inducements and issued coercive threats while other US leaders vehemently denied the United States would engage in such activities.

There are several benefits the United States can offer to recalcitrant states. Within the nuclear nonproliferation regime, nuclear technology supplied by the United States or its allies has long been used as an inducement to bring more states into the regime. In the 1970s, the United States sought to induce Argentina and Brazil to conclude safeguards agreements with the IAEA in exchange for the US supply of nuclear technology and material.[18] The United States also provided many benefits to Ukraine during its process of denuclearization following the end of the Cold War. While hundreds of millions of dollars in US aid was used to remove nuclear weapons and material, the United States also offered Ukraine security assurances, at a price. As one former senior Clinton administration official stated in a meeting, "Those security assurances will not be extended until Ukraine accedes to the NPT."[19]

COERCION

For states that have still not adhered, the United States may employ threats in the form of warning a state about the possibility of the US government removing benefits it has already supplied, such as military or economic aid.[20] These threats are often implicit, but at times they are made explicit. To issue an implicit threat, US diplomats may subtly remind foreign officials of the benefits they already receive from the United States in the same conversation in which the officials are requesting commitment to a new initiative. In this case, it is implied, not stated, that these benefits could be rescinded if the hegemon is unhappy with the behavior of the target state. A former US State Department official explained that "there are ways to have these conversations" so that, while no explicit threat is made, representatives of the target state clearly understand the risk of not adhering.[21] Or the United States may pressure the target state in other ways, such as threatening its ability to join international organizations or suggesting withdrawal of support for a policy of interest to the target state.

The United States may determine that it can do little to affect the cost-benefit assessment of some states. Their governments often have an adversarial relationship with the hegemon and see domestic benefits from noncooperation. Usually, US leaders will still attempt to persuade these state diplomatically, though sometimes the United States will pause its attempts at influencing these states, if further effort at the time appears fruitless.

In exceptional instances, the United States will issue clear and explicit threats to the target state to compel its commitment. This tool is rarely used in the case of multilateral treaties and agreements because of the risks involved. Explicit threats undermine the legitimacy of the initiative and hurt the reputation of the United States. But in cases where the stakes are high enough, such as the 1995 NPT extension decision, the hegemon may determine that threats are warranted. These threats are rarely publicized, for the reasons described above, but diplomats unhappy about the threats may allude to them in public or through leaks to the press.

In 1995, when NPT parties were scheduled to vote on the future of the treaty as required by NPT article 10, US leaders campaigned hard to persuade states to support the indefinite extension of the treaty. In the final weeks before the vote, some foreign diplomats implied that US leaders made explicit threats to bring their—previously unsupportive—states around to the US-favored position.[22]

Though the use of force has not explicitly been used to expand membership in the nuclear nonproliferation regime or promote regime adaptations, the US willingness to use force against weaker states has had an effect on the regime in at least one case. As described in chapter 3, the potential for military force appears to have influenced Cuba's decision to join the NPT in late 2002.

To summarize, when a nonproliferation agreement or activity is established, the US foreign affairs bureaucracy begins to employ a series of tools to bring about universal adherence. The first set of tools, those in the category of low-cost diplomacy, include cables that instruct US foreign diplomatic staff to engage in meetings with foreign leaders. Similar meetings will occur with ambassadors serving in Washington, DC. The United States will also send démarches directly to the target government, requesting cooperation with the particular initiative. The United States will continue to try to persuade all states to join the new initiative at bilateral and multilateral meetings. For those that remain uncommitted, the United States will engage in high-cost diplomacy, such as appeals from high-level leadership. If necessary, the US will move on to employ positive inducements in the form of military or economic aid. For the most resistant states, the previous tools are unlikely to work, and occasionally US leaders will suspend its persuasive activities and hope for a more advantageous time in the future. Importantly, the United States often will coordinate with its closest allies in deploying these tools of persuasion.

Intervening Variable

What determines whether specific persuasive tools will influence states' considerations of their adherence to the nuclear nonproliferation regime? The answer is a state's level of embeddedness within the overall US-led global ordering project. When US leaders request regime adherence, all states engage in their own cost-benefit assessment about complying with the request. Their assessment is largely driven by their position vis-à-vis the US-led global order. Theoretically, at a given time, all states exist on a spectrum of how embedded they are within this order. For the sake of simplicity, states are divided into four categories: highly embedded, moderately embedded, weakly embedded, and antagonistic.

On one side of the spectrum, US allies are most embedded within the US-led order. Not only are these states protected by US security commitments; they benefit from trade with the United States, and for the most part, they share US values of democracy and liberalism and maintain similar preferences on a wide range of foreign policy issues.[23] When US officials ask allies to adhere to new nonproliferation agreements, they are more likely to join and join more quickly than other states. The message that a new agreement or new effort is a high priority of the United States is often sufficient to attain commitment. Because of the system of global order the United States provides for these states, Washington holds a position of authority or "rightful rule" in the international system. Aligned states thus have some sense of obligation to comply with US wishes about the rules of the international system; coercion is rarely required.[24] As long as the request appears reasonable, these states will do what they can to honor the request. This grouping of states know they broadly share foreign policy preferences with the United States due to their embeddedness in the US-led order, so they would not expect the request to run contrary to their interests and values. Because they benefit from the international order, they are interested in supporting its maintenance by adhering to agreements committing to elements that strengthen the order. After adherence, these high-embedded states often then join US efforts to persuade other states to join agreements; they become key players in order building.

Discussing the relationship between the US government and its allies during the Obama administration, one European diplomat explained that any request from the United States automatically gets a "plus-1" in consideration; the diplomat elaborated, "The US is the biggest partner we have, the leader of the free world. We are happy to be part of the free world."[25] Because this diplomat's country values what the US-led order represents and what it provides, that state tries to comply with most US requests. The cost-benefit assessments of US allies and partners are simplified by their relationship to the United States and its system of international order.

Moderately embedded states, those in the middle of this spectrum, are not formally aligned with the United States but either receive US benefits in the form of military or economic aid or share liberal values and foreign policy preferences with the US-led order. Some states may benefit from US aid, but they may be illiberal and nondemocratic. Others may share liberal democratic political values with the United States but not receive US aid or the commitment of a formal security alliance. In general, these moderately embedded states are likely to be slower than allies and partners in acceding to US requests fo[...] elements of the nuclear nonproliferation regime.

The va [...] rom the United
States an [...] th the US-led order illun [...] from the United
States ai [...] eements. For example, I [...] adership for decades, a [...] ommitted to the
nonprol [...] n the form of aid
or secui [...] the United States,
and the [...] s in line with the
US-led [...] lership, the more
difficul [...] ersuade states to
join ne [...] resort to higher-
cost dip [...] nd coercion.

Farth [...]. These states get
some li [...] trade, or security.
Becaus [...] the international
system [...] military and eco-
nomic aid, most states receive some [...] stem of order created and led by the United States. These states, however, see limited advantages relative to other states, they share few foreign policy preferences with the United States, and they may be hurt by the rules intended to uphold the US-led order.

The final set of states are on the farthest side of the spectrum, US antagonists, such as Cuba or North Korea. These states are least likely to join elements of the nuclear nonproliferation regime. They find US global leadership to be anathema to their interests and thus reject many efforts affiliated with US leadership, such as nuclear nonproliferation agreements. They share few foreign policy preferences with the US-led order and are often considered US adversaries.

Table 1.1 indicates the measures used to determine the level of embeddedness within the US-led order.

It is worth noting that the description of the tools described above is not meant to suggest that nonhegemonic states in the international system have little agency over their nuclear proliferation policies or that only dominant states are concerned about nuclear nonproliferation. The fact that US persuasion is usually required to bring about most states' commitment to new nonproliferation rules in no way means that states do not value the particular initiative or nuclear nonproliferation generally. Rather, it means that most states have less *relative* interest than the United States. As described above, the dominant states in the international system have the greatest strategic interest in promoting nonproliferation globally. It is for that reason that the United States has been the primary champion of new nonprolifera-

Table 1.1 Factors of embeddedness within the US-led order

Embeddedness factor	*Sources*
Benefits from the hegemon	
Alliance with the hegemon	Relevant treaty texts
High levels of trade between the state and the hegemon	Organisation for Economic Cooperation and Development[a] World Trade Organization[b]
Provision of military and economic aid	US Agency for International Development[c]
Political values shared with the hegemon	
Foreign policy concordance with the US-led order	UN General Assembly Voting Data[d]
Liberal political values	Freedom House scores[e] Polity IV scores[f]

[a] Organisation for Economic Cooperation and Development, "Stats," accessed October 17, 2021, https://stats.oecd.org/.

[b] World Trade Organization, "WTO Data," accessed October 17, 2021, https://data.wto.org/.

[c] US Agency for International Development, "Foreign Aid Explorer: The Official Record of U.S. Foreign Aid," accessed October 17, 2021, https://explorer.usaid.gov/.

[d] Voeten, Strezhnev, and Bailey, "United Nations General Assembly Voting Data," The authors argue their ideal point "estimates consistently capture the position of states vis-a-vis a US-led liberal order." Bailey, Strezhnev and Voeten, "Estimating Dynamic State Preferences from United Nations Voting Data."

[e] Freedom House, "Freedom in the World," "Comparative and Historical Data," accessed October 17, 2021, https://freedomhouse.org/report/freedom-world.

[f] Monty G. Marshall and Keith Jaggers, "Polity IV Project: Political Regime Characteristics and Transitions, 1800–2013," George Mason University and Center for Systemic Peace, accessed October 17, 2021, http://www.systemicpeace.org/polity/polity4x.htm.

tion rules. Even though many other states prioritize stopping proliferation, especially within their own regions, the majority of states require a request from the United States before they commit to a new nonproliferation regime initiative. Nor does a theory of regime adherence based on US leadership mean that states do not have agency over their nonproliferation regime decisions. When states receive requests from the United States, they assess the costs and benefits of commitment based on their relationship with the hegemon. It is simply the case that some states, based on their level of embeddedness, are more likely to see benefits, while others are disinterested or see costs. The United States then must work to alter that latter assessment.

Based on this argument that the United States has been the most important actor in sustaining the nuclear nonproliferation regime, some readers may be considering examples of US presidents—such as Richard Nixon—who were not fully committed to nuclear nonproliferation. It is true that although the United States has been the most important actor in promoting global nuclear nonproliferation, US administrations have differed in their prioritization of the regime. At times, nonproliferation policies have been caught up in partisan debates. At other times, especially during the Cold

Table 1.2 The hegemon's tool kit for regime building

Category of tool	*Tools of influence*	*Tools employed*
Low-cost diplomacy	Requesting commitment via diplomatic meeting with the target states	
	Sending the target state demarches	
	Adding pertinent language to final documents at international forums involving the target state(s)	**Highly embedded states**
High-cost diplomacy	Sending personal appeals to target state's leadership from hegemon's leadership	
	Making appeals in person from the hegemon's leadership to the target state's leadership	**Moderately embedded states**
Positive inducements	Offering the target state military and economic aid or membership within an organization	
	Assisting on a particular global issue of interest to the target state	
Coercion	Making implicit threats to the target state to reduce military or economic aid, to withdraw support for joining international organizations, or to withdraw support for specific policies of interest	**Weakly embedded states**
	Making explicit threats to the target state to reduce military or economic aid	**Antagonistic states**
	Threatening the use of force	

War, presidents have undermined US nonproliferation goals in the service of other strategic imperatives, such as countering the Soviet Union. For instance, during the Cold War, the United States showed differing levels of support for Nuclear Weapons Free Zones (NWFZ)—regional groupings of states that vow not to acquire weapons or station weapons on their territory. Latin American states created the first NWFZ, the Treaty of Tlatelolco, following the terror of the Cuban Missile Crisis. The right to create these zones was then enshrined in article 7 of the NPT. The United States has promoted adherence to the Latin American NWFZ, especially for states

that were not yet in the NPT, such as Brazil, Argentina, and Cuba. In contrast, Indonesia wanted to establish a similar zone in Southeast Asia during a tense period of the Cold War in the 1980s. Washington pressured Jakarta to stop the effort over concerns that nuclear-armed US surface ships and submarines would not be permitted to pass through important territorial waters in the region.[26]

In another example, prioritizing a beneficial relationship with the Pakistani government in the 1980s while the Soviets were fighting in Afghanistan meant overlooking Islamabad's nuclear weapons program until it was too late. Prior to the Soviet invasion of Afghanistan, US leaders had sent over three hundred démarches to governments around the world in an attempt to stop sensitive nuclear exports to Pakistan.[27] The United States also placed economic sanctions on Pakistan over the suspected program. However, US leaders deemed the Cold War competition more important than stopping Pakistan's program in the early 1980s. US leaders continued to warn Pakistani leaders about pursuing nuclear weapons,[28] but they did not cut off aid during a period when their program made great strides.

In the 1990s, the United States failed to ratify the CTBT, a treaty banning all nuclear explosions. Nonnuclear states had been calling for this treaty since before the NPT was founded, but it only became reality when the Clinton administration supported negotiation of the treaty in the 1990s. Clinton saw clear nonproliferation benefits in discouraging states from testing nuclear devices. Republicans in the Senate failed to support the treaty's ratification in 1999, however, an indication of the growing partisanship that would overtake US domestic politics. But this Senate rejection of the CTBT is not fully inconsistent with a hegemonic-led regime. The regime built around the NPT is one that privileges the United States as an official nuclear weapon state. In contrast, the CTBT treats all states the same—they are all banned from testing weapons. While some security analysts would (and did) say the CTBT benefitted the United States disproportionately because it had conducted so many tests in the past and a ban on tests might preclude some states from developing advanced weapons, others argued the United States needed to maintain the option to test. The United States has kept this option open while fully supporting the CTBT's international monitoring system and has encouraged other states to join. In other words, US leaders have the benefits of dissuading and detecting nuclear explosions through this treaty, while not facing similar constraints.

What about that states that are not members of the NPT and have had close relations with the United States? Israel and Pakistan have been US partners at times since the NPT entered into force. How do we make sense of the fact that these states remain outside of the nonproliferation regime when it is such high priority to the US government? Both cases will be discussed in chapter 2, but it is worth noting a few points here. In the case of Israel, three different US administrations tried to halt suspected Israeli nuclear

weapons development, as would be expected by a theory centered on the key role of the United States in promoting the nonproliferation regime.[29] The United States was not aware of the extent of the program during the 1960s, however, and Israel likely possessed nuclear weapons before the NPT was adopted in 1968. Though US leaders were unable to stop this effort, they came to an agreement with Israeli leaders in 1969 to dampen proliferation pressures among Israel's neighbors. Israel would not test a nuclear weapon and would maintain a policy of secrecy about its nuclear program.[30]

In Pakistan, as discussed previously, the United States subjugated concerns about Pakistan's growing nuclear program to its Cold War contest with the Soviet Union. While the United States successfully pressured France to cancel a deal to sell Pakistan nuclear reprocessing technology in the late 1970s, US calculations would soon change. After the Soviet invasion of Afghanistan in 1979, US leaders relied on Pakistan to help counter the Soviet military in Central Asia. US leaders thus failed to pressure the Pakistani government over its nuclear program at the same time they provided Islamabad with significant military and economic aid. When the United States reinstated economic sanctions after the Cold War due to Pakistan's nuclear activities, the Pakistani nuclear program was too far along for the sanctions to affect the program or the calculations of its leaders. The Pakistani case offers evidence for the observation that when US administrations view nonproliferation as less important than other strategic goals, the regime will be weakened.

The cases of Israel and Pakistan lead to several conclusions. First, it is difficult to persuade a country to give up its nuclear program and join the NPT once the nuclear program is close to realized. Path dependency makes reversal more challenging as a program develops.[31] Second, there have been exceptional cases in which the United States, as a hegemonic power, has pursued other strategic goals that undermine its strategic goal of nuclear nonproliferation. Finally, in both cases, several US administrations did take actions to try to stop the nuclear programs and persuade the states in question to join the NPT, but these actions were insufficient or too late.

Table 1.3 summarizes the theoretical argument.

In summary, variation in states' adherence to the nuclear nonproliferation stems from variation in states' responses to US and allied efforts to persuade states to join or support elements of the regime. How states respond to these

Table 1.3 Summary of theoretical argument

Independent variable		*Intervening variable*		*Dependent variable*
US (and allied) efforts	→	Level of embeddedness within the US-led order	→	Adherence decision

efforts is determined by their level of embeddedness within the US-led order at the time of the persuasive attempts.

Observable Implications

As described above, the central theoretical argument of the book is that US efforts, at times with its allies, have been crucial to promoting widespread adherence to the nuclear nonproliferation regime. The United States has been its primary instigator and promoter. If this argument is correct, there should be several observable implications in the empirical record:

REGIME CREATION

1. The United States will lead global efforts to establish the elements of the global nuclear nonproliferation regime.
2. When US administrations believe that other strategic interests outweigh nonproliferation, the regime will be weakened.

REGIME MEMBERSHIP

3. The US and its allies will promote the universalization of the NPT and other regime agreements through the use of their tools of influence.
4. Decisions to adhere to (or support) the NPT or other regime agreements will reflect consideration of US policy preferences and persuasive tools.
5. Decisions to adhere to (or support) the NPT or other regime elements will reflect embeddedness within the US-led order.
   a. Highly embedded states will require less persuasion and will adhere relatively quickly.
   b. Moderately embedded states will require more persuasion and take a longer time to adhere.
   c. Weakly embedded states will require significant persuasion to adhere if they do so at all.
   d. Antagonistic states will rarely adhere.

Alternative Theories of Regime Adherence

This book argues for putting US leadership at the center of understanding the widespread adherence to the nuclear nonproliferation regime, but there are three important theoretical perspectives that offer alternative explanations for states' regime adherence. These perspectives include theories related to security, regime fairness, and domestic political economy. The following section discusses each of these theories in turn, highlighting their strengths and weaknesses for explaining states' decisions to join elements of the regime.

A security-based theory explaining regime participation stems from the regime's ability to solve nuclear security dilemmas.[32] From this perspective, all states seek survival in an anarchic international system, and nuclear weapons are one means of achieving security.[33] Pursuing these weapons, however, may cause others to follow suit, leading to arms racing and threats of preemptive strikes on nuclear facilities.[34] States are thus caught between two options that both could undermine their security: they could build nuclear weapons for protection and trigger their neighbors and adversaries to do the same, thus creating an arms race and inviting attack, or they could choose not to build nuclear weapons and potentially become victim to nuclear attack if their adversaries build them. The NPT allows states to solve this dilemma by providing a means by which they can credibly commit to a policy of nonproliferation if their neighbors or adversaries do the same. Indeed, before the NPT was negotiated, a 1962 UN survey of states indicated that knowing their neighbors would not develop nuclear weapons was a driving force behind supporting the notional treaty.[35] Based on this theoretical perspective, we would expect states to join the NPT and subsequent regime agreements when they are confident that current and potential adversaries are also joining and giving up their weapons. In contrast, we would expect states to reconsider their commitment to the NPT and the broader regime when their adversaries or potential adversaries are taking actions that could lead to proliferation or are proliferating. In addition, we would expect states protected by extended deterrence to join the NPT and other regime initiatives more quickly. Two of the negotiators of the NPT, George Bunn and Roland Timerbaev, argue that the existence of extended deterrence agreements was vital to some states agreeing to the treaty.[36]

Evidence presented in this book indicates that states have assessed their security interests when considering their support for aspects of the nuclear nonproliferation regime, especially when making the decision on whether to join the NPT and forgo their ability to produce indigenous nuclear weapons. But even with the confidence provided by international inspectors scrutinizing the nuclear activities of member states or by extended deterrence commitments, the security rationale for joining the treaty has often been insufficient. The United States has had to employ other tools to affect states' cost-benefit analyses. In other words, states have required more than the promise of resolving nuclear security dilemmas or extended deterrence commitments to join the regime. In addition, there are many cases in which states have continued supporting the NPT and the broader regime even when they are concerned about their adversaries building nuclear weapons. Moreover, a full account of the nuclear nonproliferation regime's membership requires moving beyond security considerations and examining the decision-making of states that were less concerned about nuclear-armed neighbors and had no interest in building nuclear weapons.

A second explanation for regime adherence emphasizes the concepts of justice and fairness. Regime theorists expect states to behave more consistently with the norms enshrined within a treaty or broader regime if the norms "are widely regarded as the result of a fair and legitimate process and if they concur with widely shared substantive notions of justice."[37] In her work on multilateral negotiations, Cecilia Albin finds that fair and just agreements promote compliance.[38] Two specific components of her formulation of justice, "balancing different principles and interests" and "the obligation to honor and comply with freely negotiated agreements," are especially relevant to the nuclear nonproliferation regime.[39] Perhaps the sustainability of the regime for over fifty years comes from the perception among members that the regime helps balance differing state interests and reflects an honoring of the agreements first established in the NPT. The NPT, after all, is made up of several bargains that can trigger ideas about fairness, especially between the five official nuclear weapon states in the treaty and the rest of its members. Arguably the most important bargain is inherent in article 6 of the NPT: nonnuclear weapon states agree to nuclear forbearance in exchange for a commitment by the five declared nuclear-weapon-possessor states to pursue good faith negotiations toward eventual nuclear disarmament. According to this perspective, states would consider the nuclear-weapon-possessor states' progress toward disarmament when assessing whether to join the NPT, make additional commitments to the regime, or remain in the regime. A second bargain enshrined in articles 3 and 4 of the treaty is that all members are supposed to have access to nuclear technology for peaceful purposes.

Albin's ideas about fairness and justice are relevant to the nuclear nonproliferation regime, but instead of perceptions of fairness causing its success, the regime has been effective despite claims by many member states that the treaty is unfair. Often nuclear nonproliferation practitioners have assumed that many nonnuclear NPT states resist committing to new nonproliferation agreements and activities because of perceived slow progress toward nuclear disarmament by the nuclear weapon states. For instance, a 2008 report from a commission assembled by IAEA director general Mohammad ElBaradei concludes that "mounting resentment" over lack of progress on disarmament by the nuclear possessor states "makes it much more difficult to agree on steps that are urgently needed to strengthen the global effort to stem the spread of nuclear weapons—even though such steps would serve the interests of all."[40]

The empirical record, however, indicates that although many states express concern over the lack of fairness in the regime, the United States and its allies have often been able to overcome these concerns and persuade states to adhere to the nuclear nonproliferation regime in cases in which the nuclear-armed states have done little to make the regime appear more fair or more just. By using other persuasive tools, including diplomatic pressure and positive inducements, traditionally the United States has been able—for the most part—to override concerns about justice by changing states' calculations about the benefits of supporting the regime.

A final alternative explanation emphasizes the role of domestic politics in regime adherence. Decisions about joining nonproliferation agreements or supporting regime adaptations may have little to do with pressure from the United States and its allies and could instead stem from states' internal politics. In a recent assessment of the role of domestic politics in all types of nuclear decision-making, Elizabeth Saunders notes three different types of actors in the "domestic circle" who could affect state decision-making. These include the state's leader and immediate circle, elite actors who can influence policy, and the mass public.[41] The most well-known domestic theory related to nuclear nonproliferation is Etel Solingen's argument that leaders and their domestic coalitions whose model of political survival relies on their state's integration into the global economy are more likely to reject proliferation and join the NPT.[42] In comparing Middle Eastern states that sought nuclear weapons to those in East Asia that did not, she finds that as East Asian governments were liberalizing economically, they rejected proliferation. Her work offers detailed evidence that certain outward-looking regimes are more likely to cooperate with the nuclear nonproliferation regime. The theory is limited in two ways, however, in explaining regime adherence. First, there are additional cases in which the mechanism for state participation in nuclear nonproliferation regime agreements is not liberalizing economies but US influence and pressure. Economically illiberal states do join regime elements, often after the US and its allies have pressured them. Second, historical evidence indicates that in several cases, the United States had to work to secure support for new elements of the regime, even from liberal states. Moreover, while Solingen provides a compelling mechanism to explain the behavior of some cases, her story is one that should be viewed as situated within the broader global context in which the United States was leading the global economic system. After all, in her cases of nuclear restraint, the leaders were most interested in improving trade relations with the United States and its allies. They wanted to become more deeply embedded within the US-led order.

Research Design

The balance of this book assesses the theories explored in this chapter. The following chapter, chapter 2, begins with the advent of nuclear weapons and chronicles the development of the nuclear nonproliferation regime. It evaluates two of the observable implications outlined above, that the United States will lead global efforts to establish the elements of the global nuclear nonproliferation regime and that when US administrations view nonproliferation as less important than other strategic goals, the regime will be weakened. The chapter also provides evidence for the argument that the Soviet Union was a lesser partner in building and promoting the nuclear nonproliferation regime.

Chapters 3, 4, and 5 present a series of semistructured, focused case study comparisons of Japan, Indonesia, Egypt, South Africa, and Cuba. These cases are selected for a variety of reasons. First, they have different levels of embeddedness within the US-led order, spanning from highly embedded Japan to antagonistic Cuba. This variation in the intervening variable allows for assessing whether it corresponds to variation in the dependent variable. The cases of Indonesia, Egypt, and South Africa have within-case variation in terms of the level of embeddedness. Within-case variation allows for holding many factors constant except for the intervening variable and dependent variable, facilitating causal identification. Second, the states are selected to account for regional differences. Nuclear weapons and nonproliferation dynamics may differ by region based on the nuclear weapon states present and the historical experience with nuclear weapons and proliferation. In addition, Japan is an important state within the global nuclear order as the only state to experience nuclear weapons in wartime and thus has unique domestic considerations for nuclear weapons policy. South Africa is another important case in the global nuclear order, as the only state that has given up its indigenous nuclear weapon program. South Africa resisted joining the regime, but since its renunciation of nuclear weapons, it has become a regional and global leader in antinuclear activities. Indonesia and Egypt have traditionally been leaders in their regions as well, including in the area of nuclear nonproliferation policies. Moreover, Indonesia is a case that is rarely covered in existing academic literature, but it has taken strong nonproliferation and disarmament positions and is a rising power in its region. Cuba's nuclear nonproliferation regime decisions have received little scholarly attention to date; the case is much less well known than that of North Korea, another antagonistic state. Each chapter focuses on these states' decisions in a different element or period of the nonproliferation regime.

Chapter 3 examines four states' decision-making processes for joining the NPT. Japan is a highly embedded state where US influence played an important part in its decision to adhere. Indonesia is a moderately embedded state during this period, while Egypt had moved from weakly embedded to moderately embedded as a result of the Camp David Accords. Cuba, an antagonistic state, has been an adversary of the United States since before the NPT's adoption and did not join the treaty until 2002, thirty-four years after the treaty opened for signature. In each case, US influence was a significant factor in the state's decision-making regarding the NPT. This chapter explores the observable implications related to regime membership while also illustrating that when US administrations view nonproliferation as less important than other strategic goals, the regime will be weakened.

Chapter 4 explores an important period in the history of the nuclear nonproliferation regime: the 1995 debate over extension of the NPT. The treaty text specifies that twenty-five years after entry into force, the treaty members must come together and decide on the future of the treaty. In the spring of 1995, NPT states had to decide on whether to extend the treaty and for how long. The United States pushed for unconditional, indefinite extension. This chapter chronicles the history surrounding this key event and examines the position of a number of states with varying levels of embeddedness within the US-led liberal order, including Japan, Indonesia, Egypt, and South Africa. Highly embedded Japan supported indefinite extension early on, though the process was not without its challenges. Indonesia and Egypt did not support indefinite extension, but for different reasons.

Table 1.4 Chapter 3 case selection: NPT ratification

The NPT opened for signature and ratification in 1968			
Japan	*Indonesia*	*Egypt*	*Cuba*
Joined—1976	Joined—1979	Joined—1981	Joined—2002
Highly embedded	Moderately embedded	Moderately embedded	Antagonistic

Table 1.5 Chapter 4 case selection: position on NPT indefinite extension

The meeting on extension occurred in spring 1995			
Japan	*Indonesia*	*South Africa*	*Egypt*
In favor	Against but did not block consensus	Against, then in favor	Against but did not block consensus
Highly embedded	Moderately embedded (trending down)	Moderately embedded (trending up)	Moderately embedded (trending down)

Table 1.6 Chapter 5 case selection: conclusion of Model Additional Protocol

The agreement became available in 1997		
Japan	*Indonesia*	*Egypt*
Concluded—1999	Concluded—1999 *(outlier case)*	Has not concluded
Highly embedded	Moderately embedded	Moderately embedded (trending toward weakly embedded)

The final empirical chapter, chapter 5, covers Japan, Indonesia, and Egypt's decision-making on the 1997 Model Additional Protocol (AP), the most stringent safeguards agreement with the IAEA. This chapter evaluates the observable implications related to regime membership as well as the expectation that the United States will lead the global effort to establish the elements of the global nuclear nonproliferation regime. As expected, Japan concluded an AP quickly. Indonesia concluded one in the same year as Japan, an unexpected outcome based on its embeddedness within the US-led order. Egypt, a weakly embedded state, has not yet concluded an AP, despite US diplomatic pressure.

Existing theories explaining why states adhere to nuclear nonproliferation agreements do not provide a full picture of how states make their decisions. These theories often overlook or deemphasize the dominant role of the United States, and sometimes its allies, in promoting this regime. Situating the nuclear nonproliferation regime within the US-led order allows for an improved understanding of the way other states operate within it and why they decide to adhere (or not). The following chapters illustrate many instances of US and allies' efforts to universalize this regime.

CHAPTER 2

How the United States Promotes the Nuclear Nonproliferation Regime

In recounting the nuclear nonproliferation efforts of each US administration during the nuclear age, this chapter serves to illustrate the two observable implications related to regime creation described in chapter 1: The United States will lead global efforts to establish the elements of the global nuclear nonproliferation regime, and when US administrations believe that other strategic interests outweigh nonproliferation, the regime will be weakened. Moreover, this chapter will demonstrate that while the Soviet Union collaborated with the United States in developing the NPT and other related agreements and prioritized nonproliferation through other policies, the Soviets played a lesser role than the United States in promoting the regime.[1]

Roosevelt, Truman, and Eisenhower

As the former US ambassador and arms controller James E. Goodby recounts, the first "international effort to establish rules about the atom bomb" was penned by Winston Churchill and accepted by President Franklin D. Roosevelt.[2] The August 1943 Quebec Agreement governed the cooperation between the United Kingdom and the United States on the atom bomb project. According to the agreement, the two states could not discuss this effort with third parties without the other's consent, and each promised a complete exchange of information. Churchill hoped for a long-lasting UK-US monopoly in atomic weapons, though scientists in both nations correctly anticipated that nuclear secrets would soon spread. Indeed, Churchill and Roosevelt both rejected pleas by the physicist Niels Bohr to tell the Soviets about the nuclear weapons program; Bohr hoped to establish some type of international control on this new and devastating weaponry.[3] The president and the prime minister wanted to prevent other states, especially the Soviets, from building nuclear weapons and thus pursued a policy of secrecy.

Harry S. Truman first learned of the Manhattan Project when he became president on April 12, 1945, following Roosevelt's sudden death. Truman warned Soviet premier Joseph Stalin of a new weapon while at the Potsdam Summit in July 1945—Truman was unaware that Soviet intelligence was well informed of the US atomic weapons program. (The US government was thus surprised when US intelligence assets detected a Soviet nuclear explosion in August 1949. The Anglo-American monopoly had lasted four years.) Concerned with additional proliferation, Congress abandoned the nuclear sharing agreement put in place by Roosevelt and Churchill and passed the McMahon Act in 1946. The act established a policy of nuclear secrecy, even with US allies, and helped spur the United Kingdom's independent nuclear weapon program.

In 1946, Truman appointed Undersecretary of State Dean Acheson to develop a plan for the international control of nuclear energy. Acheson put together a committee of consultants for the project led by David Lilienthal, the chairman of the Tennessee Valley Authority. The committee's assessment, which became known as the Acheson-Lilienthal Report, called for an international body to control all fissile material. Truman supported their plan, and the New York City financier Bernard Baruch was appointed to negotiate an agreement based on its recommendations. Baruch expanded on the Acheson-Lilienthal Report, adding a proposal that an international body, the International Atomic Development Authority, would have the power to sanction nations. In practice, the proposal precluded the possibility of a Soviet nuclear weapons program. Unsurprisingly, the Soviets rejected the plan and it was not adopted.

Global proliferation of nuclear weapons continued apace both quantitatively and qualitatively in the early 1950s. In 1950, Truman approved the development of thermonuclear weapons. Nuclear destruction would henceforth be measured in megatons. Under a policy of "atomic plenty," he would also set the United States on a course to develop thousands of nuclear weapons. The United Kingdom tested its own nuclear weapons in the desert of Australia in October 1952, and the United States tested a thermonuclear weapon a month later. The Soviets followed with a thermonuclear bomb test in August 1953. During his presidency, Dwight D. Eisenhower continued to expand the US arsenal, while also advancing delivery capabilities, including new ballistic missiles and new aircraft. By the end of the Eisenhower presidency, the United States fielded a nuclear triad: nuclear-capable bombers, intercontinental ballistic missiles (ICBMs), and submarine-launched ballistic missiles (SLBMs).

The Soviet thermonuclear bomb test in 1953 again surprised the United States with the speed at which the Soviets were advancing in nuclear technology. President Eisenhower became extremely concerned, and some in his administration felt the president needed to do more to inform the American people about nuclear dangers. A public relations campaign, Operation

Candor, aimed to share the gravity of the global situation with all citizens.[4] Eisenhower used an invitation to speak before the UN General Assembly in December 1953 to discuss the unprecedented threat of nuclear warfare while also delivering a more hopeful message about peaceful nuclear technology. In his speech, Eisenhower announced his Atoms for Peace plan. He proposed the establishment of the International Atomic Energy Agency (IAEA), to be set up under the auspices of the United Nations. Eisenhower also recommended the creation of an international fuel bank of nuclear material to be used for peaceful purposes.

US leaders shared the Atoms for Peace plan with the Soviets in early 1954. Soviet leaders were skeptical, concerned—rightly so it turned out—that sharing peaceful nuclear technology would lead to the spread of nuclear weapons. They insisted on pursuing their proposal for the complete renunciation of all nuclear weapons. US leaders told the Soviets they would move ahead with the creation of the new atomic regulatory agency with or without Soviet support, but the fuel bank idea was dropped. After a draft penned by the United Kingdom was passed to the State Department and revised, the United States convened the United Kingdom, France, Canada, Australia, South Africa, Belgium, and Portugal to negotiate on the text of the IAEA statute. The Soviets joined the negotiations in July 1955. The statute for the IAEA entered into force in July 1957.

As a former military commander who helped integrate nuclear weapons into US war planning, Eisenhower had a deep understanding of the destructive potential of these weapons. He worried about their spread, especially to smaller states, but was able to make little progress on nonproliferation or disarmament during his administration.[5] His primary efforts to address proliferation involved negotiations over a nuclear test ban treaty and the creation of a nuclear sharing arrangement with European allies, but he left office without either plan solidified. As Shane Maddock concludes, "the United States failed to develop a consistent and effective nuclear nonproliferation policy" during the Eisenhower years.[6]

From 1958 to 1960, the United States engaged in negotiations with the United Kingdom and the Soviet Union to ban nuclear tests. The international community had grown increasingly concerned about the harmful health effects from radioactive fallout. In March 1958, Soviet premier Nikita Khrushchev announced that the USSR would stop testing and then requested the Eisenhower administration join the moratorium.[7] A panel of experts appointed by Eisenhower determined that a halt to testing would benefit the United States due to its advantage in weapons development.[8] The initial talks were productive, and Eisenhower kept the process moving forward, even as many in his administration, including officials from the Department of Defense and the Atomic Energy Commission, were against a testing ban. The British representatives at the negotiations reported back to London that progress was undermined by the US insistence on linking the ban agreement to broader disarmament progress and by requiring additional technical talks.[9] The Eisenhower administration eventually settled on offering to conclude a threshold treaty, whereby nuclear tests would be limited to a certain size, but these talks faltered as well—in part due to the May 1960 incident in which a US U-2 spy plane was shot down over the Soviet Union[10]—with no agreement by the time Eisenhower left office. Historians have long debated the strength of Eisenhower's commitment to a comprehensive test ban treaty. Benjamin P. Green notes that some prominent historians consider the ban a significant goal of the administration while others argue the ban was never a serious pursuit. With more evidence available with the passing of time, Green concludes that Eisenhower was favorable to a test ban but that his interest in establishing consensus among his advisers "inhibited him from overruling the strong internal opposition to the test ban."[11]

Eisenhower's second major nonproliferation effort was a nuclear sharing scheme aimed at reducing allies' interest in proliferation. In December 1960, the Eisenhower administration proposed the Multilateral Force (MLF) at a NATO meeting.[12] According to this plan, the United States would share its nuclear weapons with NATO nations under the authority of the Supreme Allied Commander in Europe. Improving Soviet nuclear capabilities concerned many European allies, and Eisenhower's proposal offered reassurance and a way to stop allies from building their own independent nuclear capabilities. France's indigenous nuclear arsenal, first tested the previous February, provided a warning about the kind of independence allies would seek with their own nuclear weapons. The feasibility and the wisdom of the MLF proposal was challenged on many fronts and faced significant opposition from the Soviet Union. Eisenhower left office with the plan still in flux.

Kennedy

President John F. Kennedy entered the presidency "with the intention to place nuclear arms control and nonproliferation in the center of the American foreign policy agenda."[13] Kennedy achieved a few significant nonproliferation successes during his short tenure as president.

In September 1961, the Kennedy administration established the Arms Control and Disarmament Agency (ACDA), an organization charged with working on strategic arms control, nuclear nonproliferation, and disarmament. The creation of this independent organization ensured that within the US interagency progress, there always would be an advocate for arms control and nonproliferation. Whereas the State Department was sometimes known to value bilateral relations over specific US policy priorities and therefore assess nuclear proliferation on a case-by-case basis, ACDA would be more likely to advocate general nonproliferation policies regardless of the states involved. This organization increased the breadth of the US bureaucratic assets devoted to nuclear nonproliferation.

President Kennedy was greatly concerned about additional states developing nuclear weapons, though his policies to curtail specific nuclear programs saw limited success. In February 1962, Kennedy argued to British prime minister McMillian that the continued existence of an independent British nuclear arsenal would motivate German proliferation and continued French proliferation. The French test in 1960 raised concerns that the Germans would follow, something both the Americans and Soviets wanted to prevent. Kennedy went as far as to cancel the SkyBolt ballistic missile program in November 1962, a program on which the future British nuclear arsenal was based. The British allies were angry with this action, and Kennedy sought an alternative. In the end, Kennedy offered US Polaris missiles as a replacement for the abandoned SkyBolt program, and the British nuclear weapons program continued.

Israel was also a target of Kennedy's proliferation concerns. When elected, Kennedy ordered a postmortem of the intelligence community's failure to detect the Israeli nuclear program earlier. It was only at the end of the Eisenhower administration that the US government became aware of the extent of this effort that had begun by the mid-1950s. Kennedy pushed for the Israeli government to safeguard its Dimona nuclear reactor and allow Americans to inspect the facility. After visiting, American scientists reported that Dimona was used for peaceful purposes, despite doubts within the US intelligence community. It was difficult for Kennedy to speak against the report's conclusions and press Israeli prime minister Ben Gurion further about the purpose of the reactor. But then in the summer of 1963, President Kennedy went as far as to threaten the US-Israel security relationship if American scientists could not continue to visit Dimona.[14] New Israeli prime minister Levi Eshkol relented in August 1963, allowing periodic US visits to Dimona. According to the historian Avner Cohen, it was the weakness of this bilateral approach to nonproliferation that led US policy makers to consider a global nuclear nonproliferation strategy.[15]

Concluding the Limited Test Ban Treaty (LTBT) with the Soviets was Kennedy's most lasting contribution to the nonproliferation regime. The Cuban Missile Crisis brought the two adversaries together on this issue after years of stalled negotiations on a complete test ban. It was a "turning point" in US-Soviet nonproliferation cooperation[16] and what Kennedy called "a shaft of light cut into darkness."[17] China's developing nuclear weapons program, though at this point untested, also pushed the two superpowers toward a test ban.[18] By the summer of 1963, the Soviets agreed to the LTBT, prohibiting testing in the water, atmosphere, and space; nuclear tests could now only be conducted underground. The US Senate ratified the treaty in the last weeks of Kennedy's life.

Historians differ in their assessment of Kennedy's role in promoting nuclear nonproliferation. Whereas Cohen writes that "Israel was the awakening that led Kennedy to discover nuclear proliferation as a global US concern" and argues that Kennedy was the first president to truly prioritize global nuclear nonproliferation as American policy,[19] Francis J. Gavin argues Kennedy's nonproliferation approach was more ambivalent "and did little to halt proliferation."[20] While it is true that Kennedy's attempts largely failed with the British and Israeli programs, he did appear to care deeply about the issue. The formation of ACDA and the creation of the LTBT both had lasting effects on nuclear nonproliferation efforts.

Johnson

"The greatest single requirement is that we find a way to ensure the survival of civilization in the nuclear age. A nuclear war would be the death of all our hopes and it is our task to see that it does not happen."[21] With these words, President Johnson opened and closed his first National Security Council meeting after Kennedy's assassination. Over the course of his presidency, Johnson would galvanize the US bureaucracy and the international community to push forward with a global nuclear nonproliferation treaty—the treaty that would become the cornerstone of the nuclear nonproliferation regime. His commitment to stopping the spread of nuclear weapons stemmed from an appreciation of not only the assured devastation wrought by a nuclear exchange but the ways in which additional nuclear states could undermine US power and interests. He also sought to be remembered as a "man of peace" and saw the NPT as part of that legacy.[22]

In 1961, for the third year in a row, the Irish minister of external affairs Frank Aiken presented a resolution in the UN General Assembly calling for a global nonproliferation agreement. For the first time, both the Soviet Union and the United States supported the effort; on December 4, 1961, the General Assembly passed the resolution. The next year, the United States and Soviet Union began "private bilateral talks" on a possible treaty.[23] Little progress was made until January 21, 1964, when President Johnson, three months into his unexpected presidency, called for negotiating a nonproliferation agreement based on the Irish resolution within the Eighteen Nation Disarmament Committee (ENDC). This UN-sponsored committee was formed in 1961 to promote dialogue between the United States and the Soviet Union on disarmament-related issues.[24] The Americans and Soviets developed draft treaty texts; the United States submitted its draft to the ENDC in August 1965, and the Soviets submitted their own in September. Early disagreement between the two superpowers occurred over the transfer of weapons to another territory. The USSR considered NATO nuclear sharing to be "proliferation"; the United States did not.[25] Negotiations continued for over four and a half years.

Anticipation of the first Chinese nuclear test in 1964 put nonproliferation on the forefront of Johnson's policy agenda, as his advisers assumed other states, including India, Israel, Japan, and Sweden, would follow China's example.[26] Potential nuclear cascades appeared everywhere once China had the bomb. The Chinese test, in October 1964, pushed the two superpowers to cooperate more closely on a nonproliferation treaty. One of the greatest fears of both powers was the possibility of a West German nuclear weapons program, and if China's proliferation led to proliferation by new states, it was assumed West Germany would have greater incentive to develop its own program. The US plan for the MLF in Europe—a policy the West Germans enthusiastically supported and one the United States hoped would curb West German interest in an independent nuclear capability—remained a stumbling block between the superpowers, but they continued to hold high-level discussions about a potential treaty through 1964 and 1965.

Two weeks after the Chinese detonation, President Johnson commissioned a high-level group to examine US nonproliferation policy and predict the influence of the Chinese test on international politics. Johnson selected Roswell Gilpatric, a Wall Street lawyer and former undersecretary of defense, to lead the effort. The committee studied six issues and wrote four potential courses for US policy action spanning from the United States taking a laissez-faire attitude toward nonproliferation (option 1) to making it the number one US policy goal, even if this meant taking actions at the expense of allies (option 4).[27]

Elements of the US bureaucracy responded differently to the Gilpatric Report. The ACDA argued nonproliferation was the most important US foreign policy goal and should be pursued without exemptions or special cases, thus favoring option 4. The State Department was concerned about close allies and sought a policy based on country-by-country considerations.[28]

On January 21, 1965, the Gilpatric Committee issued its final recommendation, option 4: The United States should develop stronger nuclear nonproliferation policies; nonproliferation should not be approached on a case-by-case basis; and when goals clashed, nonproliferation should take precedence. The committee recommended a US effort to negotiate a nuclear nonproliferation agreement (which was already underway), a comprehensive test ban treaty, and nuclear weapons free zones. In an action memo dated June 28, 1965, Johnson accepted the report and instructed his administration to halt the further spread of nuclear weapons, and, significantly, he put the ACDA, not the State Department, in charge of enforcing the new policy.[29] Gavin concludes that the Gilpatric Committee "laid foundations for far more robust nonproliferation policy, which would eventually lead to the negotiation, in cooperation with the Soviet Union, of the Nuclear Nonproliferation Treaty (NPT)."[30]

While the Gilpatric Committee met, US and Soviet leaders were working through the difficult task of negotiating and drafting nonproliferation treaty texts. Day-to-day negotiations were conducted by George Bunn for the United States and Roland Timerbaev for the Soviet Union.[31] In September and October 1966, Secretary of State Dean Rusk and Foreign Minister Andrei Gromyko, along with ENDC cochairs from each country, engaged in intense negotiations. The two sides were eventually able to come together on a basic understanding on nuclear sharing. By December 1966, the United States accepted Soviet draft language.[32]

For two years after the US and Soviet negotiators agreed on draft NPT text, US leaders consulted regularly with key allies about the treaty. The declassified ACDA archives contain several country files with numerous cables and meeting records in which foreign leaders ask the United States to clarify the meaning of treaty provisions, respond to concerns about the requirement for nuclear safeguards, and make suggestions for alternate phrasing. European allies preferred nuclear facility inspections by the European Atomic Energy Community (EURATOM), a nuclear organization founded in 1958, and resisted the requirement for IAEA inspections. Many countries, especially those close to the United States, did play a role in shaping the final draft text of the treaty. Early US and Soviet drafts included nothing about disarmament, and the treaty was to be of unlimited duration.[33] The Japanese, Swedes, West Germans, and Italians sought a term limit for the treaty. The Japanese suggested treaty reviews every five years. Many nonnuclear weapon states, including Japan, also sought assurances in the treaty text that they would not be attacked with nuclear weapons. The two superpowers resisted putting this language in the treaty but did support a resolution on security assurances at the UN General Assembly in 1967.

Though hundreds of meetings, cables, and consultations would suggest a different US message, President Johnson wrote that at this time, he encouraged US diplomats "to avoid taking the lead or exerting pressure. Let our allies and others take the initiative."[34] This was a wishful statement, since it would have been obvious that the United States and the Soviets had negotiated and drafted the treaty between themselves, and yet it illustrated an awareness that the treaty and its goals were best served by not being perceived as directed by the United States. ACDA director William C. Foster was less circumspect about US efforts to promote the treaty. An August 29, 1967, "Eyes only for the Secretary" letter from Director Foster to Secretary Rusk states, "I hope you will inspire our 'salesmen' (ambassadors) in certain capitals to really put their hearts into their job of convincing their clients that NPT is in their interests and that the United States believes in it and wants its broad acceptance. Some of our salesmen seem to have doubts."[35]

In January 1968, the United States and the Soviet Union submitted separate but identical NPT drafts to the ENDC. The new drafts included a new amendment on nuclear safeguards, a revised article 4 ensuring all states have the right to peaceful uses of nuclear energy, and a new article 6 committing all treaty parties to pursue negotiations in good faith toward disarmament. In his State of the Union Address, President Johnson announced that he hoped to present the NPT to the Senate in the coming year. The draft text was approved by the UN General Assembly in June 1968. Only Albania, Cuba, Tanzania, and Zambia voted against the treaty. China voiced opposition, calling the treaty "a hoax and a conspiracy that would allow the United States and the Soviet Union to restrict 'the right of nonnuclear powers to the peaceful uses of atomic energy' and leave them vulnerable to nuclear blackmail."[36]

On July 1, 1968, at a White House ceremony, President Johnson and representatives of the Soviet Union, the United Kingdom, and more than fifty other nations signed the NPT. It would enter into force once forty nations, in addition to the United States, Soviet Union, and Great Britain, ratified the treaty through their national ratification procedures. After years of painstaking work, the Johnson administration and their Soviet counterparts had succeeded in creating what would be the foundation of a global nuclear nonproliferation regime. Unfortunately for Johnson, his successor would not share his vision.

A month later, in August 1968, the Soviets invaded Czechoslovakia. Presidential candidate Richard Nixon, though he claimed to generally favor the NPT, suggested delaying US ratification in response.[37] On September 17, 1968, the Senate Foreign Relations Committee recommended ratification, but the full Senate voted in October to postpone further action on the NPT.[38] According to Johnson adviser Glenn T. Seaborg, once Nixon won in November, "White House sources confirmed on Nov 27 that President Johnson was considering calling the Senate into special session in December for the specific purpose of ratifying the treaty."[39] Senate leaders would not approve this measure unless the new president-elect agreed to the session. Nixon originally supported the special session but later reneged. No special session was called.

A transition meeting between President Johnson and Nixon illustrated the import with which Johnson viewed the NPT. Johnson briefed president-elect Nixon in December 1968. Of the five topics covered with the new president, Johnson included the NPT and explained his reasons for supporting it.[40] Johnson's commitment to the NPT appeared to have only weakly affected Nixon, if at all. In the history of US nuclear policy, Nixon is an anomaly, appearing to care little about nonproliferation and at times exhibiting outright distain for the NPT. Lack of leadership on this issue in the White House did not stop the ACDA and other bureaucrats in the US government from promoting the treaty, but they lacked support from the highest levels of government.

Nixon

For nuclear nonproliferation, the Richard Nixon administration represents "lost years."[41] This administration best illustrates how the nuclear nonproliferation regime may be weakened when US leaders do not prioritize it. Nixon believed the United States should have nuclear superiority and that it could be beneficial for certain states, such as France or Japan, to possess nuclear weapons.[42] As president, he stopped pressuring Israel to give up a nuclear weapons program. He and Henry Kissinger thought little of treaties, including the NPT. (In 1,200 pages of his memoirs, Kissinger mentions the NPT once in passing.)[43] By the summer of 1974, however, India had detonated a nuclear device, and Kissinger, Nixon, and then president Ford did begin to reassess their lax approach to nonproliferation.

As a presidential candidate, Nixon issued reservations about the NPT, stating in September 1968 that the United States should negotiate a nonproliferation treaty but that he was "concerned about some of the provisions of the treaty."[44] Three days later, he endorsed the treaty but ordered the Senate to "delay ratification until the intentions of the Soviet Union toward Czechoslovakia and other nations could be assessed."[45] Once in office, Nixon's National Security Council Review Group examined the pros and cons of the treaty. In a declassified document from January 1969, the review group leaders wrote to the vice president, secretary of state, secretary of defense, and director of emergency preparedness about a meeting the next day on the NPT. They reported that they had to cast their net wide to come up with arguments against the treaty and that the con arguments presented were not necessarily representative of the people in the group.[46] Though Nixon and Kissinger were both skeptical of pursuing nonproliferation through a treaty regime, the administration's NPT review group recognized the same proliferation concerns as the Johnson administration, writing one reason to ratify the treaty: "The further spread of nuclear weapons would increase the threat of nuclear war. . . . Not only would there be the danger that some countries would prove irresponsible in the use or control of nuclear weapons, but there would be an increasing number of nuclear confrontations that could rapidly escalate local conflicts with increased danger of great power involvement."[47] According to one former US official, Nixon and Kissinger were ready to dispense with the NPT altogether, but Spurgeon Keeny Jr. and Morton Halperin persuaded the two to move forward with the treaty.[48] In an internal White House debate that was largely hidden from the State Department, Keeny and Halperin convinced Nixon and Kissinger that it would hurt US credibility to reject the treaty after the United States had led the negotiations.[49]

Having agreed to support the treaty's ratification, the Nixon administration was not interested in pressuring other states to join the treaty. In the memo introducing the NPT review group's pros-and-cons document, Kissinger told the president that a US decision to ratify did not require a decision on pressing other countries to ratify, as the Johnson administration had. The review group's final report reveals the extent of previous US efforts to promote the NPT: "For the last two years the US has carried on a continuing diplomatic campaign to persuade key countries first to support and then to sign the NPT. The key countries that have not yet signed the treaty include the FRG [West Germany], Israel, India, Pakistan, Switzerland, Japan, Australia, Brazil, Argentina, South Africa, and Italy. The reasons for these countries' reservations or objections to the treaty vary widely. The extent to which we can influence these countries or be responsive to their concerns also varies widely from country to country."[50]

The presidential memo alerting high-level officials of the US decision to ratify the treaty stated, "There should be no efforts by the US Government to pressure other nations . . . to follow suit. The Government . . . should reflect a tone of optimism that other countries will sign or ratify, while clearly dissociating itself from any plan to bring pressure on these countries to sign or ratify."[51] This statement may seem similar to the one made in the Johnson administration telling diplomats to avoid the appearance of pressuring other states, but the difference is that the bureaucracy in the Johnson administration and Johnson himself did promote the treaty; Nixon did not. As George Quester wrote in the early 1970s, "While one can of course make a mistake in applying too much 'hard sell' for something like the Nonproliferation Treaty, the Nixon Administration, at times seemed to be applying no salesmanship at all."[52]

On February 5, 1969, Nixon recommended US ratification of the treaty in a special message to the Senate, despite the continued Soviet presence in Czechoslovakia. After a round of hearings, the Senate approved the NPT 83–15 on March 13, 1969. A year later, in March 1970, the NPT entered into force. Following entry into force, the IAEA had to establish a model agreement for the NPT's safeguards requirement. As expected by a theory placing the United States at the forefront of global nuclear nonproliferation leadership, US leaders led the drafting of the resolution within the IAEA to begin work on agreement. The US representatives to the IAEA at the time reported back to Washington, "As a result of intensive consultation prior to and during the Board we were able to get the support of the Soviets for the text of our resolution."[53] Notably, the United States and not the Soviet Union drafted what would become the safeguards standard for all NPT members.

Nixon achieved NPT ratification, but he was not a strong advocate for the treaty,[54] and nonproliferation was a lower priority for him than any other US president during the nuclear age. Instead, Nixon approached nonproliferation through the US dominance of the nuclear energy market.[55] But in this period, other states, including the Soviet Union, Belgium, France, Germany, and Canada, were developing advanced nuclear energy expertise, so Nixon sought more US research into nuclear technology, especially related to breeder reactors.[56] A market-based nonproliferation policy in the early 1970s was doomed to fail, as the United States lost its industry edge soon after.[57] US market share was decreasing at the same time the 1973–1974 global oil crisis convinced more and more states to pursue nuclear energy, providing many opportunities for foreign technology suppliers.

Declassified memos and records of conversations inside the Nixon White House reveal Nixon's true feelings about the NPT. When complaining that the State Department was trying to link the Strategic Arms Limitation Talks (SALT) to the commitments made in the NPT, Nixon complained to Kissinger, "It has not a goddamn thing to do with the Nonproliferation Treaty, and the Test Ban treaty and all the rest. This is nuts. I wasn't for those things, not really." Kissinger responds, "I wasn't either." Then Nixon admits, "I supported nonproliferation because we had to." This conversation between Nixon and Kissinger concludes with Nixon adding, "Let me say, the State [Department] always puts that Nonproliferation Treaty in there. You know what the reason is? The State Department bureaucracy considers that to be theirs, Henry. Really, it's a selfish damn thing. Now listen, the Nonproliferation Treaty has nothing to do with the security of the United States of America. You know very well."[58] Despite minimal support at the highest level of government, bureaucrats from the State Department and ACDA sought ways to make the NPT more universal. In May 1969, the National Security Council Undersecretaries Committee met to discuss progress on the NPT and set out different strategies for persuading states including India, Pakistan, Argentina, Japan, Australia, and the EURATOM countries to join.[59] Promoting ENDC membership for Argentina and Japan was one means considered to help with securing NPT ratification by those states.[60] A telegram to all US diplomatic posts in December 1969, penned by the ACDA and approved by the secretary of state, encouraged all states to ratify as soon as constitutionally or politically possible. It provided an up-to-date status report on all states and noted that recent signatures from Germany and Switzerland might help convince other states to ratify. The telegram also asked for the United Kingdom's help in achieving ratification in its former colonies.[61] In another example, in February 1970, the ACDA sent a telegram to embassies of key non-NPT member states hoping to at least secure their signature on the treaty before it entered force in the next month. The memo about the telegram stated that the document "makes the point in a low-key way to avoid an impression of arm-twisting."[62]

In 1969, President Nixon did focus on the problem of one state's status as a non-NPT member: Israel. By 1968, the United States believed Israel would soon have nuclear weapons. Nixon asked for a study of options, one of which was using the sale of F-4 Phantom aircraft to induce Israeli commitment to the NPT.[63] Nixon rejected this option, in part because canceling the sale would raise questions that could lead to revealing the Israeli nuclear program. On September 26, 1969, Nixon met with Israeli prime minister Golda

Meir. The details of the meeting remain classified, but it is believed that in this meeting Nixon agreed to stop pressuring Israel to give up its nuclear weapon program and join the NPT, and Meir agreed that Israel would not publicly disclose its possession of nuclear weapons or test its capability.[64] This agreement thus enshrined Israel's policy of nuclear opacity, which continues to this day. While the United States did not stop the Israeli program, it did what it could to ensure the program did not provoke proliferation by Israel's neighbors.

On May 18, 1974, an event on the other side of the world caused the Nixon administration to change its lax attitude toward nuclear proliferation. India had conducted a so-called peaceful nuclear explosion (PNE), taking most of the world by surprise. Afterward, the US intelligence community prepared a Special National Intelligence Estimate, "Prospects for Further Proliferation of Nuclear Weapons."[65] It is notable that this type of comprehensive estimate had not been prepared since the 1960s, before Nixon was president.[66] Nonetheless, an Indian explosion was not a complete surprise to the US government. In the 1960s, the Johnson administration had engaged diplomatically with Indian leaders in an attempt to persuade them not to develop nuclear weapons, especially after China's 1964 nuclear test. As part of these efforts, the Johnson administration shared intelligence with Indian leaders about China's nuclear weapons program.[67] In 1967, Indian leaders requested US and Soviet security guarantees; the Indians were seeking protection against the Chinese nuclear program. The Soviets rejected this idea, and the Johnson administration did not think a US-only guarantee would be effective in curtailing domestic pressure for an Indian nuclear weapons program.[68] The Johnson administration decided to focus on attaining Indian adherence to the NPT, but India would have little interest in the treaty.[69] By the Nixon administration, the National Security Council circulated a document in September 1972 stating that the Indian nuclear program "provides the capability of conducting a test on short notice," and later noting the "US ability to influence events is marginal, [*sic*] Indeed, given the present poor state of Indo-US relations, an overly visible US effort could hasten, rather than delay, the day India explodes a nuclear device."[70] US-Indian relations were difficult in the 1960s but were especially strained after the United States sided with Pakistan during the Indo-Pakistani War of 1971. The United States cut off aid to India in 1971, calling it the "main aggressor" in the conflict.[71] Thus, in the lead-up to the Indian test in 1974, the United States had very little leverage over India to influence its nuclear activities.

Five days after the Indian nuclear test, on May 23, Nixon had Kissinger request a study of US nonproliferation policy and the NPT. "It should consider specifically whether the United States should press for renewed support for the treaty by those now party to it and accession to the treaty by those not yet signators [*sic*], and if so how and to what extent."[72] The Indian test caused sufficient anxiety in Nixon that he was willing to consider granting greater support to NPT promotion. Nixon had never been very interested in nonproliferation, but it is true he was also preoccupied with other pressing priorities, especially Vietnam, SALT, and the growing Watergate scandal. The Indian PNE brought nonproliferation to the forefront.

A month after the Indian test, a meeting on the NPT indicated the change in nonproliferation policy from Johnson to Nixon in terms of NPT promotion. At Undersecretary Joseph J. Sisco's State Department Principals' and Regionals' Staff Meeting on June 24, Sisco mentioned having just been at a meeting to discuss the US approach to nonproliferation. On the topic of that meeting, he asked, "Should this government renew what was its historic policy—and we have really eased off under this administration since 1969—we used to take the lead in trying to get adherence to the NPT. I think we have relaxed on this in fashion I frankly have not liked."[73]

In July 1974, administration leaders were still grappling with US nonproliferation policy. A background paper for a July 11 meeting led by Secretary Kissinger made statements including "it is still in the US interest to abate the further spread of nuclear weapons" and "we still have time and influence to deter states from acquiring independent nuclear explosive capabilities."[74] The background paper goes on to note that additional nuclear weapons acquisitions by other states would lead to "diminishing American influence."[75] On the NPT, it states, "A US policy of relative indifference to the NPT at this juncture can seriously damage our ability to cope with nonproliferation, while reinvigorated efforts on the treaty's behalf could help prevent such serious damage and help compensate for the set-back represented by the Indian explosion."[76] Top Nixon officials were beginning to realize that the nonproliferation regime was weakened when it did not have full US support.

US government papers and reports in response to the Indian nuclear explosion appear to have finally convinced Nixon of the importance of nonproliferation and perhaps even the NPT as one means of promoting this policy goal. As the Watergate scandal enveloped Nixon, an August 2 memo called for the United States to take increased action on the NPT in the months leading up to the 1975 NPT Review Conference.[77] This strategy document to the secretary from the director of the ACDA listed the two most important steps as "approach[ing] crucial NPT holdouts at high levels with a view toward securing early ratification decisions" and "find[ing] some visible ways in which preferential treatment can be given to NPT parties such as areas as the availability of commercial nuclear facilities, fuel, and technological support, and possibly, credit terms."[78]

As Nixon resigned and Ford became president in those difficult weeks of August 1974, the Nixon administration seemed to be evolving on its position toward nuclear nonproliferation, or at least Kissinger was. But for most of its tenure, the Nixon administration was at odds with the argument that dominant states care most about nuclear nonproliferation and will expend resources preventing the emergence of new nuclear states. The efforts of the Johnson administration meant that the ACDA and State Department continued to promote the NPT while serving under Nixon, but these officials were hampered by the limited support they received from the highest levels of government. Since Nixon, US presidents may have approached the problem in different ways, but by and large they all promoted nuclear nonproliferation and the NPT. Why was Nixon different?

Joseph Nye writes that, ironically, after the NPT was established, both the Soviet Union and the United States decreased their focus on nuclear nonproliferation. The Soviets had been primarily concerned with West German proliferation, and the NPT made this contingency much less likely. Nye writes that Nixon thought Johnson had prioritized nonproliferation at the expense of its allies. He sought to be less "dogmatic" in his approach.[79]

Nixon and Kissinger were leading the United States through a period in which the country was perceived to be in decline—the military budget was decreasing, and the president and his closest adviser expected the world to become increasingly multipolar. A confidential draft of the president's 1972 *Annual Review of Foreign Policy* (which unsurprisingly did not mention nuclear nonproliferation) discussed Europe's economic growth and noted that relations "are now essentially multipolar."[80] In this geopolitical context, it perhaps makes sense for Nixon to have thought it might not be so bad if certain allies, such as Japan, proliferated. Consistent with a theory of US hegemonic leadership, a perception of waning global reach could change a leader's calculus about the dangers of horizontal proliferation. As Gavin writes of this period, "US prospects in the global order were dim."[81] US power was in decline, and the United States might need its allies to take on a greater burden of global security. James Cameron and Or Rabinowitz's characterization of Nixon's approach to nonproliferation as "benign neglect and geopolitical pragmatism" is consistent with this explanation.[82]

Most of the states that Nixon considered potential proliferators were US friends or allies. Nixon encouraged French proliferation, did not discourage Israeli proliferation, and refused to pressure the Japanese to join the NPT.[83] Though this was still a unique perspective among most American presidents of the nuclear age, Nixon was perhaps hoping to improve the US global position through this limited proliferation by American friends. It was the Indian nuclear explosion, an unexpected development from a less developed, nonaligned nation, that led his administration to reconsider its laissez-faire approach. According to one former ACDA diplomat, it was the May 1974 explosion that truly initiated modern US nonproliferation policy.[84]

Perception of US decline is not the only plausible reason why Nixon was different than other US presidents when it came to promoting nuclear nonproliferation. After all, President Carter also led the United States during a period of assumed US decline and strongly promoted the NPT. Nixon and Kissinger were also unique among US executives in seeing great political utility for nuclear weapons. Nixon wished for nuclear superiority for the United States, taking the lesson of the Cuban Missile Crisis to be that the United States prevailed because of its superior arsenal.[85] He bemoaned the parity between the two superpowers he inherited, preferring to possess a destabilizing first strike to the strategic stability advocated by arms controllers.[86] Nixon and Kissinger wanted new and more flexible war plans, recognizing that Kennedy and Secretary of Defense Robert McNamara's "flexible response" was primarily a rhetorical shift from Eisenhower's "massive retaliation."[87] Nixon sought more nuclear weapons options—this would allow more opportunities to exploit nuclear risk but also was expected to enhance nuclear deterrence by providing greater credibility of use.

Moreover, the attitude with which Nixon approached nuclear weapons suggests that he did not perceive the same danger from nuclear use as other presidents did. Many scholars have chronicled Nixon's "madman" theory, in which engaging in risky and threatening nuclear actions would bring about US goals by making the adversary perceive that Nixon might be just crazy enough to use nuclear weapons.[88] In October 1969, Nixon ordered a secret nuclear alert to convince the Soviets and the North Vietnamese that the United States might consider nuclear use in the Vietnam War.[89] Similarly, four years later in October 1973, Kissinger ordered the nuclear alert level raised to DEFCON 3 to warn the Soviets against intervening unilaterally in the Middle East.[90]

Perhaps it was because Nixon and Kissinger saw great utility in nuclear weapons that they were skeptical that a treaty, or US nonproliferation policy generally, would be able to convince nations to forgo nuclear weapons. In some cases, horizontal proliferation might even improve US security by bolstering its allies and friends at a time of perceived US decline. Furthermore, his flippant remarks about nuclear weapons suggest he did not see them as a grave danger the way Johnson did or as Carter and Reagan would in the future. In taking this approach, the Nixon administration lost an opportunity to strengthen the NPT in the early years of the treaty. His presidency illustrates how the nuclear nonproliferation regime can be weakened when the United States does not prioritize it.

Ford

President Ford increased US promotion of nuclear nonproliferation relative to Nixon, though he still would not give it the same priority as subsequent administrations. Toward the end of his presidency, the election of 1976 and his opponent's emphasis on nonproliferation led Ford to focus attention on this area.

Initially, President Ford supported Nixon's market-based approach to nonproliferation. But the recently concluded sale of eight West German reactors and reprocessing technology to Brazil, a non-NPT member, had illustrated the limits of such a policy in a world of alternative nuclear suppliers. US leaders attempted to pressure Bonn to seek assurances from Brasília that the reactors would only be used for peaceful purposes.[91] The Ford administration did find success a few years later in pressuring the French and South Koreans not to move forward with a sale of reprocessing equipment to Seoul. A study prepared by the Office of International Security Affairs in the Department of Defense in early 1976 reads: "We have strongly indicated to the Koreans that we will not support this effort and that acquisition of such a plant could affect our fundamental relationship. We have told the ROKs in the firmest terms that we will withdraw US support for their nuclear energy programs if they continue ahead with plans to acquire the reprocessing plant. There are signs that the Koreans will change their position. It is essential to persist."[92]

By the end of his presidency, Ford acknowledged that the United States was no longer the dominant supplier it once was: "While we remain a leader in this field, other suppliers have come to share the international market. . . . In short, for nearly a decade the US has not had a monopoly on nuclear technology. Although our role is large, we are not able to control worldwide nuclear development."[93]

The major nonproliferation achievement of the Ford administration was in creating and promoting an adaptation to the regime: the Nuclear Suppliers Group (NSG). Henry Kissinger, "in great secrecy," initiated the creation of what was first called the London Suppliers Group to coordinate export guidelines in reaction to India's PNE, which was developed using technology provided by the United States and Canada.[94] In the fall of 1974, US leaders began consulting with the Soviets about a suppliers' conference as well as issues related to the security of nuclear material.[95] According to a declassified State Department telegram sent to the US Embassy in Moscow in October 1974, "The Soviets have also recognized the need for more international attention to physical security of weapons grade materials, although they have indicated they would not take the initiative on this subject."[96] Here we see a stark difference between the United States and the Soviet Union—through the nuclear age, the US bureaucracy was consistently taking initiative to improve global nonproliferation policy, while the Soviets were happy to go along.

At the first meeting on nuclear supply in London in 1975, the United States gathered together the major nuclear exporters: Great Britain, France, the Soviet Union, West Germany, Canada, and Japan. At a second meeting a year later, additional supplier states joined, including Belgium, East Germany, Sweden, Czechoslovakia, the Netherlands, and Italy. Next, Switzerland and Poland joined and acceded to the guidelines. In some ways, this effort was a continuation of a market-based solution to nuclear proliferation, only this time the United States was coordinating all nuclear exporters to establish limits and guidelines on potentially dangerous supply. In the context of the oil crisis, renewed global interest in nuclear energy, and an increasingly competitive nuclear marketplace, the United States needed to persuade the other exporters to come to consensus on supply rules, lest it be the only supplier making such demands on its customers.[97] The formation of the NSG was one of the first ways in which US leaders recognized a weakness of the nascent nuclear nonproliferation regime and established an institutional fix. While an ad hoc body of NPT nuclear exporters, the Zangger Committee, had previously established a list of exports that required safeguards, the organization had many faults, including that it did not include France, which was a nonmember of the NPT at the time.[98] The NSG, in contrast, included all major exporters. It was a controversial adaptation however, as many nonnuclear NPT members saw the NSG as undermining portions of articles 3 and 4 of the NPT. In the NPT, nonnuclear states are promised that "nothing in this Treaty shall be interpreted as affecting the inalienable right of all the Parties to the Treaty to develop research, production and use of nuclear energy for peaceful purposes without discrimination."[99] Nonetheless, the NSG has been successful in setting standards that mitigate the transfer of the technologies most suited to nuclear weapons development.

Another significant nonproliferation effort in this period was conducting the first NPT Review Conference. The treaty declared the parties would meet five years after entry into force "in order to review the operation of this Treaty with a view to assuring that the purposes of the Preamble and the provisions of the Treaty are being realized."[100] The United States proposed that members should come together in Preparatory Committee meetings prior to the Review Conference to establish the rules and procedures for the meeting. The Preparatory Committee met three times. During these meetings, it was evident that NPT members held divergent ideas about the purpose of the review. Nonnuclear weapon states wanted to use the review to highlight the lack of disarmament progress by the nuclear weapon states in the treaty. The positions of the three depository states were coordinated through the United States, and the British took on the leadership of these tasks. According to one history of the preparations for the 1975 NPT Review Conference, "The Soviet Union kept a low profile . . . and never brought any drafts to the negotiating table of the depositaries."[101] The Soviets would become more cooperative as the process moved forward, with the three depository nations consulting before each meeting. NPT parties were able to agree on the leadership of the Review Conference, the committee structure for the meeting, the decisions-making rules, and rules on participation in the conference ahead of time through the Preparatory Committee meetings. Fifty-eight of ninety-five NPT members participated in the conference.[102] Though the Review Conference was deeply divided over disarmament progress, a theme that would continue at all subsequent conferences, the members were able to come up with a consensus Final Declaration under the leadership of conference president and Swedish diplomat Inga Thorsson two hours after the meeting was supposed to conclude. US representatives reported back after the meeting that "the idea of a second review conference in 1980 received widespread support (other than from the Soviet Bloc)."[103] Indeed, this Soviet attitude appears consistent with George Quester's description of Soviet behavior in the 1970s: "At the meetings of the IAEA, or in the NPT Review Conference, or at sessions of the U.N. General Assembly on the proliferation topic, it apparently has been typical for Soviet delegations to compare strategy and tactics very closely with the United States, indeed sometimes (where the Soviet delegation had not the time to make its own assessment) even letting the American delegation decide how some other nation's proposals should be responded to."[104]

The year 1976 saw increased interest in nonproliferation in both Congress and the White House. In June 1976, Congress passed the Symington Amendment, which prohibited the United States from providing economic and military assistance to any country that imported nuclear reprocessing or enrichment technology. That same summer, a committee convened by the White House and led by the deputy administrator of the Energy Research and Development Commission, Robert W. Fri, spent six weeks studying the nation's nuclear policy, resulting in a fifty-page report.[105] Ford accepted the report's recommendations and announced a number of policy changes and initiatives in an October 1976 speech held five days before the presidential election. Ford felt added political pressure to address this issue at a time when his opponent, Jimmy Carter, was making nonproliferation one of his signature issues. In his speech Ford explained, "In short, for nearly a decade the U.S. has not had a monopoly on nuclear technology. . . . Action to control proliferation must be an international cooperative effort involving many nations, including both nuclear suppliers and customers."[106] He touted his administration's leadership in developing the NSG and said all states should understand "that the US believes that nonproliferation objectives must take precedence over economic and energy benefits if a choice must be made."[107] Ford called for a hold on the development of a new US reprocessing plant until "uncertainties are resolved."[108] He also asked all nuclear suppliers to be very cautious when considering the supply of reprocessing or enrichment technology, delaying the supply of such technology for at least three years. He announced that US supply would be based on a number of considerations, with adherence to the NPT or maintenance of full-scope safeguards listed as favorable factors.

In sum, the Ford administration emphasized nonproliferation more than its predecessor. During this period, the Fri Report echoed the previous findings of the 1965 Gilpatric Report that the United States should prioritize nuclear nonproliferation. Ford's renewed attention on nuclear proliferation stemmed from several sources: the Indian nuclear test, South Korea and Taiwan seeking reprocessing technology, and electoral pressure based on Carter's emphasis on proliferation during the 1976 election. In leading the creation of the NSG, the Ford administration created a significant adaptation to the regime.

Carter

President Carter had unique experience when it came to nuclear technology—he was a nuclear engineer who had worked on nuclear submarines and participated in the 1952 evaluation of a nuclear meltdown at Chalk River, a reactor in Ontario, Canada. Carter zealously championed nonproliferation during his presidency, especially by promoting the NPT. Though he found some success, his methods sometimes frustrated and alienated American industry as well as US friends and allies. Carter is remembered for being a staunch proponent of nuclear nonproliferation, but two of his major efforts began during the last years of the Ford administration: curtailing the US fast breeder reactor program and creating more stringent export legislation for nuclear technology.

Nuclear nonproliferation was one of Carter's primary campaign issues. In a speech in September 1976, Carter announced that as president he would stop the development of the Barnwell reprocessing plant in South Carolina, then under construction, until it was safe and necessary and would only allow its operation if it were on a multinational basis.[109] Carter historians Burton I. Kaufman and Scott Kaufman connect Carter's emphasis on nuclear nonproliferation to his commitment to morality and human rights as well as the potential for the spread of nuclear weapons to undermine US power. They write, "Nuclear proliferation and the spread of atomic weapons posed their own threats to human life. Additionally, the spread of nuclear arms endangered US security by giving enemy states and possibly even terrorists, access to atomic weaponry."[110] In his inaugural address, he promised, "We will move this year a step toward [our] ultimate goal—the elimination of all nuclear weapons from this Earth."[111]

At times, Carter failed in his attempts to pressure states regarding the acquisition of sensitive nuclear technology. In February 1977, Carter asked German chancellor Helmut Schmidt to halt a $4.7 billion sale of nuclear technology, including enrichment and reprocessing facilities, to Brazil because the technology could be used to make nuclear weapons.[112] The German chancellor refused to budge. Carter also upset Tokyo by asking the government to stop building a reprocessing plant at Tokai Mura, part of their national nuclear power generation program. Carter was again concerned that reprocessed material could be made into nuclear bombs. If Japan engaged in reprocessing, other states might follow its example. Like Schmidt, Prime Minister Takeo Fukuda refused Carter's pleas. Carter eventually backed down in both cases, though he did succeed in convincing France not to sell a reprocessing plant to Pakistan.

On April 7, 1977, the administration announced its new nonproliferation policy.[113] Carter declared the United States would no longer reprocess nuclear fuel. Reprocessing nuclear fuel is one avenue for developing weapons-grade plutonium, and therefore Carter wanted to set a global example by no longer engaging in this practice. He also canceled the US breeder reactor research program, previously delayed by President Ford, because breeder reactors produce more plutonium than they use and thus are considered a major proliferation threat. He pledged that US facilities would increase production of enriched uranium, so the United States would be a steady source of supply. Carter also announced his administration would convene an international forum to study alternative fuel cycles that would generate power while limiting proliferation risks. Over fifty states would participate in the International Fuel Cycle Evaluation (INFCE) effort over three years, but no revolutionary alternative fuel cycle was found.

On April 27, 1977, Carter sent a bill to Congress with his nuclear nonproliferation plan. His bill called for stricter export rules but was a bit less severe than a bill under consideration in Congress, where nonproliferation was also a high priority.[114] In 1978, members of Congress passed, by a wide margin, the Nuclear Nonproliferation Act of 1978. The final bill, signed in March 1978, went further in its restrictions than Carter had requested.[115] The nuclear industry largely opposed the act, which required more stringent guidelines than the NSG required for US nuclear exports. To be eligible for nuclear cooperation with the United States, states had to accept IAEA full-scope safeguards on all nuclear facilities and not manufacture or acquire any nuclear explosive devices. If current contracts did not comply with these rules, they had to be renegotiated or terminated.

Nuclear technology suppliers in both the United States and abroad were angered by the new US policies. At home, the policies meant the US nuclear industry was less competitive because it was limited in the technology it could sell. Abroad, allies and partners were suspicious that these policies were meant to help US industry at their expense. They thought the United States was trying to curtail and stigmatize technology they were developing to maintain both an advantage in nuclear sales and in energy development. The United States was wealthier than many other nations in terms of its energy resources, and trying to stop breeder reactors seemed to indicate other states could not "catch up" with the United States in energy production.

While some US allies were upset by Carter's nonproliferation efforts, they did agree to continue working together as nuclear suppliers to set rules for reducing the risks of nuclear technology transfers. By September 1977, the fifteen members of the NSG, originally convened by Kissinger, agreed to guidelines for future sales of nuclear technology. They required supplier states to seek assurances from buyers that materials and technologies would not be used for nuclear explosive devices, that material would be protected against theft or sabotage, that imported facilities and materials would be under IAEA safeguards, and that the same rules would apply if the materials or technology were sold to another country. If there were a suspected violation, the supplier states would meet and consider sanctions. The United States and some critics of this agreement would have preferred that supplier nations agree to require full-scope safeguards on states receiving their exports—which would mean inspection of a nation's entire nuclear infrastructure—but they were unable to find agreement. By 1978, the suppliers agreed to language that was published by the IAEA in INFCIRC/254, which became known as the "trigger list." Items on the list could only be exported if certain IAEA safeguards were in place. The NSG did not reconvene again until 1991 in the aftermath of revelations about the Iraqi nuclear program.

Carter faced a major nonproliferation challenge in the summer of 1977, when the Soviets reported to US officials that South Africa appeared to be preparing a nuclear test site in the Kalahari Desert.[116] Two years before, the Ford administration had cut off the supply of US fuel to South African reactors, due to congressional concerns about potential weapons proliferation.[117] The US intelligence community confirmed the nuclear test preparations, and the Carter administration issued a threat, telling the South African government that any test would jeopardize relations with the United States and the "Western Powers."[118] The South African government denied having a nuclear weapons program, and the US government tried to persuade it to join the NPT. To encourage NPT membership, the United States promised fuel for South Africa's nuclear reactors if they were under IAEA safeguards. Carter continued to push South Africa to join the NPT for the rest of his administration using low-cost diplomacy, high-cost diplomacy, positive inducements, and coercion, but his gambits failed, and it would later be revealed that South Africa went on to build six nuclear weapons.[119]

While South Africa continued its clandestine nuclear weapons program, Carter did find success in persuading other countries to join the NPT. He engaged in direct diplomatic outreach (i.e., high-cost diplomacy) to several states, including writing letters to the leaders of Indonesia and Sri Lanka, asking them to ratify the NPT. A 1980 Government Accounting Office report gave President Carter and Vice President Mondale credit for bringing both states into the NPT.[120] During the course of Carter's presidency, the regime was strengthened through the expansion of NPT membership to Indonesia, Sri Lanka, Bangladesh, Tuvalu, Cape Verde, St. Lucia, the People's Democratic Republic of Yemen, Barbados, and Turkey.[121]

While the United States was using diplomacy and other tactics to expand NPT membership, the Soviet Union appears to have taken a more laissez-faire approach. Warsaw Pact states quickly joined the NPT—likely illustrating that their foreign policy decisions were heavily influenced by Moscow. But other states in the Soviet orbit were not so quick to join. For example, North Korea, Algeria, and Cuba, all Soviet satellite states, joined the treaty quite late, in 1986, 1995, and 2002, reflecting either limited influence of the Soviets or a lack of interest in persuading these states to join the NPT.

The contrast in Soviet word and deed regarding the promotion of the NPT was explained by Gloria Duffy in the late 1970s:

> Soviet advocacy of the NPT—virtually every Soviet article on nuclear exports and nonproliferation begins with an exhortation to nonsigners to accede to the Treaty and to signers to uphold its principles—might be understood in terms of a more general Soviet foreign policy impulse. Perhaps the genesis of vigorous support for the NPT has its roots in a bureaucratic system which cranks out such prefaces automatically. Perhaps it is a Soviet effort to avoid real constraints on its own actions by offering recognizably toothless but rhetorically appealing arms control proposals. Or possibly Soviet leaders wish to gain recognition for Moscow by reminding the world that the NPT was signed in Moscow, partly at Soviet prodding. Advocacy of the NPT . . . is part of the same foreign policy impulse that gives rise to periodic Soviet proposals for General and Complete Disarmament at the United Nations. Such proposals seem to serve some abstract, internal function for the Soviet political system, but they should not be taken seriously as an indication of Soviet nonproliferation.[122]

Carter prioritized nonproliferation, and the NPT specifically, more than most US presidents, and yet he was not immune to the conflicting pressures faced by hegemonic powers when two policy priorities conflict. The president's nonproliferation policies had to take a back seat to more immediate strategic necessities when the United States reestablished previously cut-off military and economic aid to Pakistan after the Soviet invasion of Afghanistan.[123] In a secret January 1980 memo, National Security Adviser Zbigniew Brzezinski passed on advice from the US ambassador to Afghanistan that the United States still had "considerable time to work on nonproliferation in Pakistan" and should thus "first deal vigorously" with the Soviet threat.[124]

The Carter administration was more effective in curtailing the nuclear ambitions of another potential proliferator: Taiwan. The Taiwanese pursued nuclear activities through the 1970s that indicated an interest in a bomb program. After pressure from both the Ford and Carter administrations, Taiwan stopped its program. The Carter administration insisted that Taiwan dismantle some of its nuclear facilities and convert its heavy water reactor.[125]

President Carter was unique in his nuclear knowledge among US presidents. He prioritized nuclear nonproliferation from the beginning of his election campaign through the end of his presidency. He made many policy changes to promote nonproliferation and took personal interest in the NPT. His policies frustrated allies and industry leaders, and he faced many difficulties accomplishing his nonproliferation goals, and yet he succeeded in expanding membership of the NPT.

Reagan

President Reagan's approach to nuclear nonproliferation evolved from his candidacy through his two administrations. As a presidential candidate, he argued that the United States should not prevent other states from developing nuclear weapons, saying, "I just don't think it's any of our business."[126] Within an hour of making that statement—and likely after meeting with campaign advisers—Reagan announced he supported American efforts to stop proliferation but did not think the United States could necessarily succeed in doing so. In the first year of his presidency, when asked about the US role in preventing proliferation, he told reporters: "We're opposed to the proliferation of nuclear weapons and do everything in our power to prevent it."[127] A year later, he stated, "We must go at the matter of realistically reducing—if not totally eliminating the nuclear weapons—the threat to the world."[128] He would go on to talk about eliminating nuclear weapons more than 150 times during his presidency.[129] While the Reagan administration worked to expand membership in the NPT, Reagan's tenure also illustrates that when the United States focuses on other priorities, the regime weakens. In this case, focusing on the Cold War competition led the United States to expend less effort countering the evolving Pakistani nuclear weapons program.

Reagan established his nuclear nonproliferation policy in contrast to Carter's approach. In one of his first policy speeches on nonproliferation as the newly elected president, and in National Security Decision Directive 6, he declared that many allies and friends had in recent years "lost confidence in the ability of our nation to recognize their needs," and thus "we must reestablish this Nation as a predictable and reliable partner for peaceful nuclear cooperation under adequate safeguards."[130] Like Nixon, Reagan saw the nuclear supply market as an important means of US nonproliferation influence.[131] He preferred to evaluate states on a case-by-case basis, distinguishing between risky and nonrisky states by allowing the sales of nuclear technology in areas "where it does not constitute a proliferation risk."[132] His nonproliferation speech illustrated an important understanding about nuclear weapons proliferation when he argued the United States should focus efforts on reducing the global instability and insecurity that caused proliferation in first place. This argument was highlighted by ACDA director Eugene V. Rostow, who "insisted that arms control efforts must be accompanied by greater attention to problems of world order."[133] On the Reagan administration's approach, one historian has concluded, "It was evident that if the new administration shares the overall nonproliferation objectives of the Carter administration, it intends to use significantly different means in trying to attain them."[134]

On June 10, 1983, the ambassador-at-large for nuclear affairs Richard T. Kennedy reported to Secretary of State George Shultz on the Reagan administration's nuclear nonproliferation successes to date, listing twenty different accomplishments including policy statements, the promotion of nuclear safeguards, bilateral consultations, and improved export controls. Most of the details of the memo remain classified, but on the topic of the NPT, the memo reads, "The Administration has conducted and is continuing an active diplomatic initiative to encourage countries not yet party to the Treaty to ratify this central instrument of the international nonproliferation regime. In 1981, Egypt became a party. During 1982, four additional states became parties—Papua New Guinea, Nauru, the Socialist Republic of Vietnam, and Uganda."[135]

The administration had proliferation failures as well. Pakistan continued to receive military and economic aid for its support of the US effort against the Soviets in Afghanistan, despite concern that it was building a nuclear weapons program. According to government officials, during this period attempts to curtail the Israeli nuclear program were "essentially dropped from the US agenda of significant issues to be addressed in bilateral negotiations with Israel."[136] The administration also entered into a nuclear cooperation deal with China in 1983 when China joined the IAEA. Critics of the deal noted China's nuclear assistance to Pakistan and Argentina, two states of proliferation concern. The Reagan administration also favored Iraq in the eight-year Iran-Iraq War, turning a "blind eye" to many of the nuclear-related procurements made by the Iraqis during these years.[137]

According to the historian Walton L. Brown, US nonproliferation policy shifted from "vigilance" under Carter to "laxness" under Reagan, in part because the all-consuming nature of the competition with the Soviets took priority over other potential threats.[138] In the nuclear realm, President Reagan was concerned foremost with pursuing arms control with the Soviets. He successfully negotiated the Intermediate Range Nuclear Forces (INF) Treaty in 1987, eliminating for the first time an entire class of nuclear weapons, and then spent four years pursuing Strategic Arms Reduction Treaty (START) negotiations. Reagan saw the connection between pursuing nuclear arms control with the Soviets and stemming global nuclear weapons proliferation. In talking points he wrote himself for a September 1984 meeting with Soviet foreign minister Andrei Gromyko, in which he was trying to revive arms control talks, Reagan writes, "We both know that other countries have turned to nuclear weapons and more are quietly working to achieve that goal. The danger of such proliferation is the possibility of accidental war brought on by neither of us but triggering a conflict that could ultimately involve us both. But what if we who have the power to destroy the world should join in saving it? If we can reach agreement on reducing and ultimately eliminating these weapons, we could persuade the rest of the world to join us in doing away with all such weapons."[139]

As Reagan sought to contrast his nuclear nonproliferation policies with those of his predecessor, he focused on becoming a reliable technology supplier and at times supported allies at the expense of nonproliferation goals. But as expected, Reagan spoke positively about the NPT and promoted its universality. His major contribution to reducing nuclear risk, however, came in the form of significant bilateral nuclear reductions with the Soviets, the most lasting nuclear legacy of his two administrations.

Bush

President George H. W. Bush initially maintained Reagan's nonproliferation policies, but like administrations before him, external events raised the specter of dangerous nuclear proliferation, and his policy focus shifted. It was during Bush's administration that a National Security Staff member was assigned full-time to the issue of nonproliferation. Bush's prioritization of this issue resulted in several successes during his administration.

The break-up of the Soviet Union in 1991 left three new nuclear weapons possessing states in its wake; Kazakhstan, Belarus, and Ukraine retained Soviet nuclear weapons on their sovereign territory. Concern for the future of these weapons, along with Soviet fissile material and nuclear scientists, brought about an unprecedented nuclear nonproliferation effort by both the Bush and Clinton administrations. In exchange for giving up nuclear weapons and material, the three states received compensation, aid, and assistance from the United States and Russia.[140] Ukraine delayed the deal to relinquish its weapons, however, and the Clinton administration would take up that challenge.

As the Soviet Union was breaking apart, several prominent academics and policy officials raised alarm about the security of Soviet nuclear weapons and materials. The Senate overwhelmingly passed the Soviet Nuclear Threat Reduction Act in November 1991, sponsored by Sam Nunn and Richard Lugar, providing $400 million for dismantling nuclear and chemical weapons. The program would come to be known at the Cooperative Threat Reduction Program, or the Nunn-Lugar Program.

Another challenge surfaced after the 1991 Gulf War, when dismantling the previously unknown Iraqi nuclear weapons program became one of Bush's priorities. Ten years earlier, in 1981, Israel had bombed Iraq's Osiraq nuclear reactor in an attempt to delay or stop an Iraqi nuclear weapons program.[141] In the years after the attack, the Iraqis established a clandestine uranium-enrichment program with technology from foreign manufacturers.[142] Discovered only after the Gulf War, the Iraqi nuclear weapons program, like the Indian explosion in 1974, was a significant wake-up call. According to Brown, Iraq's clandestine program reflected the "consequences of complacent nonproliferation policies during the 1980s."[143] This discovery also illustrated the weakness of Comprehensive Safeguards Agreements with the IAEA, the safeguards agreement required for NPT members. Iraq had been inspected consistently for ten years by IAEA officials, who, per the safeguards agreement, were only allowed to inspect locations declared by the Iraqi government. Clever diversionary tactics and subterfuge allowed the Iraqi program to proceed quite literally under the noses of inspectors.[144] After the Gulf War, in a process detailed in chapter 5, the international community and the IAEA, led by the United States, began developing a new safeguards agreement, the Model Additional Protocol, which became available to states in 1997. The new agreement—a significant adaptation to the nuclear nonproliferation regime—allows inspectors to access all nuclear-related locations from mines to waste sites within a state and permits short-notice inspections.[145]

President Bush had several other nuclear nonproliferation successes during his tenure. France and China joined the NPT as nuclear weapon states in the early 1990s. China joined the NPT for several reasons, including the treaty's increasing universality—a trend to which US diplomacy was paramount. In addition, the United States had made NPT accession a condition of finalizing a bilateral Nuclear Cooperation Agreement with the Chinese and presented the NPT as a means to improve China's chances of the United States extending Most Favored Nation trade status to Beijing.[146] South Africa, the target of crippling sanctions against its apartheid regime, transitioned to a more democratic state, gave up its nuclear weapons program, and joined the NPT.[147] After the Bush administration removed nuclear weapons from South Korea in 1991, North and South Korea signed a joint declaration in which they agreed (among other things) not to manufacture, store, or possess nuclear weapons on their soil.[148] At home, President Bush ordered the unilateral reduction of thousands of US nuclear weapons through his Presidential Nuclear Initiatives, overseeing one of the largest reductions of nuclear weapons in history.[149]

Clinton

After his election in November 1992, president-elect Clinton was asked about his foreign policy priorities for his first one hundred days. He listed "working hard to stop the proliferation of weapons of mass destruction—nuclear, biological and chemical," along with pursuing further nuclear reductions with the Russians, continuing the Middle East peace process, and promoting the global economy.[150]

From the Bush administration, President Clinton inherited the challenge of promoting NPT accession in the three former Soviet states with nuclear weapons. Ukraine was the biggest obstacle, as the other two inheritor states, Kazakhstan and Belarus, did not claim ownership of the weapons on their soil and assured the United States they would give them up.[151] As the Bush presidency ended, the Ukrainian parliament delayed its promised ratification of START and the NPT and held out for increased US aid and security guarantees.[152] Clinton resolved this impasse with a trilateral deal inked in January 1994 in which Ukraine received approximately $175 million worth of aid and security assurances from the United States.[153] In November 1994, the Ukrainian parliament voted by an overwhelming majority to ratify the NPT after receiving assurances from the United States, United Kingdom, France, and Russia of promises of payment for their nuclear weapons and additional aid.[154]

The next proliferation challenge for the Clinton administration was the suspected nuclear weapons program in the Democratic Peoples' Republic of Korea (DPRK). In 1993, the DPRK announced its intention to withdraw from the NPT, and the state's efforts to hide its nuclear activities from IAEA inspectors suggested that another NPT member had developed a clandestine nuclear program while under IAEA safeguards.[155] After sixteen months of negotiations led by US ambassador Robert Gallucci, the United States and the DPRK agreed to a deal, the Agreed Framework, under which the DPRK would freeze its nuclear program and the United States and allies, including South Korea and Japan, would provide two electricity-producing light water reactors and annual shipments of $50 million worth of fuel oil. In addition, the United States and North Korea would begin low-level diplomatic relations.[156] After five years, the North Koreans would allow inspectors at two of its suspected nuclear weapons sites. This deal would ultimately fall apart under the next administration, though it did delay the North Korean program for several years.

Two final nonproliferation accomplishments of the Clinton administration were both treaty related: negotiating the CTBT and securing indefinite extension of the NPT. In 1993, President Clinton took a meaningful step toward ending global nuclear testing when he moved forward in seeking negotiations of a nuclear test ban. President Bush had established a US moratorium on testing in 1992, and Clinton extended this moratorium in 1993.[157] A test ban treaty had long been sought by many members of the NPT, especially the nonnuclear weapon states, and this was a step toward achieving this goal.[158] With support of the United States and other nuclear members of the NPT, negotiations for a CTBT began in 1993. The CTBT opened for signature in September 1996. The United States was the first nation to sign.[159]

Securing the 1995 indefinite extension of the NPT, as detailed in chapter 4, was the greatest of Clinton's nonproliferation accomplishments during his tenure. As stipulated in the treaty, after twenty-five years the treaty members would convene to decide on the future of the treaty. The treaty could be extended for another discrete period or become extended indefinitely. From the beginning, the United States sought unconditional indefinite extension and stridently pursued this goal, ultimately finding success.[160]

Clinton's two terms ended on a pessimistic note for US nonproliferation leadership. In May 1998, India conducted five nuclear tests, and Pakistan followed with six tests of its own, confirming for the first time that it was a nuclear-weapons-capable state.[161] In 1999, the Clinton administration failed to make the case for the CTBT, and its ratification was rejected 51–48, a rare failure of an arms control treaty in the US Senate.[162]

Bush

During his tenure, George W. Bush focused significant, high-level attention on the threat of nuclear proliferation. The devastating attacks on September 11, 2001, soon led to fears of terrorists accessing nuclear material; together with an emphasis on "rogue states" with nuclear weapons, these threats became the basis for Bush's proliferation policies. How the Bush administration approached these challenges, however, left many nuclear experts arguing Bush undermined the nonproliferation regime.

The Bush administration set out its policy for addressing the threat of nuclear proliferation in its 2002 *National Strategy to Combat Weapons of Mass Destruction*.[163] Whereas previous presidents feared additional nuclear proliferation because the United States would lose freedom of action or could be brought into small wars that could become nuclear, now a greater emphasis was placed on weapons and material in the hands of terrorists or rogue state leaders.[164] The document presented a three-pillared approach to addressing the threat of weapons of mass destruction (WMD): counterproliferation, nonproliferation, and consequence management. Though the plan did indicate support for strengthening the NPT, the IAEA, and the Model Additional Protocol as part of its nonproliferation pillar, in practice, the first pillar, counterproliferation, received greater emphasis for its connection to preemptive military action.[165]

The Bush years were marked by important nonproliferation successes. Libya gave up its rudimentary nuclear weapons program in 2003 after lengthy secret diplomacy by Great Britain and the United States.[166] A more meaningful accomplishment, perhaps, was the dismantlement of the A. Q. Khan network beginning in January 2004. For years, the father of the Pakistani centrifuge uranium-enrichment program had developed a global network of salespeople and manufacturers to sell centrifuge designs, technology, and nuclear weapons plans. Known customers of the Khan network include Iran, Iraq, and Libya.[167]

These successes were matched by more proliferation challenges in two of the states Bush labeled the "Axis of Evil" in his 2002 State of the Union Address.[168] In 2002, an Iranian opposition group in the United States revealed Iran's secret enrichment facility at Natanz, leading to IAEA inspections and a report to the IAEA Board of Governors in 2003.[169] Thus began over a decade of conflict between Iran and the United States and its allies over Iran's nuclear program and its intentions. In addition, by 2003, the Agreed Framework with the DPRK, negotiated during the Clinton administration, had broken down. The end of the deal has been a source for partisan finger-pointing, but the US intelligence community had determined by the early 2000s that the North Koreans were pursuing uranium enrichment in violation of the agreement.[170] In the same year, the Kim Jong-il regime announced that it was exercising its right under the NPT's article 10 to withdraw from the treaty, the only state to have done so.[171]

Because of the focus on the nexus between terrorism and weapons of mass destruction, and concerns about rogue states and global proliferation networks, President Bush undertook a number of new initiatives. In May 2003, the administration created the Proliferation Security Initiative (PSI), a global effort to encourage the interdiction of shipments of illicit WMD and WMD-related material around the world. This is a voluntary, informal organization by which states sign on to a Statement of Interdiction Principles; it is not a formal treaty organization.[172] With over one hundred state signatories, the PSI has a great deal of support, but it has not been without critics, including those who argue the interdictions are against the Law of the Sea.[173]

In another initiative, the Bush administration developed and pushed for UN Security Council Resolution 1540, which passed in 2004 and mandated that all UN states strengthen their export laws to prevent the spread of nuclear materials and technology and to keep these items out of the hands of terrorists.[174] The means of enforcing this mandate—through the UN Security Council (UNSC)—led some UN members to complain about the origins of the resolution and resist the mandate to make what could be expensive and time-consuming changes to their legal and regulatory codes.[175] And yet the UNSC has reaffirmed 1540 in multiple resolutions since 2004, and cooperation has increased in the intervening years. Within the UN context, the Bush administration also promoted the International Convention for the Suppression of Acts of Nuclear Terrorism, a 2005 treaty that aims to have members prevent nuclear terrorism and prosecute those involved in such activity. Finally, the Bush administration founded the Global Initiative to Combat Nuclear Terrorism (GICNT) in 2006, a voluntary partnership of states cochaired by the United States and Russia, which seeks to prevent, detect, and respond to nuclear terrorism.

The PSI, UNSC Resolution 1540, and GICNT illustrate initiatives that were US directed and distinct from the formal, institutionalized agreements within the nuclear nonproliferation regime. Indeed, while the Bush administration prioritized countering the threat of proliferation, the administration was criticized by the traditional arms-control and nonproliferation communities for its distain for the traditional means of pursing arms control and disarmament. In what many nonproliferation experts saw as a blow to the NPT, the Bush administration pursued a nuclear cooperation deal with India, permitting India to import US nuclear technology despite its nonmembership in the NPT. One of the benefits of joining the NPT for nonnuclear states is access to peaceful nuclear technology as spelled out in article 4. Critics argued that if non-NPT states received similar benefits, it weakened the NPT regime.[176] To make this exception for India, the United States had to exert great pressure on members of the NSG, as they had to agree to a waiver. The Bush administration argued that this effort helped nuclear nonproliferation by bringing a significant portion of India's nuclear infrastructure under IAEA safeguards.

One key aspect of the extant nonproliferation regime championed by the Bush administration was the Model Additional Protocol (AP), the more stringent IAEA safeguards agreement developed in the late 1990s. In a 2004 speech, President Bush announced a new policy that US nuclear supply would be conditional on a state's adoption of the AP.[177] He also sent the AP to the Senate for advice and consent, improving the US position to press other states to conclude the safeguards agreement.

The Bush administration also pursued a different approach to arms control than its predecessors. Bush was comfortable with unilateral US reductions, while Russian president Vladimir Putin pushed for a more traditional bilateral arms control agreement. The two parties signed the Treaty between the United States of America and the Russian Federation on Strategic Offensive Reductions (SORT) in June 2003. The deal cut the US arsenal in half, a major reduction. SORT was different from previous bilateral arms control agreements in several ways. It was a brief treaty—fewer than five hundred words, compared to the tome that was START—requiring the United States and Russia to bring deployed nuclear weapons to the treaty limits of between 1,700 and 2,200 weapons on December 31, 2012. The treaty neither prohibited numbers from going up after that day nor prevented the powers from maintaining large stockpiles of nondeployed weapons. The treaty also lacked verification provisions, with each side relying on START until it expired, three years before the 2012 SORT limit date.[178] In short, the George W. Bush administration significantly reduced the US nuclear arsenal, but did so in a nontraditional manner.

The most controversial legacy of the Bush administration in general, and for nuclear nonproliferation in particular, was the 2003 war in Iraq, which was ostensibly fought to keep Saddam Hussein from threatening US interests with weapons of mass destruction.[179] The war led to the loss of thousands of American and Iraqi lives, incurred costs over a trillion dollars, destabilized the region, and brought about the rise of the Islamic State. This use of force had mixed effects on nuclear nonproliferation. As chapter 3 speculates, the war in Iraq likely pushed Cuba to join the NPT. The war may have also helped encourage Libya to move forward in giving up its nuclear program in 2003 and Iran to halt its weapons program for a period in the fall of 2003.

In contrast, the war likely persuaded North Korean leaders of the value of nuclear weapons in preventing the US from pursuing regime change in their country, as one of the other members of the Axis of Evil.

Obama

President Barack Obama sought to distance himself from some Bush administration nonproliferation policies, while he continued others. Both presidents cared deeply about the risks of nuclear proliferation and nuclear terrorism, but Obama differentiated his presidency by reaffirming the US commitment to multilateral mechanisms for addressing proliferation, like the NPT, while also continuing to promote participation in the PSI, the global implementation of UNSC Resolution 1540, and the GICNT.

In Prague in April 2009, President Obama stated the United States would "take concrete steps toward a world without nuclear weapons."[180] This speech helped create a more positive atmosphere for the 2010 NPT Review Conference, where the parties to the NPT were able to come to consensus on a final document. The document was unique in incorporating action plans for each of the three pillars of the NPT, creating something of a scorecard to measure NPT progress.[181] One US effort at the conference attempted to convince other parties of the wisdom of strengthening the withdrawal clause of the NPT, with the idea that states should not go unpunished for using the treaty to import nuclear technology and pursue weapons programs, and then withdraw from the treaty (as the North Koreans did).[182] This effort continues the US pattern of US leaders, Democrat and Republican, seeking to innovate and alter the regime as weaknesses become apparent.

The fear of nuclear terrorism remained high during the presidential election of 2008. In his campaign, Barack Obama set the ambitious goal of securing all the world's nuclear material within four years.[183] One means of achieving this goal was leading a series of four Nuclear Security Summits, the first of which was held in Washington, DC, in 2010. In these summits, a selected group of approximately fifty states were invited to discuss the challenges of securing nuclear material. Though the content of the conferences was important, the major benefit of the summits has been the promises or "house gifts" offered by states to take specific steps such as giving up stocks of highly enriched uranium or passing more restrictive export laws. Though the goal of securing all the world's fissile material in four years proved overly ambitious, significant progress was made in securing nuclear material and improving security for such material.

The Obama administration also explicitly connected its commitment to bilateral strategic arms control with the Russians to its nuclear nonproliferation goals. With START expiring on December 3, 2009, the Obama administration worked quickly with its Russian counterparts to negotiate a new bilateral arms control treaty. The New START agreement entered into force in February 2011, limiting the United States and Russia to 1,550 deployed nuclear warheads, 700 deployed delivery vehicles, and 800 total deployed and nondeployed delivery vehicles by February 2018. New START was intended to be step one, as the US administration had plans for pursuing limits on so-called nonstrategic nuclear weapons, or tactical weapons, but a souring of US-Russian relations—including accusations of Russian cheating on the INF Treaty[184]—undermined this ambitious agenda.

At the end of his presidency, the Obama administration's nonproliferation agenda lost steam. There was little hope for CTBT ratification by the Senate; the 2015 NPT Review Conference ended without a consensus document; there was still nuclear material to secure; and the Russians showed little interest in continuing bilateral nuclear arms control talks. One bright spot for the Obama administration was concluding the Joint Comprehensive Plan of Action, popularly known as the Iran nuclear deal, in July 14, 2015.[185] After a long and painstaking diplomatic process, Iran and the UNSC's five permanent members plus Germany (P5 + 1) agreed to several provisions to limit their potential production of fissile and agreed to stringent inspections in exchange for reductions in economic sanctions.

Trump

As a presidential candidate, Trump criticized the Joint Comprehensive Plan of Action with Iran, and in May 2018, the United States pulled out of the deal. A year later, Iran began engaging in a series of actions that were prohibited under the agreement. Trump's other major nonproliferation challenge was addressing the DPRK's pursuit of nuclear weapons and missile technology under the Kim Jong-un regime. High-level summits between President Trump and Kim Jong-un in Singapore (2018) and Vietnam (2019) yielded little. The Trump administration did not extend the bilateral nuclear reduction treaty with Russia, New START, before leaving office. This lack of action, along with the loss of the INF Treaty in August 2019, seemed to signal an impending period without traditional bilateral arms control.

Finally, during the Trump administration, many nonnuclear states signed and ratified the Treaty on the Prohibition of Nuclear Weapons (TPNW). The NPT's nuclear weapon states continued to criticize this new treaty aimed at the complete disarmament of nuclear weapons. In the waning weeks of the Trump presidency, the United States sent a letter to parties of the TPNW requesting that they withdraw from the new treaty, arguing "we believe that you have made a strategic error and should withdraw your instrument of ratification or accession."[186] Nonetheless, the treaty received its fiftieth ratification in October, triggering entry into force of the TPNW on January 22, 2021, two days into the Biden administration.

Many are the ways in which the United States has served as the nuclear nonproliferation regime's architect since the beginning of the nuclear age. With the IAEA, the NPT, Comprehensive Safeguards Agreement, the NSG, the Model Additional Protocol, and UNSC Resolution 1540, among others, the United States led the world in creating, drafting, and promoting new elements of the regime. Several of these efforts were adaptations made to the regime after weaknesses became apparent. The foundation for this global leadership is in the vast US bureaucracy devoted to nonproliferation. US government officials working on nonproliferation across the interagency include personnel at the Departments of State, Defense, Commerce, Treasury, Energy; across the intelligence community; and formerly within the ACDA. The United States has also been the largest funder of the IAEA since its inception.[187] US resources devoted to promoting nuclear nonproliferation dwarf the efforts of all other states.

The story is not always simple, however, and the history summarized above also illustrates that when US administrations view nonproliferation as less important than other strategic goals, the regime will be weakened. The Nixon administration is the best example, but the Reagan administration also became less focused on Pakistani proliferation due to the Soviet threat in Afghanistan. At times, the US emphasis on nonproliferation diminished only to be reinvigorated. External events, such as India's 1974 nuclear explosion or revelations about Iraq's clandestine nuclear program in 1991, spurred renewed action. In addition, the means of addressing proliferation have varied over time and by administration. Some presidents preferred to address proliferation on a case-by-case basis, implicitly sending the message that some states are more trustworthy with nuclear technology than others. Some presidents attempted to rely primarily on US nuclear supply to address proliferation, while others relied more on the institutional mechanisms of the nuclear nonproliferation regime. Nonetheless, over each successive administration since the NPT entered into force, a legion of bureaucrats and diplomats continued to push the universalization of the treaty. In subsequent years, the United States expanded the regime with new initiatives to address weaknesses in the treaty. As one US official stated, the United States usually "writes the first draft and finances the effort."[188]

Conventional wisdom emphasizes the cooperation between the Soviet Union and the United States in terms of nuclear nonproliferation. As aspiring global hegemons during the Cold War, the adversaries shared a strategic interest in preventing the establishment of new nuclear weapon states. And yet the historical record indicates again and again that it was the United States that took the lead in promoting nonproliferation through multilateral, institutional means. The US and its ally the United Kingdom drafted the statute for the IAEA, and US officials drafted the first version of the IAEA safeguards agreement in the early 1970s. US leaders founded the Nuclear Suppliers Group and established the Preparatory Committee system for the NPT Review Conferences in the mid-1970s. After the Cold War, the United States continued to promote regime adaptation, providing leadership for establishing the Model Additional Protocol safeguards agreement in the 1990s, after revelations of Iraq's clandestine nuclear weapons program indicated significant weaknesses in the extant IAEA safeguards regime. Though the United States has not ratified the treaty, it was the Clinton administration's leadership (and capitulation to an idea other states had promoted for decades) that allowed the Comprehensive Test Ban Treaty negotiations to move forward in the mid-1990s. In addition, the United States expended the most energy in promoting the indefinite extension of the NPT in 1995. The Bush administration and Obama administration added informal elements to the regime, including the 2003 Proliferation Security Initiative (PSI), the GICNT, and the 2010–2016 Nuclear Security Summits. As stated by one former US official who worked on US nuclear nonproliferation efforts for decades during the Cold War, "We did not look to the Soviets for leadership or innovation."[189]

Table 2.1 Observable implications related to regime creation

Observable implication	*Examples*
1. The United States will lead global efforts to establish the elements of the global nuclear nonproliferation regime	• 1957 International Atomic Energy Agency (with the United Kingdom) • 1963 Limited Test Ban Treaty (with the Soviet Union and the United Kingdom) • 1968 Treaty on the Non-Proliferation of Nuclear Weapons (NPT) (with the Soviet Union) • 1971 IAEA Comprehensive Safeguards Agreement • 1975 Nuclear Suppliers Group • 1992 Revision of Nuclear Suppliers Group guidelines • 1995 Indefinite Extension of the NPT • 1996 Comprehensive Test Ban Treaty • 1997 Model Additional Protocol • 2003 Proliferation Security Initiative • 2004 UN Security Council Resolution 1540 • 2006 Global Initiative to Combat Nuclear Terrorism • 2009 Revision of Nuclear Suppliers Group rules
2. When US administrations believe that other strategic interests outweigh nonproliferation, the regime will be weakened	• Nixon administration disinterest in promoting the NPT • Failing to strongly counter Pakistan's nuclear program during the 1980s due to the war in Afghanistan • Failure to ratify the CTBT in 1999

The historical record also indicates that US leaders did more to universalize the NPT and safeguards agreements than the Soviets did. While the Soviet Union instructed the other Warsaw Pact states to quickly join the NPT, it did less to persuade many other states to join. For example, North Korea, Algeria, and Cuba, all Soviet satellite states, joined the treaty quite late, in 1986, 1995, and 2002, reflecting either limited influence of the Soviets or a lack of interest in persuading these states to join the NPT. Instead of promoting universalization of the regime by encouraging the states under its influence to ratify the NPT, the Soviet Union focused more on specific countries of proliferation concern. At the time the NPT was established, the Soviet Union was occupied with keeping West Germany free of nuclear weapons. In the 1970s, the Soviets expressed great concern to the United States over South Africa's nuclear program and its nonmembership in the NPT. Thus, the Soviet Union allowed US leaders to focus on universalization of the regime and regime maintenance while it focused on areas of particular strategic interest. It appears as though the Soviet Union may have been free riding on US devotion to the promotion and maintenance of the nuclear nonproliferation regime.

Though the Soviet Union cooperated with its adversary, the United States took the lead when it came to developing and promoting the nuclear nonproliferation regime. Because of US leadership in this area, the other states in the international system associated the nuclear nonproliferation regime with US global leadership and the postwar US ordering project. As a result, states' relationships to the broader US-led order are key factors in whether states join nuclear nonproliferation agreements and support regime adaptations and in how much work the United States must do to persuade them. Table 2.1 summarizes the findings from this chapter related to the regime-creation observable implications discussed in the previous chapter.

CHAPTER 3

Slow but Successful US Promotion of the NPT

Exploring the processes by which Japan, Indonesia, Egypt, and Cuba decided to join the NPT offers an opportunity to assess the three observable implications related to regime membership presented in chapter 1: the United States will promote universalization of the NPT and its subsidiary agreements through the use of its tools of influence; state decision-making about joining the NPT and its subsidiary agreements will reflect consideration of US attempts at influence; and decisions to adhere to or support nonproliferation regime elements will reflect embeddedness within the US-led order. While the alternative theories related to security, domestic politics, and fairness find some relevance, in each of the four cases, the actions of the United States were an important factor in the states' decisions to join the NPT and conclude their Comprehensive Safeguards Agreement with the IAEA, as required by the treaty.

As anticipated by a theory of regime adherence predicated on US leadership, US officials began promoting the NPT abroad even before the complete draft text was finalized. After three years of bilateral negotiations and consultations with allies, on August 24, 1967, the United States and the Soviet Union presented identical, though incomplete, drafts of the NPT to the United Nations' Eighteen Nation Committee on Disarmament (ENDC). The following day, the US State Department sent the draft treaty text to all of its embassies around the world via cable with talking points for meetings with foreign governments. In the classified cable, US diplomats were instructed to go to leaders at "the highest level deemed appropriate" and explain that the US government "attaches great importance" to concluding the NPT and achieving widespread support for the treaty.[1] The US campaign for the universalization of the NPT had officially begun, despite ongoing negotiations regarding the nuclear safeguards required for all nonnuclear signatories and the nuclear weapon states' commitment to nuclear disarmament. Over the next year, these issues would be finalized in article 3 and article 6 of the treaty. The text was adopted by the UN General Assembly in June 1968. On

July 1, fifty states, including the United States and the Soviet Union, signed the treaty. Later that day, the US State Department sent a cable to all diplomatic posts, listing the states that had signed, and asked diplomats to thank the signatory states "and urge ratification as soon as possible."[2]

Japan and the NPT

States highly embedded within the US-led order are expected to ratify the NPT sooner than other states. Indeed, highly embedded states Canada, Denmark, and Norway were among the first states to sign and ratify the NPT.[3] Japan was also a highly embedded state during the period of its NPT ratification based on several indicators. First and foremost, the United States provided for Japan's security. Japan's post–World War II constitution prohibits offensive military capability, and thus US protection became the basis of Japanese security. In 1951, the United States and Japan signed the Mutual Security Treaty, in which Japan granted the United States the right to maintain a military presence in Japan "so as to deter armed attack upon Japan."[4] In 1960, the two states signed the Treaty of Mutual Cooperation and Security, which committed the United States to defend Japan and provided for US bases and ports.[5] The United States affirmed its support for Japan during Prime Minster Eisaku Satō's term via the 1965 Satō-Johnson Joint Statement and further reaffirmed the security relationship with the 1967 Johnson-Satō Joint Communique.[6]

Beyond providing for its protection, helping the postwar Japanese economy thrive was a key US strategic goal.[7] The United States was especially accommodating toward Japan in terms of exports to the United States because it sought to prevent Japan from trading with communist countries. To bolster trade after the war, the United States provided aid to Southeast Asian nations that were then encouraged to buy Japanese products.[8] Postwar economic policies in Japan in tandem with US efforts to promote the Japanese economy were markedly successful; by 1968, Japan was the world's third-largest economy.[9] Trade would become a source of friction for the two allies at times during this period, however. Most significantly, a dispute over textiles during the Nixon administration resulted in the Japanese capitulating to US demands and a postwar low for US popularity among Japanese citizens.[10] Despite these kinds of hiccups, Japanese exports to the United States grew an average of 10 percent annually from the mid-1950s through the 1970s.[11] In addition, the United States provided significant aid to Japan from 1946 to 1966 to help rebuild the country. A majority of the aid came in the form of military assistance, training, and education.[12]

Drafted by senior US army officials with input from local legal experts and officials, the postwar Japanese constitution established a parliamentary system enshrining liberal political values, including provisions protecting civil rights. From 1952 to the present, Japan has received a 10 Polity score, indicating the highest possible democracy measure.[13] According to Freedom House, Japan has been coded as "free" since the organization's assessment of political rights and civil liberties began in 1973.[14] UN General Assembly voting data from 1968 to 1976 indicate that Japan voted in alignment with the US-led order on a broad number of multilateral issues, scoring well above the global average on this measure.[15]

During the period in which the Japanese government deliberated over joining the NPT, 1968 to 1976, Japan was highly embedded in the US-led order, and thus we would anticipate that Tokyo would have joined the NPT quickly with other states in this category. Instead, Japan signed the treaty in 1970 but then delayed its ratification; it concluded its Comprehensive Safeguards Agreement with the IAEA in 1975 and ratified the NPT in 1976. While Japan's decision-making process illustrates US persuasion through the use of its tools of influence and reflects consideration of US attempts at influence, Japan is an outlier case due to its high embeddedness and slow adherence. Multiple factors led to a slower ratification than we would expect: mixed signals from US administrations about the importance of Japanese ratification during this period, concerns about how the NPT might affect the nuclear energy industry, and the influence of political factions concerned with Japanese national security on one side and superpower disarmament on the other. The case illustrates that at times US leaders tried to influence Japanese decision-makers with positive inducements, a tool that is more likely to be employed with weakly and moderately embedded states. The Japanese case also speaks to the difficulty of persuading states to join the NPT in the early days of the treaty. Nonetheless, this case demonstrates the key role of the United States in the eventual Japanese decision to ratify the treaty.

When developing the NPT, the United States and the Soviet Union were especially concerned about Japan's proliferation potential due to its advanced industrial status and its proximity to two nuclear neighbors. US leaders consulted widely with Japanese leaders over the course of drafting and negotiating the treaty. Japanese negotiators advocated for additions to the text, including the establishment of the five-year reviews.[16] Declassified documents from the ACDA, State Department, and White House during the Johnson administration reveal almost constant discussion with Japanese officials to allay their concerns about the treaty.[17] Because Japan was not a member of the ENDC, the body responsible for negotiating the treaty after the United States and USSR submitted draft texts, Japanese officials relied on bilateral communication with the United States to offer their input and express their concerns.

By 1967, American leaders interpreted widespread political and public support for the NPT in Japan, but some reservations existed. Concerns about the inequality enshrined in the treaty, the preservation of a potential Japanese nuclear option, and the need to avoid disadvantaging the nascent Japanese nuclear industry were consistent topics in bilateral discussions with US leaders.[18]

Japan did not adhere as would be expected for a highly embedded state after initial US requests seeking universal NPT participation, such as the diplomatic meetings that resulted from State Department cables sent in the summer of 1967. A telegram to the Tokyo embassy from the ACDA in November 1967 during the Johnson administration indicated a desire by some US officials to step up pressure on the Japanese government: "While obviously we cannot trade our providing security assurances as a reward for adherence to NPT, we nevertheless need whatever bargaining leverage we can muster to induce broad adherence."[19]

High-cost diplomacy also failed to persuade Japanese leaders in these early years. With the 1967 Johnson-Satō Joint Communique reaffirming the security relationship between the two nations, the United States tried to ensure Japan's signature of the NPT through the agreement's text.[20] The text reads in part, "[Japanese and US leadership] took note of the importance of reinforcing the authority and role of the United Nations as a peace keeping organization, of promoting arms control and a reduction of the arms race, including the early conclusion of a Nonproliferation Treaty."[21] The inclusion of the NPT in the 1967 text did not bring about swift ratification by the Diet, however, in part because of mixed signals from the United States after Johnson left office. Lower-level US officials pushed for Japan's ratification, while the Nixon White House equivocated on the issue.

Japanese vice foreign minister Nobuhiko Ushiba made it clear in September 1968 that Japan would not ratify the NPT until the US Senate did. Japanese leaders said they planned to submit the treaty to the Diet in December 1968, but it would be "embarrassing for Japan to become embroiled in a debate over the treaty against a backdrop of US indecision."[22] Though the Johnson administration negotiated and championed the treaty, the president was unable to achieve US ratification during his last months in office. President-elect Richard Nixon did not support holding a special session of Congress for a ratification vote in the lame-duck period after his November 1968 win, thus delaying US action at a time when the Japanese government appeared ready to support ratification. In a counterfactual case in which the Johnson administration achieved US ratification, it appears possible Japan could have followed shortly thereafter, and the expectation that a highly embedded state would join the treaty after low-cost diplomatic outreach would find support. Instead, Nixon delayed the US NPT vote. In subsequent years, Nixon did not promote the treaty as Johnson had. As detailed below, the delay in Japanese ratification until 1976 can in part be explained by the reduction in high-level US interest in the NPT when the Nixon administration came to power. Japanese leaders perceived that the United States no longer cared about their NPT ratification for much of the early 1970s.

Without clear US support for the treaty, NPT detractors gained prominence and the treaty became much less popular in Japan among the government and the public in the late 1960s and early 1970s. Nuclear industry leaders and some government officials thought the NPT and its required safeguards could hurt Japan's civilian nuclear industry, an important development for a state with significant energy needs. In a 1967 conversation between Japanese foreign minister Takeo Miki and secretary of state Dean Rusk, Miki reminded the secretary that Japan required 100 million tons of oil annually, almost all of which was imported. As a result, Japan planned to become a "great power in the peaceful use of nuclear energy and the NPT must not prevent this."[23] In November 1967, American diplomats in Japan reported that many in Japan's nuclear industry "wish that NPT would go away."[24] Japanese officials expressed concerns about industrial espionage, lost time due to compliance with safeguards, and restraints on building new nuclear infrastructure.[25] US officials reported that there were some in Japan who wanted to reserve the nuclear option but that most of the treaty criticisms stemmed from the nuclear industry. Voices opposed to the NPT gained prominence in the following years, with the scholar George Quester recounting in 1970, "Almost no one in Japan is at all enthusiastic about NPT. All opposition parties have taken stands criticizing the treaty. A significant part of the governing Liberal Democratic Party [LDP] is also quietly unhappy about the treaty. Public opinion, to the extent that it is aware of the issue, is negative. So also is business and Japan's major newspapers."[26] During the Nixon administration, these detractors were not targeted with any high-cost US diplomatic actions to counter their concerns.

Tokyo's reluctance to ratify continued as the NPT's entry into force loomed in 1970. Once the treaty entered into force based on ratification by the three depository states (the United States, USSR, and the United Kingdom) and forty additional states, Japan would no longer be able to join through the two-step process of signature and ratification and would only be able join through the single step of accession. The Japanese government asked the United States if an exception could be made, so they would be able to take the lesser step of signing the treaty even after entry into force. This abnormal treaty procedure required approval by all three treaty depositories. When US officials asked their British counterparts about an exception for Japan, they rejected the idea.[27] Seeing that the window would soon close on the opportunity to sign only, Japan signed the NPT in February 1970. With its signature, the Japanese government set out three conditions for future ratification: progress on nuclear disarmament, the provision of security for the nonnuclear weapon states, and equality in the nuclear energy field.[28]

In the following years, with the absence of a strong message from US president Nixon favoring Japanese ratification, Tokyo had little incentive to ratify a treaty that was unpopular among so many of its constituents. ACDA and State Department officials continued to encourage Japanese leaders to ratify the treaty during the Nixon years, but they found minimal cooperation from the president and his adviser Henry Kissinger. Lower-level US officials implored Kissinger to make a statement on the importance of Japanese NPT ratification when he visited the country in 1972. The ACDA acting director wrote to Kissinger in April that year, noting the assumption among Japanese leaders that the United States cared little about their NPT ratification: "The specific need for such a reaffirmation of support by you in Japan is pointed up both by recent Japanese press articles and persistent reports from diplomatic sources that the Japanese are under the impression that the US is no longer particularly interested in their adherence to the NPT. They cite the absence of any mention of the NPT in the Nixon-Satō talks and in the President's 1972 Foreign Policy Report. This impression is being exploited by the Japanese opponents of the treaty."[29]

In June 1972, Undersecretary of State for Political Affairs U. Alexis Johnson made a similar request to Kissinger about his upcoming trip to Japan.[30] Press coverage of the trip, however, indicates Kissinger did not make a public statement on the NPT to Japanese audiences.[31] In a conversation with President Nixon after the trip, Kissinger complained, "On my trip to Japan, the State Department was bugging the daylights out of me and I was getting briefing papers, letters, planted questions, if I would publicly support the Nonproliferation Treaty in Japan and squeeze the Japanese government."[32] Nixon responded that he hoped Kissinger did not do this, and Kissinger assured him by saying, "I didn't. I sort of mumbled around where ever the ambassador was present. But I told Satō and Fukuda privately that what you said in San Clemente is our policy."[33] Kissinger was referring to a meeting in San Clemente, California, in January of that year in which Prime Minister Satō asked Nixon if the Japanese government should proceed toward NPT ratification. Nixon reportedly told the prime minister, "Each nation should handle this problem in the light of its own circumstances. It is not a matter for us to decide and we respect the right of each nation to decide for itself in the light of its own desires. The United States . . . is not exerting pressure. In fact . . . Japan might take its time and thus keep any potential enemy concerned." Then Nixon quickly asked Satō to "forget the preceding remark."[34] Not only did Nixon refrain from urging Satō to seek NPT ratification, he suggested that Japan might want to avoid ratification to make their adversaries think they could be pursuing nuclear weapons!

This theme was evident again during Prime Minister Kakuei Tanaka's trip to the White House in the summer of 1973. Over two days, the leaders discussed a broad range of security and economic issues. On the first day, Nixon acknowledged that Japan would not develop nuclear weapons, even though it could have them, and proceeded to refer to Japan as a political "pygmy" three times. The president appeared to be pushing Tanaka to commit to Japan taking on a more militarized role in the world, as Nixon explained at the time: "His own fundamental view is that an economic giant cannot remain a political pygmy, which is contrary to the laws of nature. An economic giant, he stressed, could never remain a political pygmy. The time for decision is now, but not in the form of a treaty or policy decisions about security forces. He said that we need to know, as a friend, what a forward-looking leader like the Prime Minister sees as the role Japan will play in the world."[35] Notably, President Nixon never mentioned the NPT in this conversation, in which nuclear weapons and atomic energy were discussed several times. Instead, he seemed to prod Japanese leaders into considering a bomb program.

Nixon's actions surrounding the NPT were directly at odds with the efforts of his ACDA and State Department at the time; these officials regularly expressed their concerns about Nixon and Kissinger's reticence regarding Japanese ratification. A January 1973 State Department memo from Executive Secretary Theodore L. Eliot to Kissinger expressed alarm that NPT progress was slowing and that key states, including Japan, had made no recent progress toward ratification. He wrote "despite repeated references by United States' officials to our full support for broad adherence to the Treaty, Japanese officials continue to indicate that they are not convinced of this because of the lack of a high-level US statement on the subject."[36] After the prime minister's meeting with Nixon in the summer of 1973, they would have remained unconvinced.

Despite the lack of clarity coming from the US government, Japanese officials explored the implications of joining the NPT. They were especially eager to ensure that their nuclear industry received similar treatment to its European competitors in terms of the frequency of inspections under their safeguards agreement.[37] In several conversations with their IAEA and US counterparts, Japanese officials stated that they sought an arrangement equal to EURATOM's safeguards agreement.[38] European nations had established the European Atomic Energy Community (EURATOM) in a 1957 treaty. The 1973 Comprehensive Safeguards Agreement between EURATOM and the IAEA took into account the European agency's long-standing role in monitoring Europe's nuclear facilities. Under that agreement, European inspectors would check the information sent to the IAEA and carry out inspections with the agency. EURATOM's inspection activities meant that the IAEA could reduce its man-hours in Europe. A breakthrough for Japanese NPT ratification occurred in late 1973 when the Japanese government announced that, based upon ongoing negotiations with the IAEA, they were satisfied they could achieve a fair safeguards agreement. This was a crucial development for Japan's NPT ratification. To achieve this sense of parity with EURATOM, Japan eventually set up its own domestic inspectorate in April 1977, which cooperates with the IAEA.[39]

At the point in December 1973 when the Japanese government was convinced it would not be disadvantaged by its NPT safeguards agreement, the Tanaka government thought it could pursue NPT ratification.[40] It would take another two and a half years to achieve ratification, however, as the government continued to be uncertain about US preferences and battled with domestic opponents of the treaty. During this period, Prime Minster Tanaka was replaced, and in December 1974, Takeo Miki became prime minister. In this position, Miki worked tirelessly to achieve NPT ratification. He had long shown favorability toward the treaty even when public opinion soured on the treaty in the late 1960s and early 1970s.[41]

To achieve Japanese NPT ratification, three distinct hurdles had to be overcome: convincing all Japanese leaders of the US interest in its ratification, achieving the support of Japan's nuclear energy industry, and persuading the hawkish faction of the LDP to approve the treaty. The latter two obstacles relate to the domestic political economy and security theories; however, consistent with expectations of a regime adherence theory based on US leadership, the United States was involved in addressing each of these obstacles.

US INTEREST IN NPT RATIFICATION

Even after the Tanaka government's December 1973 announcement that it would begin preparations for NPT ratification, the Nixon administration continued its ambivalence about promoting the treaty in Japan. In a May 1974 meeting between US and Japanese delegations at the White House, the participants discussed the Indian nuclear test that had occurred three days before. Nixon appeared to have been chastened somewhat by the unexpected nuclear explosion but still did not mention the NPT in his comments, saying that he "did not want to attempt to dictate to Japan on this matter but that, philosophically speaking, there will be an increasing danger of world-wide nuclear war if more and more nations acquire a nuclear capability. . . . Nations, whatever power they have, must reject the use of nuclear weapons."[42] A couple of months later, in a July 1974 discussion with the newly appointed US ambassador to Japan, Ambassador James Hodgson asked Nixon, "Another thing—are we serious about the NPT?" Nixon responded, "Go through the motions. This is our position, but you have seen the country. You know our position."[43] Nixon maintained this stance even as those at the State Department and ACDA continued to worry about the sustainability of the NPT after India's nuclear explosion if industrialized countries like Japan did not join soon. In a strategy meeting from August 1974, the ACDA director presented a classified document titled "Nonproliferation: Strategy and Action Program." This document identified Japan as a country whose ratification was "crucial" to "the continued viability of the treaty."[44] In a discussion of "Italy, Japan and others whose adherence to the NPT is especially important," the document states, "Japan appears to have new doubts both about our interest in their ratification and in whether the treaty will be commercially advantageous to Japan."[45] To combat this perception, the memo recommended high level démarches to Japan, indicating that NPT ratification would facilitate civilian nuclear cooperation, a clear example of an attempt to persuade the Japanese government with messages from high-level US officials and positive inducements. Within days of this July 31 meeting, Nixon had resigned and Gerald Ford became president.

Somewhat surprisingly, nuclear nonproliferation was listed prominently in the Nixon administration's transition binder for Gerald Ford. (Given Nixon's record on this issue, it is reasonable to suspect that the text was written by ACDA or State Department officials.) One nonproliferation policy goal is laid out as follows: "Support the Nonproliferation Treaty, particularly in the period leading up to the NPT Review Conference scheduled for May 1975, by working with other Treaty proponents to gain the adherence of non-parties, such as Japan and Italy, and by adding to the benefits which adherence bestows (e.g., improved credit terms for the purchase of nuclear materials and equipment)."[46] The Ford administration did not appear, however, to take this recommendation to heart.

President Ford visited Japan in November 1974, the first sitting American president to do so. Secretary Kissinger accompanied him. Ford appears to have continued with Nixon's NPT ambivalence toward Japan. According to declassified records on the two days of meetings with Japanese prime minister Tanaka, the NPT was not discussed. The only mention of the NPT in the declassified record occurs at a press conference in Japan on November 20, when Secretary Kissinger was asked by a journalist if the United States had received an explanation as to why the NPT had not yet been put before the Japanese Diet for ratification. Kissinger responded that this had not been explained and concluded by stating, "The United States favors the ratification of the nonproliferation treaty."[47] This otherwise bland statement was noteworthy, as ACDA officials and members of the State Department were unable to convince Kissinger to convey the same message during his previous visit to Japan in 1972.

Even with Kissinger's clear assertion of support for the NPT, the Japanese still perceived US hesitancy. After all, the NPT had been brought up by the press, and Japanese officials were not directly asked to join the treaty during the visit. Moreover, the joint US-Japanese statement following Ford and Kissinger's visit discussed the importance of nuclear nonproliferation but failed to mention the NPT: "The United States and Japan recognize the need for dedicated efforts by all countries . . . to prevent the further spread of nuclear weapons or other nuclear explosive devices while facilitating the expanded use of nuclear energy for peaceful purposes."[48] On this trip at least, Ford appeared to have maintained the Nixon administration's policy of not engaging in high-cost diplomacy regarding NPT ratification. A cable months later confirms that Japanese leaders noted this disinterest in promoting the treaty. A February 1975 cable to Kissinger from the US embassy in Tokyo reads, "Some key Japanese leaders feel they have never gotten a clear indication of our position. These leaders include Nakasone, who as SecGen is important in the LDP's decision making process. He has been interpreting your discussions with him last November as an indication that the US has no special interest in or concern over Japan's ratification."[49] A few days later, from Tokyo, Ambassador Hodgson practically begged US leaders to make a strong statement to the Japanese about the NPT.[50] The next day, the assistant secretary of state for East Asian and Pacific affairs and the director of policy planning reported that a Japanese deputy director of the UN Bureau, Noda, said that Japanese leaders were making the pitch for the NPT but that this effort would "benefit from a current high level expression of the importance that the US attaches to ratification. Noda was not acting under instructions of the [government of Japan] but we think it unlikely that he would have taken the initiative on this without at least the tacit approval of Vice Minister Togo."[51] The State Department officials went on to note, "Some Japanese leaders feel that they have never received a clear indication of your position on the NPT."[52] While the Japanese case of NPT ratification does not meet expectations for quick adherence of a highly embedded state, this evidence indicates that Japanese decision-making reflected consideration of US policy preferences. The problem for those seeking Japanese ratification was that US policy preferences were ambiguous during the Nixon years and the beginning of the Ford administration.

On February 25, 1975, years of pleading by US officials at the ACDA and State Department and the upcoming inaugural NPT Review Conference resulted in clear, high-level messaging from Kissinger. Deputy Secretary Robert S. Ingersoll requested a meeting on the NPT with the Japanese ambassador to the United States, Takeshi Yasukawa. In the meeting, Ingersoll told Yasukawa that Secretary Kissinger wanted to "make clear" the US position on Japanese ratification. Among several points on the importance of nuclear nonproliferation, the US diplomat said he hoped Japan could ratify the treaty in time to participate in the May 1975 NPT Review Conference. Ambassador Yasukawa said he would relay the US message to Tokyo "immediately" but asked the deputy secretary not to report their meeting as it might be construed by the Japanese press as "US pressure."[53] After February 1975, the United States reiterated the importance of Japan's ratification on several occasions through its embassy in Tokyo and in international forums.[54] Tokyo finally had a clear message from Washington, but two other hurdles to ratification remained.

JAPAN'S NUCLEAR ENERGY INDUSTRY

Securing support for the NPT from Japan's nuclear industry was another necessary step in achieving Japanese ratification. In addition to backing the Japanese government's efforts to negotiate a safeguards agreement on par with its European competitors, the United States also attempted to influence the Japanese nuclear industry by making clear that NPT membership would facilitate nuclear assistance from foreign suppliers. In early 1975, in the same month Kissinger made the US position on Japanese ratification clear, the Ford administration began using US nuclear supply as an inducement, a persuasive tool normally reserved for weakly and moderately embedded states. The US deputy secretary of state told Ambassador Yasukawa in February 1975 that ratification of the NPT would help Japan in seeking "cooperation on the peaceful uses of nuclear energy."[55] Soon after, Yoshitake Sasaki, the chairman of the Japanese Atomic Energy Commission and director of the Science and Technology Agency, and Hiromi Arisawa, chairman of the Japan Atomic Industrial Forum, publicly voiced support for the treaty.[56] With the support of industry secured, Prime Minister Miki announced in February 1975 that the NPT would be on the Diet's agenda that spring. By July, the American embassy in Tokyo reported, "Japan's industry and business community is concerned that failure to ratify the NPT will put Japan at a serious disadvantage in obtainin [*sic*] nuclear fuels and material."[57] Even with the backing of Japan's nuclear industry, Miki was unable to achieve ratification in the spring Diet session before the 1975 NPT Review Conference. The United States continued to push nuclear assistance as a reason for joining the NPT. In September 1975, Kissinger suggested that a US official should communicate to Japanese officials that joining the NPT would "simplify" the "US export of certain nuclear-related materials and equipment to Japan."[58] This message was underscored in the spring of 1976, when a visiting delegation from Canada "reportedly relayed the very real possibility of future nuclear fuel supply disadvantages for Japan if ratification of the treaty was not forthcoming."[59] In the US embassy's assessment following Japan's ratification, they attributed success in part to the argument that ratification was required to "guarantee access to nuclear supplies."[60]

PERSUADING LDP HAWKS

A final and security-related hurdle in obtaining Japanese NPT ratification was persuading several conservative LDP holdouts to go along with it. Some hawks in the party argued that Japan should reserve the right to pursue nuclear weapons in the future. One of Miki's tactics to address this concern was to seek additional security assurances from the United States. In March 1975, Ambassador Hodgson reported back to Washington that Miki would seek US assurances in order to get hardliners on board.[61] Miki then directed Foreign Minister Miyazawa to visit the United States and meet with Secretary Kissinger. In Japanese government meetings prior to the trip, leaders agreed that Miyazawa would ask the United States for "more clear-cut cooperation as to the national defense and security of Japan under the Japan-US Security Treaty structure."[62] If provided such assurances, Miki could mitigate the concerns of some of the treaty's critics on the right, enabling his government to pursue NPT ratification.[63]

On April 7, the Japanese government provided US officials with the language they would like to see in a statement from the United States. The language mostly comported with previous statements on the US-Japanese security relationship, except this time Japan requested the inclusion of a phrase indicating that the United States would "continue to provide Japan with a nuclear deterrent."[64] On the same day, Kissinger wrote to Ford, "Ratification of the NPT is being considered by the LDP. Detractors have posed as one condition for their support a reaffirmation of the US security tie to Japan. We can and should restate our commitment in standard terms without bluster."[65]

The Japanese foreign minister had a long and friendly meeting with Kissinger in Washington, DC, on April 11. In the afternoon, the conversation turned to the NPT. The foreign minister stated: "The question of security is important for Japan and I would like to talk about that. As you know we are considering ratification of the Nuclear Nonproliferation Treaty (NPT). The government will try to introduce the NPT at the current Diet session. In that connection the Diet will be discussing security. Your Ambassador and our people in Tokyo have achieved a meeting of the minds on how we can phrase a statement on the general security matter. I would like you to confirm or verify your agreement to that statement."[66]

Kissinger then agreed to the statement and said he would provide it as press guidance. It was soon released in the Japanese press: "(1) Both Japan and the US are of the judgment that the maintenance of the Security Treaty will be in the interests of both sides, when viewed from a long-range standpoint; (2) US nuclear war potential is an important deterrent power toward aggression against Japan from the outside; (3) the US attaches importance to its treaty obligations that it will take charge of the defense of Japan in case of its being attacked by nuclear or conventional weapons, and Japan will also continue to carry out its obligations based on the Treaty."[67]

This US commitment helped persuade some of the treaty's detractors in Japan. It also reiterated the importance US leaders attached to the NPT. On April 27, the Foreign Affairs Committee of the Lower House of the Japanese Diet approved the treaty.[68] Unfortunately for Prime Minister Miki, the US statement about its security commitment to Japan was not sufficient to bring all LDP skeptics on board and some continued to hinder the ratification process. On June 19, the Diet decided not to continue to pursue the NPT in the current session, as LDP objections and delays had left no time for the Upper House to consider the bill.[69]

In a demonstration of how the NPT decision fueled extreme nationalism among some Japanese citizens and in what may be the only case of NPT-induced violence, Prime Minister Miki was physically attacked in June by a member of an ultranationalist party over his support of the NPT. While awaiting the funeral ceremony for former prime minister Satō, a man punched

Miki twice in the face, knocking him over. The assault was broadcast live on television. The same day, a group of ultranationalists also attempted to open the gates of the US embassy in Tokyo. This faction opposed the treaty because of the inequality between the five official nuclear-weapons-possessing states and the nonnuclear states. After the assault, the US embassy reported back to Washington, the "obvious conclusion is the need for better security for him—and other VIP's—at least throughout this period of NPT discussion."[70]

When visiting President Ford at the White House in August 1975, Miki's planned talking points included conveying regret over his inability to achieve ratification in the recent Diet session.[71] Miki's regret indicates that by this point, Japan's leaders were aware that the United States sought its ratification. Miki and Ford held a joint press conference in which the prime minister expressed his intention to proceed with the necessary steps to bring about Japan's ratification of the NPT "at the earliest possible opportunity."[72] Both leaders "expressed their concern over the recent trend toward nuclear proliferation in the world, and agreed that Japan and the United States should participate positively in international efforts for the prevention of nuclear proliferation and the development of adequate safeguards."[73] Miki did not achieve Diet ratification that fall, as he was weakened as a leader with the opposition calling for the dissolution of his government. Miki had come to power suddenly after a corruption scandal engulfed the previous prime minister and only had a small faction of support when he came to office. His investigations into the corruption charges made him unpopular with many in his party. As a result of Miki's weak hold on power, the LDP decided not to take up any controversial bills that session. NPT ratification would have to wait until 1976.

Miki gave NPT ratification "top priority" in 1976, as concerns about nuclear supply were weighing more heavily on Japanese industry.[74] In May, during the first Diet session of 1976, the Upper House of the Diet approved the NPT.[75] Six years after signature, Japanese ratification was achieved under Miki's leadership. Afterward, the director of the Disarmament Division in the Japanese Foreign Ministry, Takanori Kazuhara, thanked members of the US embassy in Tokyo for their "moral support" through the process.[76]

With the nuclear industry's safeguards concerns met, the US promises of nuclear supply with ratification made clear (along with concerns about loss of supply without it), and most conservatives on board after Miki secured additional US security guarantees, the Diet was able to ratify the NPT. Ultimately, the Japanese government "believed that refusing to ratify the NPT was unthinkable due to the rift it would cause with the United States."[77] The United States provided too much of importance to Japan; division over the NPT was not worth harming the relationship or jeopardizing civilian nuclear cooperation. Indeed, after Japanese NPT ratification in 1976, Prime Minister Miki met with President Ford and told him, "Now that Japan has ratified the NPT, Mr. President, I wish to request the continued cooperation of the United States in Japan's development of the peaceful use of nuclear energy, on which we will have to rely increasingly in the future as a source of power."[78]

This case study of Japan's decision to adhere to the NPT aimed to assess three observable implications related to regime membership presented in chapter 2. The first expectation, that the United States will promote universalization of the NPT through the use of its tools of influence, finds support in this case. ACDA officials pushed Japanese ratification using low-cost diplomacy following the treaty's adoption. In 1975 top US officials began to use high-cost diplomacy and inducements to persuade Japan to ratify the treaty it had signed five years before. The process of persuading Japan was undermined, however, by the fact that for five years after the Johnson administration, US officials presented Japanese leaders with inconsistent and ambiguous messaging about the importance of the NPT. This reticence stemmed from Nixon and Kissinger's disinterest in the treaty and perhaps the idea that Japan should consider its own deterrent. As chapter 3 describes, US consideration of a Japanese deterrent was made during a period of presumed US decline, when the United States may not have been able to project power around the globe any longer. In that case, an ally in the Pacific region with nuclear weapons could perhaps bolster US security interests. But this idea was relatively short-lived and was never accepted among those working on nonproliferation in the ACDA and State Department.

The persistent attempts by Japanese officials to determine US policy preferences regarding their NPT ratification indicate support for the next observable implication, that decision-making about joining the NPT will reflect consideration of US policy preferences. The Japanese government did not adhere to the NPT until US policy preferences in favor of ratification were clearly communicated from the highest levels of government. Finally, as a highly embedded state, Japan would be expected to require minimal persuasion and adhere to the NPT quickly. The Japanese case does not meet this expectation; the US efforts were those more likely to be used in persuading moderately embedded states. Table 3.1 summarizes the outcomes for the observable implications related to regime membership. It is followed by a discussion of the alternative explanations for this case.

Table 3.1 Assessing regime membership observable implications for Japanese NPT ratification

State	*The US and its allies will promote the universalization of the NPT and other regime agreements through the use of their tools of influence*	*Decisions to adhere to (or support) the NPT or other regime agreements will reflect consideration of US policy preferences and persuasive tools*	*Decisions to adhere to (or support) the NPT or other regime elements will reflect embeddedness within the US-led order*
Japan	Yes	Yes	No

Each of the three alternative theories explaining adherence to the nuclear nonproliferation regime find some relevance in explaining the six-year duration from NPT signature to ratification in Japan, though they do not fully explain the decision to ratify the treaty in 1976. First, security considerations were relevant to Japan's delay in ratification. After China's first nuclear weapon test in 1964, the Japanese government commissioned a group of researchers to study the potential development of a Japanese nuclear deterrent. This nongovernmental group, issuing reports in 1968 and 1970, found that though Japan had the technical capacity to develop nuclear weapons, this course was not in Japan's best interest, as it would hurt its relations with the United States and Japanese geography meant it was more vulnerable to nuclear attack than China.[79] Nonetheless, during NPT deliberations, a minority on the right within the Japanese government wanted to maintain a nuclear bomb option and forgo treaty accession. By early 1975, when most factions supported ratification, this minority remained unconvinced and still wanted to leave the option open. According to a cable reporting back to Kissinger at this time, "While almost all major party figures and Japanese nuclear industry have supported ratification, active minority elements within the LDP remain opposed. These include such influential figures as party secretary general Nakasone, some older right-wing elements and younger nationalistic members of the seirankai group [an anticommunist group], all of whom see the issue as being whether Japan should hold open its 'nuclear option' for future generations."[80] One security concern expressed by this faction in early 1975 was the prospect of the Soviet Union gaining "military superiority" by the end of the twentieth century, an eventuality that US secretary of defense James Schlesinger had warned about in a recent speech.[81] Foreign minister Miyazawa responded to concerns over a future Soviet threat by expressing confidence in the US security guarantee, reportedly stating, "The US would do whatever was necessary to preserve the free world's security."[82] Lingering concerns about Japan's reliance on the United States for security were heightened by the US withdrawal from Vietnam: "Thoughtful Japanese across [the] political spectrum were surprised at rapid Indochina collapse, are newly concerned about Japan's security and uncertain about long run US reliability."[83]

The NPT debate catalyzed a strong nationalist element within Japan. Not only was the prime minister attacked on live television over his support for the treaty, when the Diet was voting for ratification in 1976, right-wing protestors in military uniforms stood outside singing Japanese military songs and waving World War II flags.[84] Beyond the additional security assurances provided by the United States, a former high-ranking Japanese official recalled that eventually conservative holdouts were persuaded to support ratification due to the NPT's withdrawal clause, which permits withdrawal if "extraordinary events . . . have jeopardized the supreme interests of its country."[85] In other words, if its security circumstances changed dramatically,

Japan could withdraw from the treaty and build a nuclear weapon program. The hawks within the LDP thus contributed to the six-year delay between Japan's signature and ratification, but they did not ultimately convince Japanese leaders to disavow the treaty. Proponents of the treaty in Japan's government, who realized that rejecting the treaty would be detrimental to security and economic relations with the United States, were able to mitigate the concerns of the hardliners through the reiteration of US security pledges and assurances about the treaty's withdrawal process.

Politicians concerned about fairness, justice, and the balance of responsibilities in the treaty were also relevant to the long duration of Japan's NPT ratification process; those who wanted to hold out for more significant progress on nuclear disarmament contributed to the delay in Miki's intended ratification timeline. When Japan signed the NPT in 1970, one of the three stated conditions for future ratification was progress on nuclear disarmament globally. Though the pro-disarmament group did not play as significant of a role in delaying the process as the conservative hawks, the Miki government did have to engage this faction during the ratification debates in the spring of 1975. According to the Japanese Foreign Office disarmament director, who briefed the US embassy about NPT ratification progress in March 1975, Miki's officials countered the disarmament proponents by saying if they waited until general disarmament occurred, they would never join the NPT and arguing that Japan should be making the case for disarmament in every possible international meeting, including the NPT Review Conferences. According to the official, this latter argument was "having some effect."[86] To gain the support of this faction within the Lower House of the Diet, the passage of the NPT was accompanied by a resolution with five components: reaffirmation of Japan's three nuclear principles from 1967, a call on nuclear weapon states not to threaten the security of nonnuclear weapon states, promotion of a comprehensive test ban treaty and eventual nuclear disarmament, maximization of safety in Japan's nuclear energy program, and support for global efforts to establish nuclear-weapons-free zones.[87] This resolution was not put to a vote by all members but was agreed to by all of the parties.[88]

The domestic political economy theory that outward-facing, international regimes are less likely to proliferate and more likely to join the NPT is relevant in this case, in that Japanese leaders in the LDP were outward facing and many wanted to join the treaty. Solingen argues that the Japanese government's legitimacy came from its export-led economic growth and that seeking nuclear weapons would have hampered its economy.[89] While accurate and a relevant explanation for Japan's decision to remain nonnuclear, Solingen's theory is less useful in explaining the specific timing of Japan's NPT ratification. As an outward-facing regime in 1968, why did Tokyo wait until 1976 to adhere? While it is true that Japan's developing nuclear industry wanted to be assured that its IAEA safeguards agreement would not hamper its growth, these assurances came in 1973. Japan did not ratify the NPT until the highest levels of the US government made it clear they sought Tokyo's commitment to the treaty and the US government communicated that continuing to remain outside of the treaty would hinder Japan's nuclear industry.

Indonesia and the NPT

Indonesia ratified the NPT in 1978 and deposited its instrument of ratification in 1979. The United States had a relatively close relationship with Indonesia's leadership during the early 1970s, due to military cooperation in Southeast Asia. Similar to the Japanese case, however, the Nixon and Ford administrations did not press Indonesia's Suharto regime to ratify the NPT when Jakarta's embeddedness within the US-led order was deepest. It was only under President Carter that the United States sought Indonesia's ratification. Indonesia joined the NPT at a time when US leaders were pushing hard for Jakarta's participation, engaging in high-cost diplomacy and offering inducements.

During the 1970s, when Jakarta ratified the NPT, Indonesia was a moderately embedded state within the US-led order. The period of the Nixon administration is considered by many Indonesians to be the "apex" of bilateral relations between Indonesia and the United States.[90] This was an era in which the Indonesian government received security and economic benefits from the United States due to Suharto's help in fighting communism in the region. In Cambodia, Suharto covertly provided arms in support of the US-backed Lon Nol government in the early 1970s.[91] From 1969 to 1973, Jakarta received over $210,000,000 annually in US aid (over one billion in today's dollars).[92] President Suharto largely supported US global and regional policies and institutions during this time. In a 1970 meeting, Suharto told Kissinger the Indonesians "appreciate US participation in the International Monetary Fund, World Bank, and Asian Development Bank," key elements of the US-led global order.[93] In return for Indonesian support for US strategic goals, the Nixon and Ford administrations largely ignored areas where their political values did not align, including Indonesian abuses in East Timor and Suharto's corruption. Moreover, though it was Western-leaning, Indonesia was an important member of the nonaligned movement (NAM) during this time.

Under the Carter administration, friendly relations and the provision of US military aid continued, with one difference: Carter took a greater interest in human rights and pushed Suharto to release political prisoners.[94] This change meant that the difference in political values between the two countries came into starker relief. Throughout the 1970s, Indonesia was assessed as a –7 on its Polity measure, indicating an autocratic regime, and Freedom House considered it only "partially free."[95] In addition, UN General Assembly voting data from this period suggest that Indonesia was not aligned with the US-led order across a majority of global issues. In summary, Indonesian embeddedness stemmed from the material benefits it received from the United States when the two states were in agreement about immediate, high-level strategic goals in the region, but their alignment did not go deeper and extend into political values.

Based on Indonesia's moderate embeddedness, we would expect Jakarta to have taken longer than US allies to adhere to the NPT, with US officials needing to engage in high-cost diplomacy and offers of inducements. In general, these expectations bear out in this case, though part of the delay in ratification was due to the disinterest of the Nixon and Ford administrations until after the 1974 Indian nuclear test. Indonesian ratification occurred in 1979 once the Carter administration took high-level interest in the issue and made clear that US nuclear assistance would only be available to states that were members of the NPT or otherwise had concluded full-scope IAEA safeguards.

Indonesian president Sukarno began speaking publicly about an Indonesian atomic bomb after China successfully tested its first device in 1964. US intelligence knew this possibility was far-fetched based on an assessment of existing Indonesian nuclear infrastructure, but they were concerned that perhaps Mao's communist government, a partner of Sukarno, would give the Indonesians a nuclear bomb. This rhetoric did not last long, however, as Major General Suharto wrested control of the Indonesian government from Sukarno in October 1965 after a botched coup attempt. Suharto led Indonesia until 1998. From his predecessor, Suharto maintained Indonesian's nonaligned stance, committing allegiance neither to the Soviet Union nor the West, but he did seek greater economic assistance from Western states, providing an opportunity for US leverage. In a 1967 assessment, the CIA called Indonesia's global position "Western-leaning nonalignment" since it interpreted Suharto's move to nonalignment from Sukarno's procommunist position as a means to gain additional Western aid.[96] The same CIA assessment stated, "So long as the US continues to assist in the rehabilitation of the Indonesian economy and the Indonesians retain hope of even greater assistance, their relations with the US are likely to remain as close and cordial as at present."[97]

In President Suharto, Washington found a more cooperative leader than Sukarno in terms of nuclear nonproliferation. In 1965, the new government agreed "in principle" to IAEA-managed safeguards on the nuclear technology it received from the United States.[98] The Indonesian government signed a safeguards agreement in 1967 in exchange for $350,000 in US nuclear assistance. This aid had been withheld from the previous regime.[99] In this instance, we see the first example of US leaders offering an inducement in exchange for Jakarta's nonproliferation commitment. This cooperation occurred once the Indonesian leadership became more Western leaning.

The NPT opened for signature in 1968, and Indonesia signed in March 1970, three days before the treaty entered into force. If Jakarta did not sign at that point, it could only join the treaty through the single step of accession. Like Japan, Indonesia's signature at the last minute likely indicated some support for the treaty but enough hesitancy that Jakarta preferred the two-step process of signing immediately and then adopting a more cautious approach to ratification. The Indonesian government attached reservations to its signature, stating that the treaty would only be effective if all states—nuclear and nonnuclear—joined, that the safeguards required by the treaty should not hamper economic or technological development, and that the nuclear states should guarantee that nonnuclear states would not be attacked with nuclear weapons.[100] When IAEA director general Sigvard Eklund visited Jakarta in September 1973 and asked about Indonesia's position on the NPT, the foreign minister responded that Indonesia would not move forward without more "positive assurances" from nuclear-weapons-possessing states in instances of nuclear threats.[101]

There is some early evidence of US efforts to persuade Jakarta to adhere to the NPT.[102] As with other states that had not yet joined, the US State Department "periodically" sent démarches to Jakarta about the treaty, but this low-cost diplomacy produced "disappointing results," which is expected for a moderately embedded state.[103] Available evidence suggests that the US government did not engage in high-cost diplomacy until after the Indian test in May 1974. At this point the United States and its allies, particularly Australia, pressed harder in Jakarta. Reportedly, following the Indian explosion, an Australian official asked an Indonesian official if Jakarta would ratify the NPT. Reportedly, the official "flatly" told his Australian counterpart that Indonesia would not ratify it.[104] Australia's Foreign Ministry made a strong case to the Indonesian government in favor of ratification in October 1974 during their annual bilateral meetings; the Australians reported back to the US embassy that the Indonesians "responded negatively" to their plea.[105] In March 1975, US officials raised NPT ratification with Indonesia's International Organizations Directorate deputy. The deputy is reported to have responded by saying, "Indonesia's position on NPT has not changed since 1970."[106] As anticipated, the US government and its allies then began engaging in more costly persuasive efforts. In April 1975, in an example of high-cost diplomacy by a US ally, Australian prime minister Gough Whitlam directly asked Suharto to ratify; Suharto replied that NPT ratification was "of little importance" to his government.[107] In September 1975, the Australian ambassador to Indonesia sent Jakarta a "strong recommendation that Indonesia ratify the NPT."[108] For two years in the mid-1970s, US and Australian leaders attempted low-cost and high-cost diplomacy to attempt to persuade Jakarta to adhere to the NPT, with little to show for it.

By the autumn of 1975, however, there were indications that at least some Indonesian officials were softening their position on the NPT. Foreign minister Adam Malik had begun to show interest in the treaty at the fall UN General Assembly session.[109] What might have altered his position? One hint stems from a meeting the previous spring in which the head of Indonesia's nuclear energy institute met with a US embassy science adviser and bemoaned the fact that US-Indonesian nuclear cooperation had recently fallen off.[110] The previous year, the United States announced at an IAEA Board of Governors meeting that it would give preference to NPT members for certain types of nuclear assistance.[111] At the same meeting, the Indonesian delegation announced plans for its first power reactor before objecting to preferential treatment in nuclear supply for NPT members.[112]

Like many countries around the world, following the 1970s oil crisis, Indonesia had begun to plan for a civilian nuclear power program as an alternative to relying on fossil fuels. In 1972, the National Nuclear Agency of Indonesia (BATAN) established a committee to explore the construction of nuclear power plants. In 1974, the director general of BATAN, Achmad Baiquni, announced that his organization's five-year plan called for the development of an Indonesian nuclear energy program with the first reactor set to generate power by 1985.[113] The next month, Indonesian foreign minister Malik announced that Jakarta would seek nuclear cooperation agreements with the USSR, Canada, France, and the United States but did not announce any plans regarding the NPT.

Problems with Jakarta's ambitious nuclear energy plan soon arose. First, prospectors were unable to find indigenous uranium. Then, in 1975, the state oil company Pertamina almost went bankrupt, costing the government funds that could have otherwise gone to the burgeoning nuclear program.[114] In 1976, BATAN and the National Electric Authority conducted a study with the IAEA that determined that between eight and eighteen reactors could be built on the island of Java by 1992,[115] but in the same year, Jakarta reported to the IAEA that it had decided to "postpone" its nuclear energy program.[116] Indonesia experienced a recession in the mid-1970s that further tapped its limited resources.[117] Help from the United States and other suppliers was all the more important in this context.

By the latter half of the 1970s, improvements in the economy meant a nuclear energy program was again a possibility for Indonesia. In January 1977, Canadian officials relayed to the United States that Indonesian officials said their parliament was scheduled to discuss the NPT. Reportedly, the atomic energy advocates in government were in favor of the treaty, while others in the government were opposed.[118] This evidence suggests that nuclear technology was the reason behind the renewed interest in the NPT. The following day, the secretary of state's office responded with guidance for the US embassy's approach to Jakarta regarding the NPT. The first point of persuasion suggested by the State Department implies an inducement regarding nuclear cooperation: "The USG continues to support the widest possible adherence to the treaty and the recent presidential statement on nuclear policy indicated NPT adherence would be a strong positive factor when considering future nuclear cooperation. Should GOI [government on Indonesia] ever consider increasing the level of such cooperation, they will find their efforts facilitated by being an NPT party because of the major weight US gives to NPT adherence. Last month the Canadians announced a similar policy, and a number of other states take NPT adherence heavily into account."[119] In the same cable, the secretary's office requested that allies Great Britain and Japan aid the United States and Canada in promoting the NPT to the Indonesian government.[120] Tokyo agreed to join an "oral démarche" consistent with the US and Canadian position.[121] London also pledged its support to this effort.[122] As anticipated by a theory of adherence emphasizing US global leadership, US allies joined the NPT and then cooperated with the United States to expand membership.

US and Indonesian officials engaged in a great deal of diplomatic communication about the NPT in early 1977. In February, the Indonesian ambassador to the United States told State Department officials "that the importance which the US placed on ratification of NPT was clearly understood at the highest level of GOI."[123] In March 1977, a high-ranking Indonesian defense official said the NPT would be submitted by the president to parliament but that the parliament had many items on its agenda. The official asked that US officials not publicly comment on its ratification until parliament was able to act because "parliament might not act expeditiously if it gained impression that GOI ratification request was result of American pressure."[124] In the same month, the State Department asked the US ambassador in Jakarta to request a meeting with Suharto and relay a specific message from the president: "President Carter particularly welcomes President Suharto's support for NPT, and hopes for Indonesia's early ratification."[125] In April, reports indicated that Indonesian officials feared the Carter administration would embargo nuclear energy technology; US officials reassured them that this would not happen and reiterated that NPT ratification would facilitate technology cooperation.[126] On May 11, Indonesian leaders formally decided it was in their interest to join the NPT, but the government stated that its ratification would occur in the following session of parliament, in October 1977.[127]

But when parliament went into session that fall, there were signs that members were not in fact in agreement about NPT ratification. At the UN General Assembly in November, the Indonesian delegation publicly expressed doubts about the NPT with Indonesian ambassador Sani stating there were "sufficient reasons for growing doubts about effectiveness of NPT [*sic*]" and that the nuclear powers' obligations were going "unfulfilled."[128] The NPT was not ratified in the fall 1977 session as previously promised.

In January 1978, Indonesian officials requested from the US embassy in Jakarta a list of the states that had signed and ratified the NPT, indicating that the government was continuing to study the issue.[129] Other than this request, there appears to have been little NPT activity between the United

States and Indonesia in the early months of 1978. By March, State Department officials in Washington suggested to the US embassy in Jakarta that the United States could offer Jakarta an inducement, hosting a "high-level ceremony to accept the Indonesian instrument of ratification" on July 1, as that date was the tenth anniversary of the opening of the treaty for signature.[130] But US officials soon learned that there continued to be internal debate over NPT ratification in Jakarta.

In April, an Australian official reported to his US counterparts in Vienna that in a meeting with Indonesian officials, they learned that BATAN "was [the] source of greatest opposition" to the NPT "but was overruled by higher authority."[131] Reportedly, this same official spent forty-five minutes explaining to the Australian diplomats "what is wrong with the NPT."[132] At the end of April, the US ambassador to Indonesia, Edward Masters, met with Indonesian minister of state Sudharmono, one of Suharto's closest advisers, to inquire about NPT ratification. Sudharmono said that a cabinet reshuffle was one of the reasons for the delay but that the ratification should occur in the next few months. Masters pushed for a public announcement about Indonesian ratification, but Sudharmono said that even though Suharto approved the treaty, it would be best to wait until the new cabinet had a chance to study it.[133] At this point, US low-cost diplomacy was apparently insufficient to persuade all of Jakarta's leaders to embrace the NPT.

The US government stepped up its persuasive actions in the spring of 1978, when President Carter sent Vice President Mondale on a multicountry trip that included a stop in Jakarta; the NPT was on the agenda. In an April 1978 memo to President Carter, about this high-cost diplomatic effort, Mondale wrote, "In my talks with President Suharto and Vice President Malik, I will urge Indonesia to ratify the nonproliferation treaty, I will sign an AID [US Agency for International Development] rural electrification loan and I will underline our interest in cooperating in food production and energy programs."[134] Vice president Mondale did not lay out an explicit quid pro quo regarding the NPT, but the discussion of US aid combined with encouragement of treaty ratification would surely be a more convincing message than a plea for the treaty alone. The Mondale visit combined high-cost diplomacy with implicit positive inducements that went beyond offers of nuclear cooperation. After the Mondale visit, the US embassy in Jakarta reported back on the vice president's meetings. On the topic of the NPT, the cable reads, "NPT. The Vice President explained the importance we attach to the broadest possible adherence to the NPT, and asked when Indonesia might complete the ratification process. Suharto said the Indonesian parliament had reconvened on May 1, and that he expected ratification within the near future."[135] In addition to economic aid, the cable indicates that the meeting with the Indonesians also included discussions of US military aid.

The May 1978 session of parliament did not address NPT ratification, but when the new session began on August 18, the parliament took up NPT ratification first.[136] B. J. Habibie, Suharto's minister of state for research and technology, made the case for the treaty. In explaining the need for NPT ratification to parliament, Habibie stated, "It is necessary to ratify at this time the NPT . . . as this will lead to talks on foreign aid, especially for nuclear technology cooperation." He continued, "The government . . . considers the current international situation as unfavorable for non-NPT countries to obtain aid for the development of nuclear projects. This . . . can lead to undesirable political effects. Considering the development of politics within and outside the country, Indonesia has come to the conclusion that the time has come for her to ratify the bill."[137] During this time, Suharto had approved a plan for a thirty-megawatt nuclear reactor in Indonesia; Habibie had advocated for this reactor to support nuclear research as well as to develop radioisotopes for agricultural and medical uses.[138]

In stating that the "international situation [was] unfavorable for non-NPT countries," Habibie was likely referring to the limits the United States was placing on nuclear supply. In the late 1970s, as an inexperienced state seeking nuclear technology from global suppliers, Indonesia faced a more constrained international environment than it had previously. By 1978, the Nuclear Suppliers Group agreed on guidelines, published by the IAEA, for nuclear supply to include safeguards and lists of trigger items that had to be considered carefully by exporters. In the same year, the US Nuclear Nonproliferation Act of 1978 had further tightened US nuclear exports. To receive nuclear cooperation from the US after this legislation, a state had to accept IAEA safeguards on all nuclear facilities and vow not to manufacture or acquire any nuclear explosive devices. The US government was also pressuring other supplier states to do the same through the Nuclear Suppliers Group. The Indonesian government received high-level pressure from the US vice president and was effectively offered nuclear trade as an inducement to secure NPT ratification, and yet it would still take a bit longer to achieve Indonesian adherence.

Indonesian ratification did not follow quickly on Habibie's speech to parliament in August 1978; in October, the legislators were still deliberating. One sticking point was the issue of security assurances for nonnuclear states. Habibie told parliament that the NPT did not provide those assurances but noted the existence of statements and multilateral efforts reflecting that goal and argued that parliament should ratify the NPT immediately and address the issue of assurances afterward.[139]

During this period in the fall, the US State Department continued to send the US embassy in Jakarta NPT talking points for Indonesian officials. They reminded the Indonesian government that it would be able to participate in upcoming preparatory meetings for the NPT if it were to ratify the treaty and included the fact that 106 states were now members. Other talking points referred to nuclear supply. Ratification would "facilitate negotiation of supply agreement between Indonesia, the IAEA, and US to supply research reactor fuel."[140] This talking point served as an inducement, as earlier in the year, Jakarta had requested additional fuel for its US-supplied research reactor, but the United States was delaying its response to the request. Another talking point noted that other suppliers, including Canada and the Soviet Union, were also giving special preference to NPT members when making decisions about nuclear assistance. The US government was actively encouraging all other suppliers to do the same.[141] The Indonesian parliament ratified the NPT on November 25, 1978, with no opposition. According to the US embassy cable back to the State Department, "All parliamentary factions expressed the hope that nuclear technology would increase the prosperity of the Indonesian people if peacefully used."[142]

When the Indonesian government deposited its instruments of NPT ratification in July 1979, it again included a declaration, part of which emphasized the country's need for nuclear technology:

> Indonesia today is actively carrying out its national development. With a view to supporting and accelerating the development process, including the economic and social development, Indonesia has decided from the outset to make use of the nuclear energy [*sic*] for peaceful purposes. Indonesia's efforts in developing nuclear energy for peaceful purposes in its national development, require the assistance and cooperation of technologically advanced nuclear countries. With the ratification of this Treaty, the Government of Indonesia wishes to draw the attention of the nuclear countries to their obligations under Article IV of the Treaty and expresses the hope that they would be prepared to cooperate with non-nuclear countries in the use of nuclear energy for peaceful purposes and implement the provisions of Article IV of the Treaty for the benefit of developing countries without discrimination.[143]

Within a year of NPT ratification, Indonesia concluded its Comprehensive Safeguards Agreement with the IAEA.[144] The swiftness with which Indonesia approached this agreement suggests that securing the safeguards required by the NPT—and newly required for nuclear trade with the United States and other suppliers—was an important factor in its NPT adherence. Soon after ratification, the government signed nuclear cooperation deals with a number of suppliers, beginning with France and Italy in 1980.[145] France, Italy, West Germany, and Canada competed to build Indonesia's first power reactor, and Indonesia signed a deal with West Germany for the thirty-megawatt reactor in 1982.[146]

From the available evidence, it appears that pressure from the United States and some its allies likely influenced the Indonesian government's decision to adhere to the NPT. The timing of Indonesia's ratification in the late 1970s coincided with new and direct pressure from the United States. During this period, Indonesian officials heard appeals from President Carter and Vice President Mondale as well as allied leaders, especially from

Australia. The US government concluded that this diplomatic outreach mattered. For example, a US Governmental Accounting Office study from 1980 states indicates that diplomacy was a key factor in Indonesia's ratification: "The State Department notes that Indonesia's decision to ratify the NPT came after years of low-key diplomatic effort climaxed by a personal appeal by Mondale."[147] In an after-action report on Vice President Mondale's trip, written in January 1979, the introduction to the document reads: "The record is quite favorable. Many major issues have been resolved or are near resolution."[148] "Indonesian ratification of the NPT" was on the list of favorable results in the report.[149] In the same memo, the writer notes that Mondale informed Suharto during his trip that the United States had agreed "in principle to sell A-4 aircraft" to Indonesia. Indonesia also requested $35 million in credit in FMS (foreign military sales) for fiscal year 1980, after the aid had been cut the previous year. Later in this same section, the memo addresses the NPT: "He [Mondale] urged NPT ratification. Parliament subsequently ratified the NPT. We sent special message of satisfaction."[150] It is possible the promise of military and economy aid offered by Mondale swayed some members of the cabinet, but we do not have evidence to know definitively.

The evidence for the role of the promise of nuclear technology and material in Indonesia's NPT decision is stronger. Indonesian government officials who had been strongly against joining the NPT started to change their minds when they sought a civilian nuclear program. During the late 1970s, US officials repeatedly communicated that adhering to the NPT would facilitate nuclear supply. The United States even held back nuclear fuel from Jakarta to make this point more starkly. Moreover, as soon as Indonesia joined the treaty, it began signing nuclear cooperation agreements with foreign suppliers. While we cannot be certain based on available evidence why Indonesian officials decided to ratify the NPT in 1978, the evidence suggests the offers of foreign aid, especially nuclear aid, were important factors. These tools are consistent with expectations for persuading a moderately embedded state.

Table 3.2 indicates how each regime membership implication fared in this case.

Table 3.2 Assessing regime membership observable implications for Indonesian NPT ratification

State	*The US and its allies will promote the universalization of the NPT and other regime agreements through the use of their tools of influence*	*Decisions to adhere to (or support) the NPT or other regime agreements will reflect consideration of US policy preferences and persuasive tools*	*Decisions to adhere to (or support) the NPT or other regime elements will reflect embeddedness within the US-led order*
Indonesia	Yes	Likely	Yes

Among the alternative explanations for Indonesia's NPT adherence, the security theory finds the most support in explaining the eight-year delay between its signature in 1970 and its ratification in 1978. Specifically, some in Indonesia wanted to maintain a nuclear weapons option for the country. In a meeting with Indonesia's director general for political affairs in July 1974, the US ambassador to Indonesia sought to clarify Indonesia's position on the NPT after press reports indicated Jakarta was no longer considering NPT ratification. The Indonesian director general responded that many in their country and elsewhere were "rethinking their position" on nuclear weapons following the May 1974 Indian test and noted that Iran was reportedly interested in nuclear weapons as well.[151] The next month, the Associated Press reported that Indonesia's minister for research, Sumitro, said the nuclear weapon option was "not closed."[152] Indicating possible disagreement within the government, Indonesia's Foreign Minister Adam Malik was quick to denounce these comments and said his country's nuclear program was only for peaceful purposes.[153] While there is no evidence that Jakarta made a decision to develop a nuclear weapons program in the 1970s, it may have considered whether it wanted to be constrained by the NPT in light of other states' nuclear weapons programs. In any case, by the time Jakarta was serious about a civilian nuclear energy program, it appears to have stopped any consideration of nuclear weapons, though there were Indonesian parliamentarians that resisted the NPT in the latter 1970s because they felt the nuclear weapons states had not offered strong enough security assurances to nonnuclear states.

The fairness theory does not seem to operate in this case based on available evidence. Indonesia had long campaigned for nuclear disarmament, including introducing the idea for a nuclear-weapons-free zone at an Association of Southeast Asian Nations (ASEAN) meeting as early as 1971.[154] However, Indonesia did not seek greater disarmament from the United States or other declared nuclear states in exchange for its ratification of the NPT. This theory is relevant to explaining Indonesian nuclear nonproliferation behavior in the future but does not seem to apply in this period.

The domestic political economy argument fails to explain the precise timing of Jakarta's ratification. Indonesian president Suharto inherited a weak economy when he came to power in 1966. He aimed to bring in foreign investment and led a period of economic expansion. His government relied on foreign investment and trade and can be considered outward facing in terms of Solingen's theory. Reliance on foreign trade, however, did not mean Jakarta was quick to ratify the NPT. It was not until 1978 when Indonesia ratified, a period that coincided with direct US pressure and Jakarta's renewed interest in nuclear energy.

Egypt and the NPT

Egypt is a seasoned participant in the global nuclear nonproliferation arena as a leader in the Arab world and the NAM, but it has not showed particular commitment to new elements of the nuclear nonproliferation regime. Its limited commitment, ratifying the NPT in 1981, can be attributed to a change in grand strategy, as Egyptian president Anwar al-Sadat sought to catalyze economic growth through closer ties to the United States, and to a desire for nuclear technology, which the United States had recently limited to states with full-scope IAEA safeguards agreements.

Egypt was a weakly embedded state within the US-led global order for most of the early nuclear age. When the NPT opened for signature in 1968, Cairo was aligned with the Soviet Union. Nonetheless, Egypt did receive small amounts of food and development aid from the United States during this time.[155] The Soviets pressured Cairo to sign the NPT after the Egyptians requested nuclear weapons from Moscow, but apparently they were unable to persuade Cairo on ratification.[156] Egyptian alignment changed in the mid-1970s, with Sadat's strategic turn toward the United States. While US aid increased in 1975 after Sadat rejected the Soviet Union and turned toward the United States, a significant increase came with the 1978 Camp David Accords. Egypt's regional security situation had improved as a result of the accords, and Cairo now received over $1.5 billion in annual US aid.[157]

The era of Egypt's NPT ratification, in the early 1980s, occurred in this period of significantly improved relations with the United States. In speeches from this period, President Sadat expressed very positive sentiments toward President Carter and US leadership. In a 1978 statement from the White House, for example, Sadat declared, "No other nation is more qualified to play this role as a contributor to world stability and prosperity."[158] In a 1979 speech welcoming President Carter to Egypt, after praising President Carter and his role in the peace talks, Sadat stated, "The reception you were accorded today by our masses is a testimony of the affection they have for you and for every American. Let us vow to cement the bonds of friendship and cooperation between our nations."[159] In 1981, the United States signed a Bilateral Investment Treaty with Egypt.[160]

Egypt was more positively disposed toward US global leadership at this point because of the benefits it received through the Camp David Accords and the accompanying US aid package, but Egypt did not align with the US-led order on the majority of issues facing the UN General Assembly or when it came to domestic political values. At this point, Egypt voted with the US-led order at the UN General Assembly at a frequency on par with the global average, although this measure was below average in both the preceding and following years. Freedom House considered the country "partly free" from 1975 through the 1980s.[161] During this time, Egypt was assessed as a –6 on its Polity score, indicating an autocratic government.[162] Thus, based on the available indicators, Egypt is best characterized as weakly embedded within the US-led order until the mid-1970s when it became a moderately embedded state and ratified the NPT.

As a state in the Soviet sphere, Egypt was not expected to be influenced by US pleas for treaty ratification when the NPT first opened for signature. Indeed, the Soviet Union successfully pressured the Egyptians to sign the NPT after Egyptian president Gamal Abdel Nasser requested nuclear weapons from the Chinese and the Soviets following significant losses in the 1967 Six-Day War.[163] Egypt signed the treaty in July 1968, the first day the treaty opened for signature, but it did not ratify while in the Soviet sphere. The Egyptians and the Soviets signed a formal defense pact a year later. During this period, Cairo's relations with the United States were difficult due to the government's ties to Moscow and its anti-Israeli and anti-Western stance. The United States had little leverage on Egyptian leaders at this point, but this would soon change.

Two years after Egypt's NPT signature, Nasser died, bringing vice president Anwar al-Sadat to power. Sadat cut ties to the USSR, expelling Soviet advisers in 1972 and ending the defense pact in 1976. He then began to orient Egypt toward the United States and the West with the aim of improving economic development. During this period, Egypt sought to develop a civilian nuclear power program. On a visit to Cairo in 1974, president Nixon offered to sell Egypt two six-hundred-megawatt power reactors.[164] A year later, Sadat initialed the deal in Washington.[165] The sale languished amid negotiations over nuclear safeguards on the reactors. The increased emphasis on nonproliferation in the Carter White House and in Congress in the late 1970s further delayed the deal as the Carter administration required nuclear safeguards on all US-supplied reactors.[166]

Resolving Egypt's conflict with Israel was a key goal of Sadat's changing strategic orientation. After ousting the Soviets, Sadat pursued a back channel with the US government to encourage US involvement in peace talks with Israel through his national security adviser Hafiz Ismail in February 1973.[167] US policy did not change, and despite warnings of impending war from other leaders in the region, Nixon, backed by the US intelligence community, did not expect Egypt to go to war with Israel. Sadat sought a limited war in 1973 to regain lost territory in the Sinai Peninsula and to compel US involvement in the Egyptian-Israeli conflict. This time, Sadat's plan to engage the United States in its ongoing rivalry succeeded. The 1973 conflict led to a long peace process between Egypt and Israel, culminating in the 1978 Camp David Accords brokered by the Carter administration.[168]

Cairo recognized the importance of nuclear nonproliferation to the United States, with one former official stating that Egypt's nonnuclear status "was a tool, something we could give to the US as a present."[169] Egyptian leaders hoped that Israel would commit not to acquire nuclear weapons as part of the peace process. Initially, the US negotiating position sought commitments to the NPT from both sides. For example, a September 1978 proposal drafted by the US assistant secretary of state for Near Eastern and South Asian affairs, "A Framework for Peace in the Middle East," in preparation for a Camp David summit, stated, "In all of the negotiations described above, they will arrange to guarantee the security, sovereignty, territorial integrity and inviolability and the political independence of each State negotiating peace through measures such as the following. . . . (f) The adherence by all the Parties to the Treaty on the Nonproliferation of Nuclear Weapons. The Parties undertake not to manufacture or acquire nuclear weapons or other nuclear explosive devices."[170]

There were many such draft frameworks over the course of the negotiations, and references to the NPT appear to have been dropped from subsequent versions. On September 12, 1978, as the Egyptian and US delegations at Camp David discussed the current US framework for the talks, the Egyptians noted differences among the Egyptian and US proposals. Osama el-Baz, Egypt's undersecretary for foreign affairs, stated "that in the Egyptian paper, there had been the proposal that all parties agree to the NPT. The Egyptians had assumed this would meet with enthusiastic American approval."[171] Two months later, in a letter to President Carter expressing a lengthy list of frustrations with the Israelis over the Camp David negotiations, Sadat noted among other disappointments, "The Israelis did not commit themselves to adhere to the treaty on the nonproliferation of nuclear weapons."[172] Sadat explained his willingness to move forward despite dissatisfaction with this aspect (and others) of the framework, "in the hope that these shortcomings will be remedied in the future with the progressive development of peace, as I have believed and still believe that the real peace process starts only after the signing."[173]

In the final drafting of the accords, neither Egypt nor Israel agreed to NPT accession. The Israelis had developed a nuclear weapons program a decade earlier and the Egyptians would be unlikely to unilaterally commit to the treaty within the accord framework.[174] Nonetheless, one former US official familiar with the Egyptian ratification gives credit to the Camp David process for Egypt's decision to ratify the NPT. In an interview, Dean Rust, retired from the ACDA and State Department, explains, "General diplomacy aimed at fostering stability in volatile regions is one of the most important indirect tools you have to foster nonproliferation. I am fond of saying that the Camp David Accords were one of the biggest nonproliferation events in the Middle East, as it led to a negotiated peace between Egypt and Israel. And it led Sadat to join the NPT in 1981, thus breaking a major taboo among Arabs who had continued to resist the NPT while Israel was outside the Treaty."[175]

By this reading, it was Sadat's goal of opening relations with the United States and US involvement in negotiating a peace settlement, which set the stage for Sadat to view the NPT as consistent with his interests. This interpretation aligns with that of the scholar Shai Feldman, who writes, "Having made the strategic decision to avoid the development of a military nuclear option and instead base Egypt's well-being on economic development and close ties with the United States, President Sadat decided to ratify Egypt's signature on the NPT in 1980."[176] Indeed, the movement from weakly embedded to moderately embedded within the US-led order during Sadat's administration made it more likely that the United States would be able to persuade Egypt to adhere to the NPT, but the accords were not enough. The peace treaty with Israel may have laid the groundwork, as Rust and Feldman suggest, but it was insufficient for Cairo's NPT adherence.

As expected, the United States continued its NPT diplomacy with Egypt after the conclusion of the Camp David Accords. A July 1980 Government Accounting Office report stated that "the United States suspended its efforts to persuade those two countries to become parties to the Treaty [during the Camp David negotiations]; efforts were resumed in May 1979 with US approaches to both Egypt and Israel on the question."[177] Indeed, in May 1979, as US officials discussed a bilateral nuclear cooperation agreement with their Egyptian counterparts, they explained that the United States required full-scope safeguards for any nuclear cooperation agreement. This agreement could be conducted through the NPT or outside it, but the United States sought widest possible adherence to the treaty and hoped Egypt would be able to join.[178] These US arguments had little effect initially. In reporting back to Washington in October 1979 about these negotiations, the US embassy in Cairo wrote, "Egyptian stand against ratifying NPT until Israel does has been unwavering. Even in the unlikely event that Egypt accepts full scope safeguards by U.S. as requested in the bilateral nuclear cooperation agreement, there is little chance that GOE [government of Egypt] would in foreseeable future consider ratifying NPT unless and until Israel does."[179]

In a follow-up meeting in Washington in December 1979, US negotiators illustrated the differences between the proposed US-Egypt nuclear cooperation agreement and the US agreement with Australia. The differences, explained the US negotiators, stemmed from Australia's adherence to the NPT.[180] In a second read out of the negotiations, from Washington to the US embassy in Cairo, there was the suggestion that the Egyptian view may have been changing. The US official reports, "In subsequent discussions with Under Secretary Benson, Egyptian ambassador Ghorbal indicated that Cairo is considering ratification of the NPT in connection with approval of the nuclear agreement but that such ratification and approval is linked to the availability of US concessionary financing for the project."[181] The Egyptians were unable to secure financing for their reactor, and the United States only provided special financing to NPT members; Carter was not willing to make an exception. It appears that with the US-Egypt nuclear cooperation deal finalized and the prospect of acquiring nuclear technology becoming a reality, the Egyptian government was willing to consider the NPT as a means to secure financing for their civilian nuclear program.

Soon after, in 1980, Sadat appointed a government commission to investigate the possibility of NPT accession. A minority of commission members wanted Egypt to pursue nuclear weapons, either within or outside of the NPT, while the majority favored nonproliferation and NPT adherence. Sadat announced in December 1980 that Egypt would join the NPT.[182] Egypt then signed a deal to buy two reactors from France. After ratification on February 16, 1981, Egypt began negotiating with Great Britain and Germany for reactors and sought to reopen its dormant reactor deal with the United States. Seven years after Nixon's offer and four months after Egypt's NPT ratification, Washington signed a deal to supply two reactors in June 1981.[183] The flurry of activity in seeking nuclear reactor deals immediately after NPT ratification suggests that Egypt's decision was primarily caused by realizing that the price of nuclear supply from the United States and its allies was adherence to the NPT.

As a moderately embedded state in the late 1970s and early 1980s, it is expected that Egypt would have eventually been persuaded to join the NPT after considerable diplomatic efforts by US leaders as well as the offer of inducements. In fact, multiple factors related to US global leadership—including a negotiated peace settlement with Israel, low- and high-cost diplomacy, and a desire for civilian technology matched with a US inducement for reactor financing—pushed Egypt in this direction. Egyptian leaders recognized the importance of the NPT to the United States, the successful US-brokered Camp David Accords created a security environment more favorable to ratification, and the United States made clear it would only help fund Egypt's program if it adhered to the NPT. Table 3.3 indicates how the Egyptian NPT case fits with the observable implications related to regime membership.

The delay from Egypt's 1968 NPT signature to its 1981 ratification could indicate a potential hedging strategy driven by security concerns. After all, Egypt has long viewed nuclear weapons through the lens of the Israeli program, and Egypt did build a nascent nuclear program in the 1950s.

Table 3.3 Assessing regime membership observable implications for Egyptian NPT ratification

State	*The US and its allies will promote the universalization of the NPT and other regime agreements through the use of their tools of influence*	*Decisions to adhere to (or support) the NPT or other regime agreements will reflect consideration of US policy preferences and persuasive tools*	*Decisions to adhere to (or support) the NPT or other regime elements will reflect embeddedness within the US-led order*
Egypt	Yes	Likely	Yes

Egypt began its civilian nuclear program in the mid-1950s and left open the option to develop nuclear weapons. Nasser founded the Atomic Energy Establishment (AEE) in 1955 and the Center for Nuclear Research in 1957. The director of AEE, Nasser's cabinet secretary, Ibrahim Hilmy Abdel Rahman, asked other members of the AEE board in 1955 about the purpose of their nuclear research. Should they pursue nuclear weapons? He was told to focus on peaceful uses but that "the program should be organized in a way that would preserve a military option."[184] Rahman sought peaceful nuclear cooperation agreements from the Soviet Union in 1956 and 1958.[185] The agreements provided for equipment, training of Egyptian physicists, and a two-megawatt nuclear reactor at Inchas, which went critical in 1961. Egypt also sought nuclear reactors in the early 1960s, for what one official called "a plutonium route to nuclear weapons."[186] These projects were halted after Western banks refused to finance them amid deteriorating relations with Egypt. The Soviets declined to provide reprocessing technology when asked by the Egyptians in 1964.[187]

With limited indigenous nuclear infrastructure and growing awareness of a developing nuclear program in neighboring Israel,[188] Egypt requested nuclear weapons from both the Soviet Union and China in the 1960s.[189] These requests were denied. Despite some level of interest in nuclear weapons, Egyptian leadership never mobilized sufficient resources to develop an indigenous nuclear program.[190] Philipp Bleek calls the efforts to secure nuclear weapons by the Egyptians "half-hearted."[191] Jim Walsh concludes, "The historical record leaves little doubt that the government repeatedly sought the acquisition of nuclear weapons, and yet it never made the kind of national commitment that would have made the bomb a reality. There was no equivalent to the Manhattan Project. . . . Instead, there was drift, delay, and missed opportunities."[192]

The 1967 Six-Day War devastated Egypt's economy: Cairo saw reduced oil revenue due to lost territory and had to pay significant costs to rebuild its conventional military forces. Nasser again considered nuclear weapons after the war, according to Walsh, but the cost of a program was prohibitive for Egypt's weakened economy.[193] The available evidence indicates that any real consideration of an Egyptian nuclear weapons program ended by 1973. Without a serious effort to develop a nuclear program, it appears that Egypt was not pursuing a hedging strategy, delaying NPT adherence because of its weapons aspirations.

Security is related to this case when it comes to Israel, however. According to Gawdat Bahgat, Egypt signed the treaty in 1968 expecting that perhaps its adversary, Israel, would feel pressure to do the same.[194] Egyptian leaders also initially thought the two states could join the NPT together as part of the Camp David Accords. Neither hope panned out, but it is likely that the Camp David Accords changed the security environment enough that Egyptian leaders could seriously consider the NPT, despite Israel's non-NPT status and probable nuclear weapons program. However, the more proximate cause for NPT adherence was the US inducement of providing financing for Egypt's reactors.

There is no evidence from primary or secondary sources to support the fairness theory in this case. Egypt's reluctance to ratify the NPT does not appear to have been based on concerns about a lack of disarmament progress by the five established nuclear states. Nonetheless, Egypt did refer to nuclear reductions once it joined the treaty, attaching a statement to its NPT ratification that expressed disappointment in the lack of disarmament progress by both the United States and the Soviet Union: "Egypt wishes to express its strong dissatisfaction at the nuclear-weapon States, in particular the two super-Powers [sic], because of their failure to take effective measures relating to cessation of the nuclear arms race and to nuclear disarmament."[195] Nonetheless, this dissatisfaction did not ultimately keep Egypt from ratifying the treaty and does not appear to be a factor in the lengthy period from NPT signature to ratification.

At first blush, the domestic political economy theory appears consistent with the Egyptian NPT case. Egyptian adherence occurred after a change in grand strategy; Sadat rejected Nasser's alignment with the Soviet Union and his economic policies in favor of free trade and foreign investment. In other words, Sadat turned toward the West as his survival strategy. But Sadat did not join the NPT when he began this grand shift in the 1970s. He only joined the treaty when the US made it difficult to build his civilian nuclear program as a non-NPT member.

Cuba and the NPT

Cuba was the last current member of the NPT to join the treaty, adhering in the fall of 2002. Due to the perceived threat of Cuba throughout the Cold War—a communist country a mere one hundred miles from the continental United States—the US government sought to undermine the Cuban government throughout most of the nuclear age. The United States ended diplomatic relations with Cuba in 1961, following the 1958 revolution that brought Fidel Castro to power. Soon after, the United States imposed a total trade embargo on Cuba and prohibited any aid to the country as part of the 1961 Foreign Assistance Act. The Cuban government was aligned with the Soviet Union during the Cold War; its political values diverged sharply with those of the United States. During this period, Cuba consistently scored a –7 Polity score, indicating an autocracy,[196] and was labeled "not free" by Freedom House.[197] UN General Assembly voting data indicate Cuba was far below the global average in foreign policy concordance with the US-led order.[198] Some US aid does show up in US AID's "Cuba" designation beginning in 1990,[199] following the end of the Cold War, though much of this aid supported civil society groups promoting democracy and human rights and flowed to organizations outside of Cuba.[200] The Cuban government rejected direct aid from the US government on several occasions.[201] For all of these reasons, Cuba is coded as an antagonistic state toward the US-led order from the early 1960s through 2002, the year of its NPT accession.

Though it became a member of the IAEA with the organization's founding in 1957, Cuba would go on to maintain an adversarial position toward global nonproliferation and disarmament efforts. In 1965, Cuba was one of five countries to abstain from a UN General Assembly resolution calling for disarmament.[202] When the NPT was adopted in June 1968 via UN Resolution 2373, Cuba was one of four states to vote against it.[203] For decades, Cuba refused to join the NPT and similarly refrained from joining the Latin American Nuclear-Weapons-Free Zone, known as the Treaty of Tlatelolco. The United States was especially keen on Cuban ratification of Tlatelolco because the treaty prohibited states parties from stationing nuclear weapons on their soil and thus would mitigate against another Cuban Missile Crisis. Moreover, Cuba's accession would help bring Tlatelolco into force.[204] In 1969, US internal documents noted that the Cuban government refused to join Tlatelolco ostensibly because "US nuclear weapons remain in Puerto Rico, the Canal Zone and 'and other Latin American areas.'"[205]

Because Cuba moved into the Soviet sphere of influence after its 1958 revolution, the United States expected the Soviets to pressure Cuba to join nonproliferation agreements. US leaders were usually disappointed by Soviet efforts, however. For example, in a 1967 discussion between US secretary of state Dean Rusk and Soviet minister of foreign affairs Andrei Gromyko on the draft NPT and their strategy to promote it, Rusk asked about the Cuban position on the 1967 Treaty of Tlatelolco. According to the US memo of the conversation, "Rusk expressed the hope Gromyko would use Soviet influence to get them to join the Latin American agreement."[206] The response was unsatisfying to Rusk: "Gromyko said he didn't know much about it. The Soviet Union had not been consulted. The question does not relate to the Soviet Union."[207] The Soviet Union appeared to have done little to persuade the Cuban government to join the Treaty of Tlatelolco or the NPT.

The Soviet Union did insist that Cuba conclude a safeguards agreement with the IAEA to secure Soviet-supplied nuclear technology. In 1976, the Soviets initially agreed to provide Cuba with twelve nuclear power reactors; the plan was later reduced to two. Cuba concluded a safeguards agreement with the IAEA in 1980 for these two reactors at Juragua, a peninsula between Cienfuegos Bay and the Caribbean Sea. The safeguards were limited to those two reactors only; this agreement was not the same as Cuba concluding the safeguards agreement required by the NPT. (The Cuban government suspended construction on the reactors in 1992 after the collapse of the Soviet Union.)

Early in his administration, President Carter sought to normalize US relations with Cuba. After discussions in March 1977—the first official contact since 1961—both states opened "interest sections" in the others' capitals, and Carter relaxed travels restrictions to Cuba.[208] The two adversaries were able to come to agreement on fishing and maritime boundaries. During those discussions, which can be considered high-cost diplomacy due to Carter's direct involvement,[209] US leaders suggested more significant steps the Cuban government could take to improve bilateral relations, including joining the Treaty of Tlatelolco and acceding to the NPT.[210]

In this same year, Soviet officials told the US embassy in Moscow that the "Soviet Union was trying to get the Cubans to sign the NPT, and that Moscow expected to assume the major share of the burden among the nuclear powers in getting Cuba to sign."[211] The Soviet's disarmament chief, Roland Timerbaev, reported to the United States that the Soviets were trying to persuade the Cubans to join the NPT.[212] This effort must have been handled at a high level because the following month, when the chief of the US Interest Section in Havana called on his Soviet counterparts and inquired about the NPT, a diplomat who had been there for six years reported that the Soviet embassy in Havana had never discussed the NPT with the Cubans.[213] The Soviet diplomat recounted that Cuba's permanent representative to the United Nations had previously been clear that Cuba would not join the NPT until the "Guantanamo base [was] removed, [the] Panama Canal problem settled, and [the] US embargo on Cuba lifted."[214] Each issue in this litany represented an area of Cuban conflict with the United States. Thus, even though Cuban leaders said they agreed with the content of the treaty, they perceived NPT accession through the lens of their relationship with the United States. They would not accede until relations with the United States improved, even as their patron was reportedly asking them to join. Similarly, Cuban leaders stated they would not join the Treaty of Tlatelolco due to US offenses: "(a) aggressive policies of the US toward Cuba; (b) need to denuclearize US military bases in Puerto Rico, Virgin Islands, and Canal Zone; and (c) illegal detention of Guantanamo."[215]

After the successful breakthrough in relations in the spring of 1977, the US-Cuba normalization process was soon undermined by US concerns about Cuban troops stationed throughout the African continent fighting alongside communist rebels. US officials had suggested to the Cuban government that the US embargo could be lifted once Cuban troops were out of Angola, one of twelve African nations where Cuban forces were present. By the end of 1977, US officials said normalization would be impossible if Cuba continued to maintain its large military presence in Africa.[216] President Castro responded in a December speech, arguing that the presence of Cuban forces in Africa should not disrupt relations between the United States and Cuba and that ending the embargo would be an important step along this path.[217] Castro hosted a delegation of ten US Congress members on

December 31, 1977, where he reiterated these points and addressed the topic of nuclear nonproliferation. He told the delegation that Cuba would not manufacture nuclear weapons and had no intention of acquiring them, but Cuba could not accede to the NPT on principle because the United States maintained thousands of nuclear weapons. He made a similar argument about why he would not join Tlatelolco and noted his nuclear reactors would be under IAEA safeguards.[218] Essentially, Cuba's leadership took the position that the state would abide by both treaties' prohibitions on nuclear weapons but could not join them because of Cuba's adversarial relationship with the United States. Consistent with expectations of a theory of regime adherence based on US global leadership, Castro perceived the nuclear nonproliferation regime through the lens of Cuba's relationship with the United States.

Despite Carter's efforts, US relations with Cuba worsened over the course of his administration as Cuba sent more troops to Africa and later with the arrival of a group of Soviet combat troops in Cuba.[219] In response to the reported stationing of 2,000–3,000 Soviet soldiers in Cuba, President Carter ordered a military exercise in late 1979 in which 1,800 Marines conducted amphibious and aerial landings on Guantánamo Bay.[220] Previously, the administration had considered closing the base as part of its improving relationship with Cuba. Relations worsened further under President Reagan, as his administration designated Cuba a state sponsor of terrorism for its role in supporting communist insurgencies in Africa and Latin America. After the fall of the Soviet Union, the George H. W. Bush administration increased sanctions on Cuba and tried to hinder other states from doing business with the state through the Cuban Democracy Act.[221]

In 1994, Cuba announced its intention to join the Treaty of Tlatelolco, doing so after other major holdouts, Argentina, Chile, and Brazil, joined earlier in the year. In the months following this announcement, several states, including Japan, encouraged Cuba to join the NPT as well. The Cuban position remained that that the NPT was an "unequal treaty" and that it would not join for that reason.[222] Cuba signed Tlatelolco in March 1995, during a period when nuclear nonproliferation was the focus of global attention due to the debate over extending the NPT that spring. Cuba did not follow its signature with ratification of Tlatelolco for another seven years, however. The year following Cuba's signature, President Clinton signed the 1996 Helms-Burton Act, codifying and tightening the US embargo against Cuba.

Cuba's decision to adhere to the NPT in 2002 appears to have been rooted in fears over US concerns that Cuba could possess and transfer biological weapons, contrary to Havana's 1976 accession to the Biological Weapons Convention. Cuba's advanced biomedical infrastructure, the revelations of the Soviet biological program during the Cold War, and Cuba's relations with other so-called rogue states fueled this speculation. Following a US intelligence report speculating that Cuba could have a biological weapons program based on its sophisticated capabilities, US secretary of defense William Cohen expressed concern about this possibility in May 1998.[223] In a 1999 story published in the *Miami Herald,* a former Soviet official accused Cuba of possessing biological weapons. The official repeated the accusation in a 2000 book.[224] The Cuban Foreign Ministry immediately denied the claim and stated, "Cuba does not, and will not, represent a threat for the US territory."[225] This accusation against Cuba resurfaced and gained additional salience three years later in the post–September 11, 2001, context in congressional testimony in February 2002.[226] Undersecretary of State John Bolton soon repeated the claim in a May 2002 speech:

> For four decades, Cuba has maintained a well-developed and sophisticated biomedical industry, supported until 1990 by the Soviet Union. This industry is one of the most advanced in Latin America and leads in the production of pharmaceuticals and vaccines that are sold worldwide. Analysts and Cuban defectors have long cast suspicion on the activities conducted in these biomedical facilities. Here is what we now know: The United States believes that Cuba has at least a limited offensive biological warfare research and development effort. Cuba has provided dual-use biotechnology to other rogue states. We are concerned that such technology could support BW programs in those states. We call on Cuba to cease all BW-applicable cooperation with rogue states and to fully comply with all of its obligations under the Biological Weapons Convention.[227]

In the same speech, Bolton accused Cuba of supplying dual-use technology related to biological weapons to Libya and Syria.[228] Not only did Cuba have these weapons, he argued; they were supplying them to other adversaries of the United States.

The Cuban government responded to these allegations in the same month at the Conference on Disarmament in Geneva, accusing the United States of lying and asserting that "the very essence of multilateralism was seriously threatened by the hegemonic and unilateral policy of one country which had pretensions to being the owner of the world."[229]

Four months after Bolton's speech, in what came as a "relative surprise to international nonproliferation observers," Cuba announced it would ratify the Treaty of Tlatelolco, adhere to the NPT, and conclude both a Comprehensive Safeguards Agreement and an Additional Protocol with the IAEA.[230] The offer to conclude an Additional Protocol was surprising as it was the most stringent nuclear safeguards agreement possible. Officials from the IAEA communicated to Cuban leaders that they were able to add a protocol to their safeguards agreements for states with little nuclear material (a "small quantities protocol"), which would allow Cuba to avoid IAEA inspections as long as it did not pass a specific threshold of material. The Cuban government rejected this offer to avoid international inspections. According to one former IAEA official, "Cuba was seeking transparency."[231] Cuba's accession on October 23, 2002, allowed the Treaty of Tlatelolco to finally enter into force thirty-four years after it was open for signature, as Cuba was the last holdout.

In the same statement announcing Cuba's NPT ratification, Cuban foreign minister Perez Roque said, "Cuba firmly opposed what now seems to be an 'inevitable' war against Iraq and warned that the UN would lose credibility if the US imposed such a war on the UN Security Council."[232] Though US-Cuban relations had worsened under the George W. Bush administration, the Cuban government declared it was joining the NPT "as a contribution to peace in the post-September 11 world."[233]

For years, the Cuban government had referred to conflicts with its powerful neighbor to the north in explaining its nonadherence to the NPT and the Treaty of Tlatelolco. As US-Cuban relations became tense under the Bush administration, however, with John Bolton accusing Cuba of hiding a biological weapons program and potentially sharing these weapons with "rogue states," the Cuban government decided to join several nonproliferation agreements. During this period, the United States was preparing for war with another rogue state that it accused of possessing so-called weapons of mass destruction (WMD). Bolton's accusations against Cuba and the build-up to the Iraq War suggest that the Cuban government likely joined the NPT and agreed to the most transparent IAEA inspections to appease the United States at a time when a potential military threat was quite real. In this rare case, the US was indirectly threatening Cuba with military action through its threats against Iraq. If one "rogue state" with weapons of mass destruction was going to be attacked for these weapons, it is plausible that Cuban leaders felt they could be next. Consistent with the idea that Cuba felt militarily threatened by the United States during this time, Havana began directing civil defense readiness procedures in early 2003.[234]

As a state antagonistic toward the US-led order during most of the nuclear age, it would be expected that Cuba would resist adhering to the NPT. And, in fact, it took Cuba thirty-four years to join this treaty. The US government used its tools of influence on and off throughout the years following 1968, though it also pushed the Soviet Union to take action as Cuba's patron. It is telling that the Cuban government continued to perceive the NPT through the lens of its poor relationship with the United States and was not persuaded by the Soviet Union. US diplomatic forays in the late 1970s—an example of high-cost diplomacy—failed as relations worsened. It was only when the threat of military action against Cuba over accusations of its purported biological weapons program became plausible that the Cuban government adhered to the NPT, the Comprehensive Safeguards Agreement, the Additional Protocol, and the Treaty of Tlatelolco. While the available evidence does not allow for certainty regarding the links among US accusations against Cuba, the impending Iraq War, and Cuba's NPT adherence, the timing indicates the plausibility of the connection. With the

George W. Bush administration taking military action against Iraq without UN Security Council approval, Cuba appears to have been attempting to protect itself from the same fate through a show of cooperation and transparency. After years of rejecting the NPT over relations with the United States, Cuba joined a flurry of nonproliferation agreements during a period of tense US-Cuban relations. Table 3.4 indicates how well the Cuban case of NPT adherence aligns with the three observable implications related to regime membership.

There is little evidence to support the three alternative explanations related to security, fairness, and domestic political economy when it comes to Cuba's decision to adhere to the NPT. Due to the Bay of Pigs invasion, the Cuban Missile Crisis, and countless reports of CIA plots against leader Fidel Castro, the Cuban government has long been concerned about its security vis-à-vis the United States. However, it does not appear that Cuba delayed its NPT ratification out of a desire to develop its own nuclear weapons program in response to the United States. Castro repeatedly stated that Cuba would not develop nuclear weapons and explained his refusal to join nonproliferation agreements by noting Cuba's many points of conflict with the United States. Cuban leaders viewed the NPT as part of the US-led order. Its close relationship with the Soviet Union did not facilitate its accession, even as Soviet leaders claimed on various occasions that they were pressuring Cuba to join the treaty. Cuba did the opposite of what the security theory would predict. When presented with the possibility that the United States was going to pursue military action against another state that it accused of maintaining a clandestine WMD program, Cuba quickly joined all of the agreements and even passed up the opportunity to avoid intrusive IAEA inspections as part of its safeguards agreement. In terms of the fairness theory, Cuban leaders did at times call attention to the lack of disarmament progress by the NPT nuclear-weapons-possessing states. But it does not appear that this was the primary cause of Havana's long delay in adhering to the treaty; nor did Cuba finally join because of progress on nuclear reductions. Lastly, there is little evidence of a change in Cuban lead-

Table 3.4 Assessing regime membership observable implications for Cuban NPT ratification

State	*The US and its allies will promote the universalization of the NPT and other regime agreements through the use of their tools of influence*	*Decisions to adhere to (or support) the NPT or other regime agreements will reflect consideration of US policy preferences and persuasive tools*	*Decisions to adhere to (or support) the NPT or other regime elements will reflect embeddedness within the US-led order*
Cuba	Yes	Likely	Yes

Table 3.5 Summary of chapter 3 findings

State	*The US and its allies will promote the universalization of the NPT and other regime agreements through the use of their tools of influence*	*Decisions to adhere to (or support) the NPT or other regime agreements will reflect consideration of US policy preferences and persuasive tools*	*Decisions to adhere to (or support) the NPT or other regime elements will reflect embeddedness within the US-led order*
Japan	Yes	Likely	No
Indonesia	Yes	Likely	Yes
Egypt	Yes	Likely	Yes
Cuba	Yes	Likely	Yes

ers' economic approach leading to new calculations about the NPT. Cuba remained a mostly inward-facing regime during this period.

The United States played an important part in shaping the NPT calculations of each of the four states discussed in this chapter. For Japan, renewed US prioritization of the treaty in the mid-1970s, promises of nuclear cooperation, and renewed security assurances were key factors in its decision-making. High-cost diplomacy from vice president Mondale, promises of economic and military aid, and the offer of nuclear assistance encouraged Indonesia to join the treaty. In the Egyptian case, an inducement regarding the supply of nuclear technology led Sadat to seek ratification in the early 1980s after he had rejected the Soviet Union and welcomed support from the United States. Finally, Cuba's adherence appears to have been motivated by the threat of force against another US adversary accused of possessing WMDs. While the most embedded state—Japan—joined first among these four states, it is something of an outlier compared to other highly embedded states in the time required for ratification. The least embedded state discussed, Cuba, did not join for decades. In each case, the foreign leaders became aware that the United States prioritized their adherence, and in each case, US actions helped persuade the states to join the NPT.

The alternative theories of NPT adherence related to security and fairness help explain the ratification delay in the Japanese case. Security considerations also contributed to the Indonesian delay in NPT ratification. The domestic economic politics theory is consistent with aspects of the Japanese and Egyptian cases, though it does not explain the specific timing of either ratification decision. US diplomacy and US policy appear to have been decisive factors in ratification across all four cases as shown in table 3.5.

CHAPTER 4

The Hard-Fought Battle for NPT Extension

In the spring of 1995, the members of the NPT faced an important decision about the future of the treaty. A provision in its text instructs members to decide on the NPT's extension twenty-five years after its entry into force. Entry into force occurred in 1970, so the every-five-year NPT Review Conference in 1995 became the NPT Review and Extension Conference. In the years leading up to the conference, member states disagreed over whether the treaty should be extended indefinitely or for shorter increments of time. The United States promoted unconditional, indefinite extension; some other states within the NPT favored alternative options.

What can we learn from the NPT extension decision-making processes within the governments of Japan, Indonesia, South Africa, and Egypt? These four cases illustrate several of the observable implications related to regime membership presented in chapter 1. As expected by a theory of regime adherence based on US global leadership, the US government expended great effort in trying to persuade all other NPT members to support indefinite extension. US allies also played a significant role in promoting this position. As anticipated, highly embedded Japan supported indefinite extension early on after a brief reconsideration of its policy and then promoted extension among other states. Moderately embedded South Africa was long undecided about indefinite extension but eventually helped the United States achieve this outcome. Egypt and Indonesia, both moderately embedded and trending down, were against indefinite extension for different reasons; both states complicated US efforts and offer less support for the primary theory. In addition, the evidence presented indicates some support for the three alternate theories of regime adherence.

The 1995 NPT Extension

When developing draft NPT texts in the 1960s, the Soviet Union and the United States favored a treaty of indefinite duration, similar to previous arms control agreements. During negotiations, other states pushed back against this proposition, resistant to giving up nuclear weapons indefinitely. Some states advocated for a treaty duration as short as five years. The compromise position is reflected in NPT article 10, section 2: "Twenty-five years after the entry into force of the Treaty, a conference shall be convened to decide whether the Treaty shall continue in force indefinitely, or shall be extended for an additional fixed period or periods. This decision shall be taken by a majority of the Parties to the Treaty."[1] That conference, the NPT Review and Extension Conference, convened from April 17 to May 12, 1995.

Consistent with the argument that the United States has had the greatest strategic interest in nuclear nonproliferation, the US government took the leading role in promoting indefinite extension of the NPT. The Arms Control and Disarmament Agency (ACDA) began strategizing about NPT extension in the early 1990s. One of its initial efforts toward this goal was seeking to move the 1995 meeting location from Geneva, Switzerland, where all previous NPT Review Conferences had been held, to New York City. The logic in pursuing this move was in the numbers. Due to the location of the United Nations, all NPT members, large and small, rich and poor, had representation in New York City. If the meeting were held in Geneva, some smaller states—including many states favorable to US global leadership or where US leverage would be strong—may not have been able to send representatives to vote on extension. The United States wanted to have as many treaty members as possible present to vote. Eventually, US officials successfully convinced other treaty members to move the 1995 meeting to the UN Headquarters in New York City.[2]

In the early 1990s, the ACDA began promoting indefinite extension through low-cost diplomacy in its bilateral and multilateral meetings. US leaders sought to increase support by asking existing groupings of states to make public statements in favor of extension. Close US allies were the first to publicly support indefinite extension; NATO's Nuclear Planning Group made a joint statement supporting extension as early as October 1992.[3] The UN's Western Group first met to coordinate plans for pursuing NPT extension in February 1993. By March 1993, when the three depository states met, UK representative Brian Donnelly told his US and Russian counterparts that "support for indefinite extension was growing with G7, EC [European Community] and NATO endorsement of it."[4] Many allies then began their own campaigns in support of this goal. With these states on board, the United States began a long campaign of meeting foreign leaders one-on-one to convince them of the value of NPT extension. The most active part of the US campaign began when ACDA director John Holum appointed Thomas Graham Jr. as the US ambassador-designate to the NPT renewal process, offering him the job in July 1993.[5] Graham set up an office devoted to NPT extension, headed by Susan Burk. The United States was the only country with an office with multiple individuals devoted solely to the indefinite extension of the

NPT. Together, Graham and his team traveled around the globe for a year and a half promoting indefinite extension, seeking to persuade states that a permanent treaty was in their interest.

While Graham and his team focused on low-cost diplomacy, after the conference, several participants indicated that pressure had been used to coerce smaller powers, with few specific examples cited.[6] There is some limited evidence, however, that reveals the type of pressure exerted by some US officials. For example, in January 1995, the United States had helped bail out Mexico from its peso crisis, providing billions of dollars from a US stabilization fund and organizing IMF loans. At the same time, Mexico's lead ambassador on the issue, Miguel Marín Bosch, was giving speeches against indefinite NPT extension, resulting in the Clinton administration asking the Mexican government to remove Marín Bosch from his position.[7] The Mexican diplomat was also advocating for finalized CTBT negotiations as a necessary condition for NPT extension. Mexico refused to yield to the pressure and remove the ambassador. The United States favored unconditional extension; in other words, it did not want extension held hostage to specific disarmament actions. Publicly, ACDA director Holum did not support linking US aid to the extension vote, but he did promise, "This is not one we'll forget about."[8] Venezuela and Mexico apparently felt pressure to abandon conditions and the cause of rolling NPT extensions once the NPT Review and Extension Conference began.[9] Venezuelan ambassador Adolfo Taylhardat resigned as the head of his delegation after Caracas switched its position to supporting indefinite extension. When asked why his country had changed its position from a twenty-five-year rolling extension to indefinite extension, he replied, "My only answer is that there had been too much pressure . . . applied in all directions."[10] Recognizing the import of indefinite extension for the United States, some states sought to profit off their vote. US officials who were working in government at the time indicate that some states did ask for favors in exchange for their support, but these former officials were unwilling to provide specific details.[11]

The United States faced two major challenges in achieving indefinite extension of the NPT. First, nuclear nonproliferation was not a high priority in most states around the world. US diplomats thus had to spend a great deal of time reminding leaders about the NPT and explaining the treaty's benefits for international security. In their travels, Ambassador Graham's team found that many states did not know much about the treaty. As the *Washington Post* recounted at the time, "In many of these capitals, nuclear weapons seemed to be the least of the government's problems. Some officials Graham met had barely heard of the NPT, never mind having decided how they might vote. In a sense, the NPT regime had worked so well over its twenty-five-year life that many nations now took it for granted."[12]

The second major challenge facing the United States was ensuring that the Non-Aligned Movement (NAM), with its one-hundred-plus members, did not achieve a unified position in opposition to indefinite extension. Though conceived during the Cold War as a bloc of states that was not officially aligned with either East or West, the NAM remained active after the fall of the Soviet Union and had often taken positions in opposition to the United States.[13] Many prominent NAM members favored alternatives to indefinite extension. As demonstrated below, the United States succeeded in ensuring the NAM did not have a shared position going into the conference by convincing a prominent NAM member to support indefinite extension and thus breaking unanimity in the consensus-based group.

The United States engaged in a hard-fought campaign for extension that eventually involved all levels of US bureaucracy across many different agencies and departments and included the efforts of US allies, especially the United Kingdom and France.[14] US leaders and some allies used the full persuasive tool kit from low-cost diplomacy to coercive threats. As former ACDA official Dean Rust recounts, "Secretary of State Warren Christopher made clear this was one of the President's top foreign policy priorities and that a concerted diplomatic plan had to be undertaken. Weekly, then twice a week, then as we got closer, almost every day, representatives from all the State regional bureaus and the arms control agency got together to coordinate their diplomatic efforts to persuade all countries that this treaty should be extended indefinitely."[15]

According to several former US officials, they knew by the time the conference began that they had enough support to achieve extension by majority vote.[16] In the end, the majority was evident to the membership, and so the vote was unnecessary; indefinite extension of the NPT was achieved.[17]

Japan and NPT Extension

Japan was an early supporter of indefinite extension, signing on to a Group of Seven (G7) statement in 1992 and declaring its commitment to this position in the fall of 1993 at the United Nations, a year and a half before the NPT Review and Extension Conference. Its early commitment fits with the expectation for a highly embedded state, yet Japan's support was not immediate and unequivocal, however, and it came after the first change in Tokyo's government in the post–World War II period. In June 1993, before the new government assumed power, Japanese leaders sought a weaker G7 statement in support of indefinite extension, causing concern in the United States and speculation by global media outlets that Japan was reconsidering its commitment to remain a nonnuclear state. Once the new government was in place, its leaders declared their commitment to the indefinite NPT extension within weeks. Japan then became a promoter of indefinite extension among other states.[18]

Most indicators suggest that Japan can be characterized as a state highly embedded in the US-led order during the period surrounding the NPT extension debate, 1990 to the spring of 1995. The United States and Japan maintained their defense alliance, and Japan continued to benefit from its trade relationship with the United States. Trade disputes strained the relationship between the two allies at times, however, as President Clinton came to office in 1993 seeking to reduce the US trade deficit with Japan.[19] In terms of political values, Japan continued to be a free and democratic nation.[20] During the 1990s, Japan scored well above the global average on shared policy preferences with the US-led global order.[21] For reference, Japan's score is comparable to Ireland at this time. In addition, there were several visits between US and Japanese leaders during this period, in which Japanese leaders expressed positive sentiments toward the United States and its global leadership. For example, in August 1995, Prime Minister Murayama made a statement on the fiftieth anniversary of the end of World War II in which he offered "profound gratitude for the indispensable support and assistance extended to Japan by the countries of the world, beginning with the United States of America."[22] Based on all of these factors, we would expect Japan to support indefinite extension early on, with little persuasive effort required by the United States. However, two factors complicated this expectation: a significant change in government leadership in the summer of 1993 and the developing North Korean nuclear program.

As expected for a highly embedded state, Japan was in the grouping of states to first agree to support NPT extension. In his memoirs of this early period of the campaign, Ambassador Graham recalls, "First NATO, then the Group of Seven industrialized nations, and then CSCE (now OSCE) were persuaded to endorse group statements in support of indefinite extension of the NPT without conditions as the most desirable outcome for the 1995 conference."[23] Japan was part of the G7 industrialized nations.

In 1992, Japan agreed to the G7 statement: "We are firmly of the view that the indefinite extension of the NPT at the 1995 Review Conference will be a key step in this [proliferation] problem."[24] The following year, the Japanese government agreed to a weaker version of the same G7 statement at a time when the acting government was awaiting national elections, and Prime Minister Kiichi Miyazawa was unable to garner consensus among the members of the LDP.[25] On July 13, a Japanese government spokesperson even suggested that the treaty could again be extended for a fixed period, with the decision of indefinite extension considered at a later date.[26] A fixed period of extension was the preference of some in the NAM and strongly opposed by the United States and thus inconsistent with the expectation that Japan would quickly and easily commit to supporting indefinite extension. Within five days of this statement, however, on July 17, the Japanese government declared that it would announce its support for indefinite extension as "early as the fall," responding to apparent alarm from the United States.[27] The government spokesperson stated that this announcement was aimed at "dispelling concern among the United States and Asian countries that Japan intends to possess nuclear weapons in the future."[28] According to a former Japanese official who was serving in government at the time, many in Japan wanted their government to resist indefinite extension because they would lose future leverage over the nuclear weapon states in terms of nuclear disarmament; however, "Japan was persuaded under heavy pressure from the United States."[29]

In Japan's national election on July 18, the LDP lost control of the Diet for the first time since 1955. Afterward, LDP foreign minister Kabun Muto came out and announced that Japan would be ready to support indefinite extension of the NPT in the future, stating that because of the election some procedural matters had to be addressed.[30] The United States quickly welcomed this position.[31] The next day, however, illustrating the difficulty of forming a position within the new government, outgoing prime minister Miyazawa declared that Muto had spoken out of turn and was only expressing his personal views.[32] On August 2, 1993, the new vice foreign minister, Kunihiko Saito, told the press that Japan was still working out its stance on NPT extension.[33] In his first address to the Diet on August 23, 1995, new prime minister Morihiro Hosokawa stated, "The nonproliferation of weapons of mass destruction is an urgent security imperative for Japan and the whole of the global community, and I intend to support the indefinite extension of the Nuclear Nonproliferation Treaty. Going beyond that, I believe world peace depends upon the ultimate elimination of all nuclear weapons from the earth and global disarmament, and I intend to engage in more active foreign policy efforts to that end."[34]

At a speech before the UN General Assembly on September 27, 1993, Prime Minister Hosokawa again announced Japanese support for indefinite extension of the NPT, stating, "I wish to affirm that Japan supports the indefinite extension of that treaty beyond 1995." He also asserted Japan's commitment to disarmament and praised recent US-Russian nuclear reductions.[35]

The Japanese government promoted indefinite extension from August 1993 through the 1995 NPT Review and Extension Conference, a period that saw a change to a coalition government in June 1994. In UN meetings, Japan called on other states to support indefinite extension.[36] On April 18, 1995, just ahead of the conference, Secretary of State Warren Christopher and Japanese foreign minister Yohei Kono held a joint press conference in which they stated that they were "working together to try to achieve indefinite extension of the Nuclear Nonproliferation Treaty (NPT) because they both believe that it 'is absolutely essential for a solid path to the future.'"[37]

The Japanese case fits with a theory of regime adherence based on US leadership as Japan was a highly embedded state from which the United States sought and received commitment early in the indefinite extension campaign. The story becomes complicated, however, by the fact that in the summer of 1993, the Japanese government changed party leadership for the first time in the post–World War II era. When Japan appeared to hesitate about supporting indefinite extension as it was in the process of forming this new government, the United States put diplomatic pressure on the Japanese government—likely high-cost diplomacy, though the relevant documents are not yet declassified—to announce a commitment to extension. Nonetheless, by the fall of 1993, well in advance of the 1995 Review and Extension Conference, Japan was fully on board with indefinite extension and helped promote extension among other states. While high-cost diplomacy is not always required to persuade highly embedded states, it is occasionally used when the stakes are high for the United States.

In sum, the Japanese government supported NPT extension quite early, in 1992, and did eventually promote extension publicly to other states. Where the theory falls short is in terms of embeddedness within the US-led order. As a highly embedded state, Japan would be expected to be an early and consistently strong supporter of indefinite extension. But when Japan's government changed in the summer of 1993, there was a period when the new government was forming its policies and appeared to waver on its position. After US pressure, the new government came around and support indefinite extension once again. The mixed-support conclusion for the observable implication related to embeddedness stems from this short period of wavering and two of the alternative theories, those related to security and fairness. The table below illustrates how Japanese positions on NPT extension fare in terms of the observable implications.

The security theory predicts that states will reconsider their commitment to the NPT and the broader nonproliferation regime when their adversaries are proliferating. Was North Korea's nuclear program and its attempt to withdraw from the NPT in March 1993 the reason Japan appeared to struggle with the indefinite extension decision in the summer of 1993?

In the lead up to the G7 meeting in Tokyo in June 1993, the seven states were unable to agree to a strong political statement supporting indefinite extension of the NPT "in deference to Japan."[38] A news report from the period explains, "The Japanese argued that in light of their internal political problems and concern over North Korea's nuclear weapons program, they

Table 4.1 Assessing observable implications for Japanese support of indefinite NPT extension

State	*The US and its allies will promote the universalization of the NPT and other regime agreements through the use of their tools of influence*	*Decisions to adhere to (or support) the NPT or other regime agreements will reflect consideration of US policy preferences and persuasive tools*	*Decisions to adhere to (or support) the NPT or other regime elements will reflect embeddedness within the US-led order*
Japan	Yes	Yes	Mixed support

could not commit their Government to an indefinite extension of the treaty."[39] Japan also refused to allow the term *unconditional* to be used in describing the extension of the NPT.[40] The final June 1993 G7 political declaration reads, "We reiterate the objectives of universal adherence to the NPT as well as the Treaty's indefinite extension in 1995."[41] Japanese preferences were the primary reason this language was weaker than the G7's 1992 statement on this topic.[42] Japan's hesitancy was widely reported in international media, with some journalists speculating that North Korea's growing nuclear capability meant Japanese leaders were considering a nuclear weapons option in response.[43] Indeed, indefinite extension of the NPT was challenged by a small group of hawkish Diet members—"the influential minority in the right wing of the LDP"[44]—who wanted Japan to maintain the option for a nuclear weapon program in the future. Their position is consistent with expectations of the security theory in that a state will be less likely to support the regime if it is considering its own nuclear program for its perceived security needs. Furthermore, maintaining an ambiguous position on the NPT extension could provide Japan leverage against the DPRK, as Pyongyang declared in March 1993 that it would withdraw from the treaty.[45]

Ultimately this minority in the Diet failed to convince Japanese leaders to avoid committing to indefinite extension or backtracking on the government's September 1993 pledge to support the US-favored position. Though the desire by some to leave the nuclear weapon option open may have influenced the government's reluctance in the spring of 1993 to sign on to a strong G7 statement, it did not stop Japan from fully supporting indefinite extension only months later. It certainly helped those factions seeking to support indefinite extension that it appeared as though progress was being made on halting the North Korean nuclear weapon program through the Agreed Framework. In this agreement, North Korea has agreed to stop producing plutonium in exchange for two proliferation-resistant reactors and fuel oil.

Those seeking a possible nuclear option continued to influence Japanese decision-making in this period, however. It was revealed in 1999 that in 1995, the same year Japan supported indefinite extension of the NPT, its Defense Agency conducted a secret review of a Japanese nuclear weapons option in "A Report Concerning the Problems of the Proliferation of Weapons of Mass Destruction."[46] This report explored whether the US nuclear umbrella could be trusted in the post–Cold War era. The report found that the nuclear option was "not favorable to Japan," and Japan should "support indefinite extension of the treaty." On its security relationship with the United States, the report concluded: "Since the theory of nuclear deterrence remains effective, reliance on the US extended deterrent is the best choice. Based on such a precondition, what is appropriate for Japan is to start a discussion on the maintenance of the credibility of the US extended deterrent in the security dialogues between Japan and the United States beginning today, and to pursue measures to mitigate, in terms of practice, the one-sided nature of the Japan-US Security Treaty, which is the basis for it."[47]

By the time this report made the above conclusion, the Japanese government had already publicly supported the indefinite extension of the NPT for two years. Nonetheless, the 1995 Japanese Defense Agency report does show the strong influence of those in government who wanted to consider nuclear weapons. The report supports indefinite extension, primarily because of the importance of Japan's relationship with the United States and the security benefits provided by the US nuclear umbrella. In sum, while security factors can be said to have influenced Japanese thinking and the hesitancy in the summer of 1993, it was US leadership and its benefits to Japan that convinced this faction they could support indefinite extension of the NPT.

In a similar vein, the fairness theory of regime adherence is related to the Japanese government's machinations about indefinite extension, in that some government factions opposed supporting indefinite NPT extension over the lack of disarmament progress by the five NPT nuclear weapon states. Based on available evidence, this faction appears to have had more sway in the deliberations than those seeking a nuclear weapon option. They argued the treaty's five official nuclear weapon states were not abiding by their side of the bargain. Some within the Japanese government and civil society worried indefinite extension would hamper further nuclear disarmament efforts by removing a point of leverage over the nuclear possessor states.[48] For example, in August 1993, the mayor of Hiroshima led a group that called for Japan to reject the US-favored position out of concern that it would hurt future disarmament efforts.[49] In addressing the global speculation that the weakened G7 statement in 1993 was due to nuclear weapon considerations, Japanese foreign ministry spokesman Masamichi Hanabusa stated in July 1993 that Japan would continue to adhere to the three nuclear principles and that "some political forces in Japan demand that the nuclear powers fulfill their obligations under the NPT before any indefinite extension. Article VI of the treaty states that nuclear weapon states should strive for further nuclear disarmament."[50] The spokesperson went on: "Some people may justifiably raise the question as to what extent that objective has been met."[51] In a turn alarming to the United States, the spokesperson then suggested rolling extensions of the NPT, a proposal similar to the one promoted by some NAM states.[52] In September 1993, 150 prominent academics signed a petition asking prime minister Hosokawa not to support indefinite extension.[53] The disarmament faction did not ultimately convince politicians in Japan to withdraw support for the indefinite extension of the NPT, but like the LDP hawks, this faction likely played a role in the short delay in Japanese support in the summer of 1993. The prime minister's reference to recent US-Russian disarmament progress when he announced Japanese support of indefinite extension in the fall of 1993 was likely aimed at appealing to this faction.

Japan would go on to help the United States push for indefinite extension, but even at the NPT Review and Extension Conference in 1995, there was a recognition by the United States and its close allies that the Japanese government was not entirely happy with this position. As British delegate Sir Michael Weston recalled when asked about nonnuclear allies, "They had their doubts about extending a treaty which basically they were not happy with, since it did license nuclear weapons. . . . . [Japan] felt viscerally that this was not something that they wanted to do. They behaved impeccably at the conference; I'm not suggesting that they did not. But one was always worried that somehow, one's support in one's own group would evaporate."[54] Though the fairness theory finds relevance within the decision-making process in Japan, it is limited in its ability to predict Japan's final decision. Moreover, the fact that Japan followed US wishes even as many in the country did not want to support indefinite extension and lose the leverage to encourage nuclear disarmament indicates the important role of the United States in pushing indefinite extension.

Solingen's theory that liberalizing states will eschew proliferation appears less relevant to this specific case. The 1990s were a period of economic strife for Japan, known as the "Lost Decade," and the LDP lost power for the first time since 1955 due to economic weakness and an insider-trading scandal involving a number of members of the party. Japan and the United States also had several trade disputes during this period. Nonetheless, Japanese leadership was consistently outward facing across both administrations. Thus, the theory that economically liberal states will support nonproliferation is consistent with this case, but it does not explain the Japanese government's initial support, reservations, and then ultimate support for extension.

Indonesia and NPT Extension

As a leader in the NAM, Indonesia was an influential member of a grouping of states that was largely skeptical of indefinite extension. Indonesia favored a proposal for twenty-five-year rolling extensions of the NPT to maintain pressure on the nuclear weapon states to continue pursuing nuclear disarmament. Try as it might, the United States repeatedly failed to garner Indonesia's commitment. Instead, the United States focused its efforts on ensuring Indonesia could not lead a unified NAM position going into the Review Conference. To do this, the United States focused on other nonaligned states.

Based on most indicators, Indonesia is considered a state moderately embedded within the US-led order at this time, but it was trending toward weakly embedded in the period leading up to the NPT extension decision as the relationship between the two countries worsened. The one bright spot was US-Indonesian economic relations, as the United States was the second-largest trade partner to Indonesia during the 1990s for both its imports (about 11–14 percent) and exports (about 13–14 percent).[55] However, Indonesian relations with the United States during the first half of the 1990s were greatly affected by US concerns for Indonesian human rights abuses, which represented a deep conflict over political values. The United States was no longer focused on fighting communism—a key element of successful US-Indonesian relations during the Cold War—and became more concerned with President Suharto's abuses, which in turn led to growing anti-Americanism within Suharto's regime. The State Department's 1991 report on human rights around the world states that the Indonesian government was "responsible for numerous human rights abuses, including killings and torture of civilians."[56] The US cut off international military education and training aid to Jakarta, funding that supported Indonesian security, after members of the Indonesian military killed seventy-five to two hundred demonstrators in the Dili Massacre in East Timor on November 12, 1991.[57] In addition, from 1992 to 1995, President Suharto served as the secretary-general of the NAM, a grouping that was often at odds with the United States and the US-led order at this time. During this period, Indonesia is coded a –7 by Polity, indicating an autocracy, and Freedom House determined Indonesia to be "partially free" from 1990 to 1993 and "not free" from 1993 to 1995.[58] UN General Assembly voting data indicate that Indonesia had a very low foreign policy concordance with the US-led order in the early 1990s, comparable to Syria and Vietnam.[59]

As anticipated by the fact that Indonesia was trending from moderately embedded to weakly embedded within the US-led global order in the first half of the 1990s, Indonesia was reluctant to extend the NPT permanently, and the United States was thus required to engage in high-cost diplomacy and inducements to attempt to bring about its support. Indonesia's stance was significant because of its leadership position in the NAM. If the NAM, with its 111 members at the time, unified against the US-favored position, indefinite extension would be unachievable. Thus, as a number of former officials confirm, the United States and its allies maintained the strategic goal of preventing the NAM from developing a consensus position against indefinite extension.[60] For Indonesia, US diplomatic efforts failed, and US leaders, convinced that Indonesia was not going to change its position, shifted focus to winning the support of other NAM states.

US ambassador Thomas Graham Jr. visited Jakarta in February 1995 to attempt to persuade the Indonesian government of the value of NPT extension. He recalls that the Indonesians were "unmovable." They told him that if the United States insisted on indefinite extension, "it would be a difficult conference."[61] In an example of high-cost diplomacy, Graham brought a letter for President Suharto from President Clinton personally requesting support for NPT extension. The letter included an inducement. The "United States would look 'positively' on a Southeast Asian nuclear-weapon free zone—long desired by Indonesia" if they would support indefinite extension.[62] Previously, the United States had argued against this zone because it could inhibit the US Navy's freedom of action in the waters of the region. The Indonesians refused Graham admittance to President Suharto or the foreign minister, though they did accept Clinton's letter. The US offer regarding the nuclear-weapons-free zone did not appear to influence Indonesia's leadership, and Jakarta continued to support their rolling extension proposal.

Indonesia has long held ambitions to produce nuclear energy, and as discussed in the previous chapter, it had a national atomic energy agency, BATAN, at this time. When US ambassador Graham visited Jakarta to deliver the letter from President Clinton, he also met with officials from BATAN. He found that these leaders were in favor of indefinite extension because of nuclear supply concerns, but they had little leverage with the more powerful Indonesian Foreign Ministry.[63] Thus the intuition that the inducement of nuclear assistance results in regime adherence applies to this case, but those seeking to commit to indefinite extension were not powerful enough within the Indonesian government to have their preferences set policy. This would soon change, however, as the following chapter demonstrates.

The multiweek NPT Review and Extension Conference began on April 17 in New York City. The United States avoided a potential last-minute setback to its goal when a NAM conference held in Bandung, Indonesia, April 27–29, was unable to come to a last-minute consensus position on how to approach the issue of NPT extension. First, the group could not agree on calling for a vote by secret ballot at the New York conference, a position supported by Indonesia to help nonnuclear weapon states resist pressure from the nuclear powers, especially the United States. Unsurprisingly, the United States strongly opposed the secret ballot. Second, and more significantly, the NAM also failed at Bandung to agree on promoting Indonesia's proposal for rolling twenty-five-year extensions of the NPT as an alternative to indefinite extension. A policy of rolling extensions was the position Indonesia and some like-minded NAM states would champion at the conference, but the lack of a single unified bargaining position behind Indonesia's proposal severely weakened the NAM's leverage.

Over the course of the NPT Review and Extension Conference, support for Indonesia's position waned. By May 9, the *New York Times* reported, "Indonesia, which began the conference as head of a large group of nations opposed to indefinite extension, was by Friday able to get only a handful of supporters for its formal proposal calling for perpetual renewals every 25 years."[64] Indonesia's supporters included Iran, Jordan, Malaysia, Mali, Myanmar, Nigeria, North Korea, Papua New Guinea, Thailand, and Zimbabwe. Notably, the group of states aligned with Indonesia's position represents several that were weakly embedded within the US-led order.

The Indonesian position lost any remaining steam during the conference after South Africa introduced a compromise proposal. This proposal was similar to one put forth by Mexico, but significantly, it included a *nonbinding* statement of principles ("Principles and Objectives of Nuclear Nonproliferation and Nuclear Disarmament"). The principles called for the nuclear weapon states to commit to a CTBT, a Fissile Material Control Treaty (FMCT), and systematic and progressive efforts toward disarmament. These principles were not legally binding, making this compromise position much more appealing to the nuclear weapon states who sought unconditional extension. The compromise also included a commitment to strengthen the treaty's review process ("The Strengthening of the Review Process of the Treaty"), by adding regular preparatory committee meetings in the three years before each five-year NPT Review Conference.

Randal Rydell and 1995 conference chair Jayantha Dhanapala recount that a key contribution to the emerging consensus toward indefinite extension was provided by the Indonesian foreign minister Ali Alatas, who arrived in New York after the NAM conference in Bandung disbanded. Alatas proposed a more explicit linkage between the documents "Principles and Objectives of Nuclear Nonproliferation and Nuclear Disarmament" and "Strengthening of the Review Process of the Treaty" and the proposal for indefinite extension. As a result, three parallel decisions were then presented to the entire membership "with built-in linkages although it was acknowledged that while the extension decision was legally binding the other two were politically binding."[65]

Ambassador Graham initially hesitated when considering Indonesia's linkage proposal. As he was thinking about what the US position should be, an Indonesian ambassador, recognizing that they were getting very little in exchange for indefinite extension, said, "Oh come on, Tom, give us a crumb."[66] Graham then agreed. Indonesia, leading the opposition against indefinite extension, would ultimately not oppose this compromise outcome when consensus on indefinite extension was declared. Essis Essoh's study of the 1995 NPT conference concludes, "Indonesia . . . agreed not to oppose consensus when it became clear not only that there were a majority for indefinite extension, but also that it was impossible to get more non-aligned states to support a rolling 25-year extension."[67] In other words, recognizing its position had lost, the Indonesian government chose not to oppose the final outcome, but it did not support it.

In an interview after the conference, the Indonesian ambassador Nugroho Wisnumurti bemoaned the approach used by the United States and its allies to bring about indefinite extension of the NPT: "What I feel as very disturbing is how they have reached the majority for indefinite extension. It is simply by the use of pressure tactics against smaller countries. Not all of them were being pressured. There are those that already had positions in favor of indefinite extension, but many countries complained to us about pressure with conditionalities and other types of pressures. This might lead to a bad precedent and this should be avoided in the future."[68] Later in the same interview, Wisnumurti stated: "There were other countries—members of the European Union—working in their own sphere of influence, lobbying and in some cases putting pressures on various countries. I even heard complaints from Western countries, 'smaller guys' in the Western group, that felt the pressure was too hard. This kind of arm twisting is unacceptable. This is very undemocratic."[69]

Though US attempts to influence Jakarta were not successful in changing Indonesia's position on extension, US leadership is the best explanation for the outcome of the conference. As Mexican ambassador Miguel Marín Bosch put it, the reason the nonnuclear weapon states were not able to get more from the nuclear weapon states was twofold: "a) the divided nonaligned . . . b) the situation we are living everyday. . . . It is a unipolar 1946 world—there is only one superpower."[70]

Indonesian decision-making surrounding the NPT extension demonstrates mixed support for a theory of regime adherence based on US global leadership. The United States did attempt several tools of influence, including high-cost diplomacy and an inducement to persuade Jakarta to back indefinite extension, and thus the observable implication related to US tools of influence finds support. But Jakarta rejected these US efforts and maintained its principled position in favor of rolling extensions; Jakarta's decision did not reflect US preferences or tools. Indonesia was trending toward weakly embedded within the US-led order in this time, and thus it is anticipated that it would take longer and require more costly tools to bring the southeast Asian state on board. This finding indicates mixed results for the US-based theory of regime adherence in that Jakarta's rejection of the US position is consistent with a state weakly embedded in the regime, and yet it would be expected that eventually the United States could persuade Indonesia to support its position. Jakarta never supported extension; it only decided not to oppose consensus when it realized its position had lost. Table 4.2 summarizes the outcomes for observable implications related to regime membership in this case.

Table 4.2 Assessing observable implications for Indonesian support of indefinite NPT extension

State	*The US and its allies will promote the universalization of the NPT and other regime agreements through the use of their tools of influence*	*Decisions to adhere to (or support) the NPT or other regime agreements will reflect consideration of US policy preferences and persuasive tools*	*Decisions to adhere to (or support) the NPT or other regime elements will reflect embeddedness within the US-led order*
Indonesia	Yes	No	Mixed support

There is no evidence to suggest that Indonesia was motivated to oppose indefinite extension of the NPT for reasons connected to its security or domestic political economy. When examining the grouping of states that opposed indefinite extension along with Indonesia, however, we see there may be some truth to the security theory for states aligned with Indonesia at the NPT Review and Extension Conference. Opposing indefinite extension was a vote both for making the treaty contingent on future decisions and arguably for weakening the treaty regime. At the time, many analysts considered that anything but indefinite extension would be a significant blow to the treaty. The supporters of Indonesia's alternative proposal, those that wanted to avoid enshrining the NPT indefinitely, included Iran, Jordan, Malaysia, Mali, Myanmar, Nigeria, North Korea, Papua New Guinea, Thailand, and Zimbabwe. Three of these states, North Korea, Myanmar, and Iran, would later have or be suspected of having nuclear weapons ambitions. In terms of domestic political economy, the main area in which Indonesia was embedded within the US-led order at this time was in its trade relations. Trade and openness to the world economy did not push Jakarta in the direction of supporting indefinite extension of the regime.

Instead, the fairness theory of regime adherence best explains this case, as Indonesia's position supporting twenty-five-year rolling NPT extensions stemmed from its desire to maintain disarmament pressure on the five NPT nuclear weapon states. Leading up to the 1995 conference, Indonesia and the NAM made clear they sought concrete progress on disarmament in exchange for extending the NPT indefinitely. At the September 1994 NPT Preparatory Committee meeting, Indonesia submitted the NAM's position on the treaty to the conference chairman. The letter noted that there were "fundamental shortcomings" in the NPT and that the success of the 1995 Review and Extension Conference would be aided by greater achievements in nuclear disarmament, nuclear weapon states cooperation with nuclear-weapons-free zones, progress on the Comprehensive Test Ban Treaty, security assurances for nonnuclear weapon states, progress on a Fissile Material Cut-Off Treaty, and fewer "unjustified" limitations on nuclear technology.[71] Many nonnuclear weapon states, especially in the NAM, recognized the 1995 conference as a rare opportunity to be able to pressure the nuclear weapon states over disarmament.

The deep-seated frustration within the Indonesian Foreign Ministry over nuclear disarmament progress was evident at the NPT Review and Extension Conference during the committee debates. Joseph Pilat recalls that after a US ambassador spoke about everything the United States had done to date in the area of NPT article 6 (the disarmament commitment), a young Indonesian diplomat stood up and essentially accused the ambassador of being a liar. Pilat recalls, "The young diplomat was very angry. . . . I hadn't seen that kind of emotion [before]."[72]

In the end, concessions to Indonesia and its like-minded partners included promising progress on the CTBT, adding the nonbinding principles document at the Review Conference and supporting a spring 1995 UN General Assembly resolution on security guarantees for nonnuclear weapon states. Whether these limited actions were sufficient for Indonesia not to block consensus or whether it simply had no options once it was evident the majority favored indefinite extension is unclear. The nonnuclear weapon states received no legally binding commitments from the nuclear weapon states in exchange for securing indefinite extension of the treaty. Former Mexican ambassador Marín Bosch wrote afterward, "In exchange for the indefinite extension of the NPT (which all five nuclear-weapon states favored strongly) the non-nuclear states got almost nothing."[73]

South Africa and NPT Extension

Unable to obtain Indonesia's support for indefinite extension, US officials sought to ensure that there was not a consensus position among the 111-member NAM. To achieve this goal, the position of another nonaligned state was key: South Africa. US leaders put a great deal of effort into gauging and influencing South Africa's evolving position in the months leading up to the NPT Review and Extension Conference. South Africa eventually came to support indefinite extension in April 1995.

South Africa is assessed to be moderately embedded in the US-led order during the period leading up to the 1995 NPT Review and Extension Conference. The South African government received significant aid from the United States and assurances of more in the wake of its transition to democracy in the early 1990s. The United States provided $35 million to support the first democratic election in April 1994 and promised $600 million in investment and aid after the election.[74] In November 1994, President Clinton announced the establishment of a joint commission to promote cooperation between the two nations to be led by South African deputy president Thabo Mbeki and US vice president Al Gore. However, South Africa was also a new and powerful member of the NAM in this period, a grouping that often opposed the United States within the United Nations. In addition, though the new South African government aspired to democratic political values, US and South African leaders diverged over the new South African government's interactions with the illiberal states Cuba and Libya. UN General Assembly votes are unavailable for South Africa in the early 1990s because South Africa's apartheid government was suspended from the UNGA from 1974 to 1993. The scores in 1994 and 1995 indicate a moderate level of foreign policy concordance.[75] Based on its moderate embeddedness within the US-led order, we would expect that the United States would have to use its more costly and targeted tools of influence to bring about South Africa's support for indefinite extension but that South Africa would eventually support extension. In this case, the United States put extra pressure on South Africa as part of its strategy to ensure the NAM did not have a unified position against indefinite extension.

South Africa's position on NPT extension must be understood in the context of its democratic transition and the renunciation of its secret nuclear weapons program. The South African government decided to destroy its nuclear weapons in 1989, during the period when President F. W. de Klerk was also dismantling the apartheid government and pushing forward democratic reforms. At the time, de Klerk only told the United States and the IAEA about his country's bomb program.[76] As Helen E. Purkitt and Stephen F. Burgess recount, "De Klerk took dramatic steps to end weapons of mass destruction in part because he wanted to bring South Africa back in line with the United States, the West, and international law."[77] The South African government acceded to the NPT in July 1991. Two years later, in 1993, the government officially announced publicly that South Africa had previously been in possession of six nuclear weapons. The IAEA then entered the country to verify its nonnuclear status. Democratic elections were held in April 1994, with the long-banned African National Congress (ANC) winning the majority of votes.

Over the course of 1994, members of the international community scrutinized South Africa's position on NPT extension; in fact, its government did not develop an official position until April 1995. Based on a February 1994 conference organized by the ANC and the nongovernmental Environmental Working Group to establish the new government's nuclear policy, it seemed that South Africa might follow many other NAM members and favor rolling NPT extensions. Abdul Minty, an ANC leader in the nuclear policy field who would become one of South Africa's most important diplomats on nuclear issues, sounded very much like other NAM leaders when he stated at the conference that "[the NPT] is a discriminatory treaty where the nuclear weapon states have very little pressure on them to get rid of their weapons. . . . Our efforts must, of course, go to make sure that that does not continue to operate in such a discriminatory manner."[78]

In April 1994, the ANC's Nelson Mandela was elected president in South Africa's first democratic national election. In the following month, South Africa joined the NAM at a ministerial conference in Cairo. In August 1994, Ambassador Graham and Susan Burk visited South Africa as part of a multicountry trip to the African continent to promote NPT extension. The US team made their pitch about the importance of extending the treaty for international security and the security of South Africa. Graham recounts that the new South African government had not yet made up its mind about extension, though they made clear they were committed to the treaty and nuclear nonproliferation.[79]

NPT Preparatory Committee (PrepCom) meetings for the 1995 NPT Review and Extension Conference were held in May 1993, January 1994, September 1994, and January 1995, spanning the change in South Africa from the apartheid regime to the new democratic government. South Africa sent representatives to all four meetings, although they only sent local New York representatives to the first one in 1993. From the second NPT PrepCom on, the meetings were covered by a small office in what would come to be known as the Department of International Affairs, which included Tom Wheeler, Peter Goosen, Tom Kellerman, Frank Land, and Jean duPreez. Abdul Minty, a member of the ANC, served as an adviser but was not yet officially employed by the government. The office did not initially have much changeover from the old government to the new.

During the PrepCom process, Goosen requested a document from South Africa's Office of the Chief State Law Advisor outlining the legal options for extending the treaty based on NPT article 10.2. The South African delegation then presented that legal document publicly at the fourth NPT PrepCom in January 1995. South African lawyers had outlined three options: indefinite extension, extension for one additional fixed period, or extension for additional fixed periods.[80] The document further explained two options for fixed periods: they could be automatic unless parties sought to end the treaty, or each fixed period could require a vote of the parties for the treaty to continue.[81] As former South African diplomats recall, they did not yet have an official government position on extension at the fourth NPT PrepCom, but South Africa became associated with the third option in the document: fixed periods of extension.

Though some South African officials had expressed personal and unofficial views on extension in 1994, those in the highest levels of the South African government had not made a decision on NPT extension as late as February 1995, two months before the conference. When President Clinton sent a letter to President Mandela on the topic in mid-February 1995—one of many examples of high-cost diplomacy in this case—the legal adviser to Deputy President Mbeki called duPreez's office and asked what the letter was about.[82] Mandela had charged Mbeki with making the decision on NPT extension. The call from Mbeki's legal adviser gave duPreez's small office the opportunity to request a decision meeting with Mbeki. Before that meeting occurred, however, in March 1995 Mbeki visited Washington, DC, and met with Clinton and Gore. According to the US ambassador to South Africa at the time, Princeton Nathan Lyman, Clinton made the NPT extension "the main topic of conversation" when he met with Mbeki. Lyman writes that Clinton "emphasized the tremendous importance the United States accorded to this matter."[83] In terms of diplomatic effort, the United States was putting a full-court press on Mbeki and his delegation.

On April 1, 1995, approximately a dozen individuals, including Deputy President Mbeki, met to discuss South Africa's position on NPT extension.

Rusty Evans, the Department of Foreign Affairs director general, chaired the meeting. Members of the group presented Mbeki with several options, including alternatives to NPT indefinite extension promoted by Mexico, Indonesia, and Nigeria. According to duPreez, Minty made a strong argument in favor of South Africa taking a position in line with other NAM states, such as a one-time extension for twenty-five years or rolling extensions.[84] In the end, Mbeki made the decision to support indefinite extension. Those at the meeting recall that Mbeki said that "human beings have the right, and it's almost as if it's a human right, to have their life not to be threatened by weapons of mass destruction."[85] Goosen recalls that he and duPreez then were instructed to come up with what they would ask for from the nuclear weapon states in exchange for South Africa's support of indefinite extension. Despite this "ask," the South African government "decided that the proposal for a set of 'Principles' was not conditional for [their] support for indefinite extension of the Treaty."[86] Goosen and du Preez spent the rest of the weekend developing their position, which was subsequently mentioned in letters responding to Gore and Clinton. South Africa's ask would become the set of principles to accompany indefinite extension and the stronger review process for the treaty described above.

In an April 4 letter from Mbeki to Gore, Mbeki notes the importance of the treaty and then writes, "South Africa therefore supports the view that the NPT should be extended indefinitely."[87] He goes on to explain that though extension should not be held hostage to conditions, a "mechanism" should be found to address the complaints of many nonnuclear NPT states about the lack of disarmament progress, the lack of formal security assurances for nonnuclear states, and the perceived challenges in securing peaceful nuclear technology. Mbeki offered the idea of adopting "Principles for Nuclear Nonproliferation and Disarmament" at the conference. The principles would set out "general obligations" and be a "yardstick" by which members could assess the treaty moving forward. The principles could be adapted at each subsequent NPT Review Conference.[88] This suggestion would have the effect of strengthening the review process for the treaty. Gore responded to Mbeki with a letter on April 13, welcoming further discussion on a strengthened review process as long it did not hurt efforts to extend the treaty and offering to meet with South African ambassador Alfred Nzo at the upcoming conference in New York.[89]

As discussed above, the South African delegation at the NAM Bandung conference in April 1995 made clear it was supporting indefinite extension, and thus the NAM was unable to establish a consensus position with which to challenge the United States and its partners. South Africa's intervention was thus an important component of achieving indefinite extension. Ultimately, many smaller NAM states supported indefinite extension as well, but the most important factor in the lack of unity in the consensus-based NAM was South Africa's dissent.

At the beginning of the NPT Review and Extension Conference, South African ambassador Alfred Nzo presented the principles and revised Review Conference ideas in his opening speech. Presenting the two documents at the beginning of the conference was Nzo's decision, one that other participants considered instrumental to the conference outcome in favor of indefinite extension. Sven Jurschewsky, a member of the Canadian delegation at the conference, recalls that Nzo's speech was key in "creating a certain psychological momentum." He remembers, "We knew we were going to have a good result because the psychology had been created."[90] In the end, these ideas were adopted as two separate documents along with indefinite extension.

On the question of whether the United States influenced South Africa's decision on NPT extension, there is quite a bit of disagreement, with South African officials understandably claiming that their leaders were not influenced by US pressure. It is evident, however, that the US government employed several tools to attempt to influence the new government's position.

The United States engaged in numerous examples of high-cost diplomacy in trying to persuade the South African government to support indefinite extension. Several US officials made clear in person and through personal letters that they prioritized extension and sought South African support. Beyond the visit by Graham and Burk in 1994 and several visits from US embassy officials, Graham asked General Colin Powell to send a letter to Nelson Mandela requesting support.[91] Colin Powell was one of the Americans most admired by Mandela according to intelligence collected by Graham's team; Powell sent the letter.[92] President Clinton also asked Mbeki for support during the deputy president's visit to the White House in March 1995. Moreover, Gore was known to have developed a close relationship with Mbeki. They served together on the US–South African bilateral commission that Clinton publicly introduced in November 1994, but their relationship began earlier when the vice president reportedly established a back-channel connection with Mbeki.[93] Gore personally asked for Mbeki's support on indefinite extension, according to former US officials.[94] NPT Review and Extension Conference chair Dhanapala affirmed the importance of this interpersonal relationship: "A special link on key [NPT Review and Extension Conference] issues is said to have been established between US Vice President Al Gore . . . and South African Vice President Thabo Mbeki, ensuring South Africa's support for an indefinite extension of the NPT. This was an undoubted diplomatic triumph."[95] Ambassador Lyman concludes, "I think Thabo Mbeki made the decision in the context of the overall relationship [with the United States], the promises of the binational commission, and other forms of cooperation."[96] According to Graham, the decision to support indefinite extension had been made by Mbeki "after a long internal debate about whether South Africa's national interest lay in supporting indefinite extension or the NAM position."[97]

The import of South Africa's position on extension meant the US government went beyond high-cost diplomacy—it issued threats as well. According to one news report at the time, the United States had lobbied South Africa in the months before the NAM's Bandung conference, telling South Africa that its tentative support for rolling twenty-five-year NPT extensions "called into question its 'nonproliferation credentials' and its right to gain membership in an exclusive nuclear exporters trade group [the Nuclear Suppliers Group, or NSG]."[98] Former South African diplomat duPreez alluded to stipulations set by the United States during negotiations over South Africa joining such groups. He stated, "There were negotiations to enter the NSG [Nuclear Suppliers Group] and the MTCR [Missile Technology Control Regime], and the US support for that was critical and they laid down some conditions."[99]

Many of those who served in South Africa's government at the time strongly dispute that they were unduly influenced by the United States. Noting other instances when he witnessed South African leaders oppose US wishes later on, duPreez argues, "Whether [Mbeki] did so to satisfy the United States, I would dispute. I think he just saw the bigger picture. . . . So, I don't think that this was as a result of pressure. This was as a result of see[ing] the bigger picture. See[ing] the bigger picture of the way South Africa is, see[ing] the bigger picture of what this treaty means."[100]

Despite what duPreez argues, with the United States offering significant aid and investment to the transitioning nation and making some small threats, it is unlikely Mbeki would not have at least factored in the personal requests made by both Clinton and Gore into his consideration of "the bigger picture." In 1993, the US Overseas Private Investment Corporation signed an agreement with South Africa to foster foreign investment. This agreement would lead to hundreds of millions of dollars for South Africa.[101] The United States has remained the single largest foreign investor in the country, representing approximately 40 percent of total foreign investment since the democratic transition.[102] Moreover, the US Agency for International Development (AID) had pledged $600 million to South African development in 1994 before the conference.[103] As Mbeki made his decision about NPT extension, the US–South African bilateral commission was just getting started. This commission would lead to additional investment and aid for the newly democratic state.

The United States also helped South Africa with nuclear assistance and with its interest in becoming a recognized nuclear supplier. In April, as the NPT Review and Extension Conference was beginning, South Africa became a member of the Nuclear Suppliers Group, an important step for a country that sought to promote its peaceful nuclear industry after dismantling its nuclear weapons program. US support was integral to South Africa's entry into this grouping. Four months after the NPT conference, the United States signed a nuclear cooperation agreement with the South Africans, allowing the state to purchase US nuclear technology.[104] When President Clinton announced the nuclear deal, he noted that South Africa played a "decisive role in the achievement of indefinite NPT extension—a top US foreign policy and national security goal."[105] In the mid-1990s, the United States was the only state that could provide such a significant amount and array of benefits to South Africa. Over the 1990s, US aid and investment in South Africa was worth $10 billion.[106] While there is no direct evidence of the connection, it is difficult to fathom that in this context, personal appeals from the US president and vice president about a specific policy priority would not be positively considered by Mbeki. In his study of the role of South Africa in the NPT extension process, Onderčo concludes, "The US's cooperation with South Africa would not have been possible without the leadership of Thabo Mbeki, who clearly expected a future benefit for his country from the relationship with the US."[107]

When it came to the indefinite extension of the treaty, Mbeki had to weigh South Africa's interest in nonproliferation along with the competing positions of the NAM and the United States. South Africa's decision was costly; one former official noted that South Africa was "a pariah within the NAM for quite a while" after supporting indefinite extension.[108] Pariah status stemmed not only from South Africa's role in preventing a NAM consensus position but from being perceived as a lackey of the United States. South African officials were very sensitive about this perception. After the 1995 NPT conference, the South African Department of Foreign Affairs director general, Rusty Evans, told his US counterpart, "It was important that SAG not be put into position of appearing to be bending under USG pressure."[109]

The South African case provides mixed results for the three observable observations related to regime membership. The United States did indeed promote NPT extension using several tools of influence, including low-cost and high-cost diplomacy as well as implicit inducements and threats. While we cannot know for certain why Deputy President Mbeki made the decision to support the US-favored position of indefinite extension, it would appear likely that the personal pleas from President Clinton and Vice President Gore and the significant aid the United States was providing and promising to provide in the future would affect Mbeki's calculation. This was a costly decision for South Africa as it was unpopular among many of the powerful NAM nations and risked making the government look like it was beholden to the United States. Based on South Africa's moderate embeddedness during this time, it is expected that the United States and its allies would be able to persuade South Africa to come on board with high- and low-cost diplomacy. While these efforts may have been sufficient, the United States was not taking any chances in ensuring South Africa supported indefinite extension. For that reason, the United States also engaged in more costly tools like inducements and threats. While much of the US aid would likely have flowed to South Africa regardless of the extension debate, this level of economic aid would have likely shaped the calculations of South Africa's leadership. Table 4.3 summarizes the outcomes for observable implications related to regime membership.

As a state that had just given up its indigenous nuclear weapons program, there is no evidence that South Africa's position on NPT extension aimed to weaken the treaty to preserve a nuclear option. Instead, the alternative explanations that find resonance with the South African case are the theories related to fairness and domestic political economy.

In terms of the fairness theory, when Mbeki made the decision to support indefinite extension, he told his team to think of what they were going to ask the nuclear states for in exchange for South Africa's support. After all, the support of South Africa—a new NAM member and former nuclear weapon state—was an important prize for the United States in the campaign for indefinite extension. What they asked for eventually became the two additional documents agreed on at the NPT Review and Extension Conference. The first, "Strengthening the Review Process for the Treaty," established that there would be three ten-day PrepCom meetings, with the possibility of a fourth, in the years leading up to the five-year NPT Review Conferences. These longer meetings would provide additional time for the treaty members to "to consider principles, objectives and ways in order to promote the full implementation of the Treaty, as well as its universality, and to make recommendations thereon to the Review Conference."[110] The document also suggested the creation of subsidiary bodies within the three main NPT committees to provide a more "focused consideration" of issues. Finally, the enhanced review process required the treaty members to look forward and back, to assess progress and make goals for the future. The second document, titled "Principles and Objectives for Nuclear Nonproliferation and Disarmament," reemphasized many goals of the original treaty text, including progress on nonproliferation and disarmament, access to peaceful nuclear technology, universal adherence to the NPT, a ban on nuclear testing, and security assurances to nonnuclear weapon states.[111] While the review process for the NPT has been strengthened and some of the principles have

Table 4.3 Assessing observable implications for South African support of indefinite NPT extension

State	*The US and its allies will promote the universalization of the NPT and other regime agreements through the use of their tools of influence*	*Decisions to adhere to (or support) the NPT or other regime agreements will reflect consideration of US policy preferences and persuasive tools*	*Decisions to adhere to (or support) the NPT or other regime elements will reflect embeddedness within the US-led order*
South Africa	Yes	Likely	Mixed support

been addressed by the international community since 1995, these two documents were political agreements only and thus not binding by international law. Many of the provisions in the principles document have gone unfilled in the years since the conference. Moreover, it is hard to argue that South Africa's support was conditional on securing agreement from the nuclear states for the objectives because the decision to support the treaty came before they started considering what they could get for their support. Certainly, the strengthened review process and the objectives documents were welcomed by those who assumed the United States was going to achieve its goal. Thus, it might be better to assess the two additional documents as a way to make the extension more palatable to reluctant states.

Nonetheless, many involved in promoting extension, including Ambassador Graham, believe that additional disarmament progress was necessary to persuade states to agree to indefinite NPT extension. Indeed, the provenance of these additional two documents—the principles and strengthened review process—is contested among several players involved in the extension process, with many taking credit for developing the idea for new requirements in exchange for NPT extension. Representatives from Canada recall that they spoke with Mexican and South African representatives in 1994 at a nongovernmental meeting about providing "unique leverage to strengthen the review process, to get some more concessions from the weapon states on nuclear disarmament, and to agree on some benchmarks against which to measure."[112] The Australian ambassador at the conference also recalls sharing his government's papers on how to improve the NPT process. John Simpson, a British academic, gave a talk to an unofficial gathering of NPT-related government officials from a variety of countries in 1993 about the idea of trading extension "for an NPT with annual reviews."[113] In recounting the events of 1995, former South African officials insist they were only doing the bidding of their own government in developing these documents. This is evidently a case of success having many fathers, but it also shows that many within the worldwide NPT community anticipated that there would have to be a disarmament price to pay in exchange for achieving indefinite extension. In order to ensure extension, they sought to have these ideas pushed forward. Based on the number of supporters going into the 1995 meeting and South Africa's decision to support extension, it seems likely that extension could have been achieved without these steps, but the atmosphere would have been more challenging.

Finally, the domestic political economy theory is consistent with the South African case but provides an insufficient explanation. South Africa was liberalizing its economy during this transition, and thus South African support for NPT extension is consistent with the spirit of Solingen's theory that outward-facing leaders would reject proliferation and join the NPT. The state was transitioning to a democracy and seeking foreign investment. It is worth noting, however, that in liberalizing and rejoining the international community after the apartheid era, South African leaders were most interested in what help they were receiving from the United States. Joining the NPT and supporting extension were part of improving South Africa's economic position because the United States put so much emphasis on nuclear nonproliferation. Moreover, the fact that South Africa was liberalizing was not sufficient to secure South Africa's support for extension. The United States had to engage in a lengthy and costly campaign involving the US president and vice president to persuade South Africa to go along with its preferred position.

Egypt and NPT Extension

Egypt was an extremely challenging case for the United States during the campaign to achieve indefinite extension of the NPT. Not only was Egypt against the US position—Egyptian ambassador Mohamed Ibrahim Shaker explicitly stated after the conference, "We were not in favor of an indefinite extension"—the United States had to actively work to keep Egypt from undermining US diplomacy with other Arab states.[114] In the Clinton administration's National Security Council's list of goals for 1995, the challenge posed by Egypt is explicitly noted within the section on achieving indefinite extension of the NPT: "Our highest priority is to work with Egypt and Israel to ensure that their current differences over Israel's non-adherence to the NPT and nuclear program do not threaten indefinite extension of the NPT at the April Review Conference. *We must make clear to Mubarak that he must delink Egyptian (and consequent NAM) support for NPT indefinite extension from his bilateral dialogue with Israel.* This is a critical issue for the US and continued Egyptian brinkmanship poses threats to our relationship."[115]

Egypt used the NPT Review and Extension Conference to focus attention on Israel's undeclared nuclear weapons program and succeeded in sidelining the conference for a day while NPT parties addressed the issue of weapons of mass destruction in the Middle East.

US-Egyptian relations were complex during this period, with Egyptian foreign policy alignment with the US-led order—as assessed through UN General Assembly voting data—lower than the period surrounding the Camp David Accords, but not nearly as low as it would become in the 2010s. The 1990s began positively as Egypt supported the United States in the 1991 Gulf War. Egypt benefited from that position when the United States lobbied other states to forgive billions of dollars of Egyptian debt.[116] Moreover, the United States continued to provide Egypt with over a billion dollars in annual aid as part of the Camp David Accords.[117] However, President Hosni Mubarak faced a difficult balancing act when it came to relations with the United States. On the one hand, Egypt received significant aid, and the Egyptian military collaborated with the US military. On the other, the United

States was linked to Israel, and Mubarak continued to focus his diplomatic attention on Israel and its position outside of the NPT. Moreover, Egypt's political values were far from aligned with that of the United States; Freedom House assessed Egypt as "partially free" in the early 1990s and then changed its assessment to "not free" in 1993.[118] Egypt's Polity score for the entirety of the 1990s was –6, indicating an autocracy.[119] Due to the combination of aid from the United States and incompatible political values, Egypt is assessed as being moderately embedded within the US-led order during this period. Based on this level of embeddedness, the theory of adherence based on US leadership would predict that it would require high-cost diplomacy and inducements to bring Egypt along. In fact, the US leaders also issued threats, and still Egypt did not come on board with the US-favored position on NPT extension.

Most of the US efforts vis-à-vis Egypt during the lead-up to the NPT Review and Extension Conference were more in line with damage control related to Egypt's intense focus on Israel rather than attempts to convince Egypt of the merits of indefinite extension. Throughout the 1980s and early 1990s, Egyptian leaders had used international forums to call on Israel to join the NPT. Egypt led Arab states in boycotting the Chemical Weapons Convention (CWC), which entered into force in 1993, until Israel committed to the NPT. The Egyptians took this position despite President George H. W. Bush's interest in the CWC and "clear signs of displeasure from—and an interest in maintaining close ties with—Washington."[120] Thus, as in the case of the CWC, for NPT extension, Egypt's concern over Israel trumped relations with the United States.

In the years before the 1995 NPT Review and Extension Conference, Egyptian leader Mubarak claimed he would only support NPT extension if Israel adhered to the treaty, and at times he sought to persuade other Arab leaders join his position. Egypt's potential to harm US efforts to gain the support from as many states as possible meant Egypt received a great deal of high-level US attention in this period and, at times, implicit and explicit threats—though not necessarily in the order described in chapter 1. Ambassador Graham visited Cairo and Tel Aviv in December 1994, seeking to persuade Egypt that indefinite extension would make it more likely that Israel would eventually join the treaty.[121] Toward the end of January 1995, Egyptian leaders again announced that they would not support indefinite extension unless Israel joined the NPT, increasing tension with the United States.[122] Cairo seemed to be able to persuade some Gulf States, including Saudi Arabia, to waver in their support of indefinite extension. In response, the United States sent Assistant Secretary of State for Near Eastern Affairs Robert Pelletreau to Egypt. He allegedly told Egyptian leaders, in a not so subtle threat, that some in Congress were thinking about reconsidering the $2.2 billion in annual aid provided by the United States due to Egyptian threats to complicate the NPT extension process.[123] (Senator John McCain had recently said something to this effect in a congressional hearing related to nuclear nonproliferation.[124]) A former US government official serving at the time of this visit indicates that Pelletreau's statement about aid was not an insignificant threat and would have been carefully vetted within the US interagency.[125] In a similar threat, one unnamed official is quoted in the press at this time saying that Mexico and Egypt could be persuaded to support the US position on the NPT if their enormous US aid packages were "held in the balance."[126] How much these threats mattered is unclear—surely the United States did not want to weaken Mubarak's regime and would have been unlikely to follow through on this threat, but that does not mean the US Congress would not have considered it or that it would not have affected Mubarak's cost-benefit assessment. Shai Feldman writes that although Pelletreau's visit "did not induce Egyptian leaders to alter their position on the indefinite extension of the NPT, it seems to have contributed to the softening of their rhetoric on that issue."[127]

Egypt continued to receive a great deal of US attention in the period right before the NPT Review and Extension Conference. In early March 1995, US secretary of state Warren Christopher visited Egypt to discuss Cairo's position on Israel and indefinite extension. After Christopher's visit, Egypt tempered its position, announcing it would not block indefinite extension while it continued to pressure Israel to join the NPT.[128] Nonetheless, later the same month at a specially called Arab League meeting, Egypt attempted to persuade eight other Arab states to sign on to a document declaring they would not support indefinite extension unless Israel joined the NPT. In another example of high-cost diplomacy, vice president Gore then arrived in Cairo to have a "blunt" discussion with Egypt and members of the Arab League.[129] Gore met with Egyptian president Mubarak to try "soften his position."[130] Mubarak then visited Washington in early April, where Clinton sought to convince him to support indefinite extension. Mubarak reportedly promised not to block consensus or try to convince other states to object to indefinite extension.[131] But throughout the conference, the Egyptian delegation continued its focus on the Middle East nuclear weapons issue.

Even after the United States and its allies had secured a majority of states in favor of indefinite extension at the NPT Review and Extension Conference, the issue of Egypt and Israel halted progress as Egypt continued to focus on naming Israel as a non-NPT state in the official conference documents. The compromise on indefinite extension had to be delayed one day while the United States, Egypt, and a small group of other states worked feverishly on a Middle East Resolution. Egypt wanted to name Israel specifically; the United States rejected this position. Concerned this development would undermine prospects for indefinite extension, President Clinton became involved from his travels in Moscow and reportedly made a phone call to President Mubarak.[132] In the end, the resolution referred to all states in the Middle East region outside of the treaty and to "unsafeguarded nuclear facilities" in the region.[133] Changes in language meant that Egypt did not want to sponsor the resolution, and thus the United States, Great Britain, and Russia became the official sponsors of the Middle East Resolution. Egypt had partly achieved its goal through the resolution; the press surrounding the conference delay made it very clear that Egypt's focus on Israel was the cause.

Egypt's strategy of holding out on agreeing to the NPT's extension for as long as possible allowed it to put a global spotlight on Israel's NPT treaty status for months. Cairo consistently used the conference to highlight Israel's nuclear weapons program, even as multiple US leaders—the secretary of state, the vice president, and the president—pressured Egypt not to harm the conference proceedings.

Egypt's position within the debate over NPT extension was unique. It used this opportunity to focus on an issue that garnered its leadership domestic and regional benefits: the status of Israel outside of the treaty. The Egyptian case does not follow all of the regime membership expectations of the adherence theory based around US-global leadership. While the United States did promote indefinite extension to Egyptian leaders using high-cost diplomacy and coercion, it was unable to achieve Egypt's support for extension. US leaders also were unable to keep Egypt from using the conference to highlight Israel. Thus, Egypt's decision on how to approach the NPT conference did not reflect considerations of US preferences and US tools. At this point in the 1990s, Egypt was a moderately embedded state trending toward weakly embedded. Egyptian resistance to the US position is more akin to the behavior of a weakly embedded state than a moderately embedded one. Coding Egypt as a moderately embedded state—versus a weakly embedded state—during the first half of the 1990s stems primarily from the vast amount of US aid that continued to flow to Cairo because of the 1978 Camp David Accords. This aid may have provided the US government less and less leverage over time if the Egyptian government assumed the United States would not fully eliminate it due to the importance of the Accords. Table 4.4 summarizes the outcomes for the observable implications related to regime membership for this case.

Table 4.4 Assessing observable implications for Egyptian support of indefinite NPT extension

State	*The US and its allies will promote the universalization of the NPT and other regime agreements through the use of their tools of influence*	*Decisions to adhere to (or support) the NPT or other regime agreements will reflect consideration of US policy preferences and persuasive tools*	*Decisions to adhere to (or support) the NPT or other regime elements will reflect embeddedness within the US-led order*
Egypt	Yes	No	No

There is little evidence that Egypt's position on NPT extension was related to consideration of a nuclear weapon program. Instead, Egypt joined other states at the conference seeking greater disarmament concessions in exchange for support of NPT extension.[134] And while Egypt has consistently called for greater disarmament progress from all of the nuclear-weapons-possessing states, it appears that in this case, Egyptian leaders were primarily motivated by the regional and domestic benefits of focusing its diplomacy on one suspected nuclear state, Israel. Domestic politics best explains Cairo's approach, but in this case, their actions were consistent with a survival strategy based not on economics but in vocal opposition to a regional adversary.

In August 1994, Egyptian foreign minister Amre Mousa made his first official visit to Israel, in which he said his primary goal was to encourage the Israeli government to ratify the NPT. This visit marked a new level of conflict between the two neighbors, one that resulted in numerous high-level meetings in fall of 1994 and spring of 1995.[135] After Mousa's visit, president Mubarak announced that Egypt would withdraw from the NPT if the issue of Israel's nuclear status was not addressed by the NPT Review and Extension Conference.[136] With the issue threatening both the ongoing Middle East peace process and the NPT Review and Extension Conference, the United States began pressuring Egypt to back off its position. Some US consideration was given to pressuring Israel to shut down its Dimona nuclear reactor or provide Egypt with a lesser gesture, such as indicating its intention to sign the NPT at some point in the future,[137] but it became clear that Israel was not going to cooperate. In fact, the Israeli government assumed the Egyptians' bluster was intended for domestic audiences, and thus it would not necessarily help if Israel did respond. From 1994 through the spring 1995 conference, relations between Israel and Egypt would be dominated by the nuclear issue.[138]

Politicians and analysts at the time assumed that Mubarak's campaign for Israel and the NPT was in part based on a desire "to mollify his domestic opposition."[139] During this period, Mubarak was facing an Islamic insurgency marked by assassination attempts and violence.[140] The intense focus on the Israeli nuclear issue provided a distraction through a popular issue. Mubarak's stance also allowed him to receive a great deal of attention from the highest levels of the US government, and at times, he was able to score domestic and regional points by showing off his lack of cooperation with the United States. As Shai Feldman concludes: "Egypt's tough position also made Cairo a key target for US appeals for requesting support for indefinite extension of the NPT. Thus, Egypt's militant position may have been intended to compensate for its domestic troubles and diminished standing in regional affairs. This strategy became increasingly apparent as the NPT campaign evolved; Egypt's position evoked strong nationalist sentiments, increasing domestic support for the Mubarak government."[141]

In addition, pointing the finger at Israel allowed Mubarak to reclaim regional leadership at a time when it was diminishing.[142] The United States was mediating peace between Israel and Syria and negotiating between Israel and the Palestinians, leaving Egypt out of both processes.[143] Egypt was also being marginalized by the Gulf Cooperation Council and the United States in their efforts to secure the border between Kuwait and Iraq in October 1994.[144] In sum, domestic political considerations appear to best explain Cairo's position on NPT extension. US leaders employed several tools to attempt to shape Egypt's behavior but were unable to stop Cairo from pursuing an agenda of highlighting Israel's nuclear status at the NPT Review and Extension Conference.

Finally, the political economy theory is not entirely inconsistent with Egypt's behavior leading up to the 1995 NPT Review and Extension Conference. Solingen writes that president Mubarak followed Sadat in rejecting nuclear weapons and favoring economic reforms. These reforms largely failed, however, indicating that Egypt remained an inward-facing regime. Inward-facing regimes are less likely to support the global nuclear nonproliferation regime. Nonetheless, the evidence indicates that Mubarak's focus on Israel as a tactic of political survival is a more plausible explanation than Egypt's domestic political economy.

Much of the evidence presented in this chapter supports a theory of nuclear nonproliferation regime adherence based on US global leadership to explain the final outcome of the 1995 NPT Review and Extension Conference. As expected of a highly embedded state, Japan signed on early to support indefinite extension, though the process was not without its challenges due to the change in the Japanese government in the summer of 1993. As states moderately embedded within the US-led order in this period but trending toward weakly embedded, both Indonesia and Egypt were against indefinite extension. For Indonesia, US pressure was not successful in bringing Jakarta around to the US-favored position, but US diplomatic engagement with

Table 4.5 Summary of chapter 4 evidence

State	*The US and its allies will promote the universalization of the NPT and other regime agreements through the use of their tools of influence*	*Decisions to adhere to (or support) the NPT or other regime agreements will reflect consideration of US policy preferences and persuasive tools*	*Decisions to adhere to (or support) the NPT or other regime elements will reflect embeddedness within the US-led order*
Japan	Yes	Yes	Mixed support
Indonesia	Yes	No	Mixed support
South Africa	Yes	Likely	Mixed support
Egypt	Yes	No	No

South Africa meant the NAM would not have a unified position behind Indonesia's proposal. US pressure was insufficient to keep Egypt from using the conference to focus on Israel, its neighbor and adversary. While US actions in total are key to understanding the ability to achieve indefinite extension of the NPT, alternative explanations find some relevance to states' decision-making processes.

For Japan, concerns about North Korea's nuclear program caused some in the government to reject extension and study a nuclear option for Japan's security. On the other side of the political spectrum, those in Japan seeking global disarmament—and thus fairness in commitments between the nuclear weapon states and the nonnuclear weapon states—were concerned that indefinite extension would not put enough pressure on nuclear states to disarm. These factions within the government and the population, along with Japan's change in government in 1993, served to complicate Japan's support for a short period in the summer of 1993. Indonesia and South Africa, though their positions on indefinite extension were different, were both motivated by a desire to see more progress on nuclear disarmament. Egypt primarily used the extension conference for domestic and regional benefit, to highlight the lack of disarmament by one state only, Israel.

The 1995 effort to extend the NPT demonstrates that when nonproliferation stakes are high, the United States uses all of its tools of persuasion—low-cost diplomacy, high-cost diplomacy, positive inducements, and coercion—to achieve its desired outcome. The high importance of achieving this time-bound outcome explains in part why the observable implication related embeddedness within the US-led order finds less support in these cases. US officials used more costly tools than would be expected for each embeddedness level because of the importance of securing adherence from as many states as possible.

Though US leaders failed to persuade the Indonesian government and were consistently frustrated by the Egyptian leaders, in the end, the outcome of the conference—extension of the NPT in perpetuity—is best explained by a multiyear diplomatic effort led by the United States and supported by states highly embedded within the US-led global order.

CHAPTER 5

Mixed Success in Promoting a New Safeguards Agreement

In the aftermath of the 1991 Persian Gulf War, international inspectors were surprised to learn of Iraq's extensive nuclear weapon program. Despite inspections by International Atomic Energy Agency (IAEA) officials for a decade, Iraq managed to build a clandestine program in rooms and buildings adjacent to inspected locations. This revelation highlighted a major weakness of existing NPT safeguards: inspectors only visited sites declared by the state. The IAEA had the legal authority to undertake special inspections outside of declared locations, but in practice, the agency had never carried one out. If a government set out to cheat on the NPT, as Iraq had done, it simply did not declare nuclear-weapon-related sites. Because of the discovery in Iraq, the United States, the IAEA, and other members of the international community began promoting a strengthened safeguards mechanism. This chapter explores the process by which the United States pushed and promoted a key adaptation to the nuclear nonproliferation regime in the 1990s. It also tests the three observable implications related to regime membership in the case of three states, Japan, Indonesia, and Egypt, as they considered whether to conclude (i.e., adopt) the new safeguards agreement.

In 1993, the IAEA Board of Governors mandated that the IAEA secretariat propose means for strengthening nuclear safeguards.[1] This effort proceeded along two tracks. First, the IAEA set about strengthening safeguards agreements based on rights they already possessed but had not put into practice (e.g., conducting special inspections, collecting environmental samples). Second, the IAEA developed a new, more stringent safeguards protocol to attach to states' previously concluded Comprehensive Safeguards Agreements.

The Model Additional Protocol (AP) was approved by the IAEA Board of Governors in May 1997.[2] From this point, states were encouraged by the IAEA to conclude their own bilateral agreements with the IAEA, adding an AP to their extant safeguards agreements. The Model AP includes several provisions to increase inspector access, including inspections across all elements of the nuclear fuel cycle from uranium mines to nuclear waste facilities, short-notice inspections, and quicker visa processing for inspectors. With an AP in force, inspectors would no longer be limited to visiting only certain locations within a state.

The conclusion of an AP agreement with the IAEA has not been a high-profile event within most states, in contrast to the highly visible and politicized 1995 NPT Review and Extension Conference discussed in the previous chapter. The decision to conclude an AP generally involves only a small group of political actors within the foreign ministry, nuclear regulators, and the state's nuclear industry, if one exists. Nonetheless, US administration officials have promoted the universalization of the AP as it significantly improves the IAEA's ability to detect clandestine nuclear activities.

Background on the Model Additional Protocol

US leadership was "instrumental" to concluding AP negotiations within the IAEA.[3] In a detailed history of the AP negotiations, Frank Houck, Michael D. Rosenthal, and Norman A. Wulf conclude that the success of the IAEA committee that negotiated the AP was in part based on "US leadership and support from the highest levels of the USG."[4] A multivolume history of the development of the AP captures the many ways in which the United States influenced the process:

> It is important to note the important role played by the US throughout the process of the development of safeguards strengthening measures and the negotiation of the Model Additional Protocol. Led by the US Arms Control and Disarmament Agency and with strong support from an interagency team, especially the Departments of Energy and State, the US supported the effort to strengthen the safeguards system from start to finish. In addition to numerous consultations with the IAEA, the US regularly consulted with friends and allies. Numerous diplomatic messages were sent to capitals to help reinforce US positions. The US also had the benefit of being able to take advantage of support from the senior-most levels of the US government, including the White House. This support played a pivotal role in the negotiations within Committee 24.[5]

The US strategy to bring about a stronger IAEA safeguards agreement was to focus first on discussing the AP with Japan, France, the United Kingdom, Russia, and occasionally China. According to a former US official familiar with the AP negotiations, US delegations met with these states because the majority of concerns with the new safeguards agreement came from states with significant civilian nuclear infrastructure, as they would be burdened by additional requirements more than others.[6] To establish an AP, it was important for the United States to get these states on board early in the process of developing the new safeguards text.

In 1996, the IAEA established Committee 24, made up of the IAEA Board of Governors, to draft a new safeguards protocol. At the first Committee 24 meeting, few developing nations showed up, except Nigeria, indicating the low priority of these issues for many states, especially those without significant nuclear technology.[7] Committee 24 met during the period from July 1996 to April 1997. Once the IAEA finalized the AP (INFCIRC/540) on May 16, 1997, states were able to negotiate their own bilateral AP with the IAEA based on the model text.

Similar to other international treaties, many (but not all) states join the AP in a two-step process of signing before ratifying and "concluding" it. Australia was the first state to sign an AP, in September 1997. President Clinton signed the US AP on June 12, 1998, but it was not submitted to the Senate for ratification until the George W. Bush administration did so in 2004. What accounts for the delay in submitting an agreement that was promoted so strongly by the United States? First, the intrusive IAEA inspections allowed under the AP were an obstacle within the US interagency process. After the 1987 US-Soviet INF Treaty and its unprecedented on-site verification protocol, many US agencies were hesitant about additional rigorous inspections. This reluctance occurred even though the United States was permitted a "national security exclusion" on US military sites due to its status as an official nuclear-weapons-possessing state within the NPT. The Department of Energy's security department was especially wary.[8] Second, the ACDA was enveloped into the State Department during this period. Key members of the former AP delegation to the IAEA were given other responsibilities when they moved over to State, or they retired as a result of the merger. Those who continued on with responsibility for the AP wanted to make sure they got the implementing legislation right before submitting it to Congress, an effort that took on greater importance after the Senate rejected the CTBT—a treaty banning all nuclear explosions—in November 1999.

According to one former US official, the United States made some overtures to other states about concluding AP agreements in the late 1990s and early 2000s, but the United States had to rely on the persuasion of allies until the US government took steps to conclude its own AP with the IAEA.[9] One early effort occurred at the 1998 G8 summit. The foreign ministers' statement from that meeting reads, "We urge all countries to conclude additional safeguards protocols with the International Atomic Energy Agency at the earliest possible date and, recognising the Agency's efforts to make the system more efficient, to ensure that it has the resources necessary to implement this dramatic nonproliferation accomplishment."[10] The subsequent 1999 and 2000 G8 statements did not mention the AP, except for calling on

Iran to conclude one in 2000.[11] The AP reappeared again in the 2001 G8 statement: "We call on all States who have not already done so to conclude appropriate safeguards agreements and Additional Protocols with the International Atomic Energy Agency (IAEA)."[12]

A 2000 report by Mark Hibbs illustrates the challenge US leaders faced in promoting the AP abroad without a US AP in place: "The Vietnamese Foreign Ministry and its disarmament bureaucracy have raised serious questions about the Additional Protocol. They objected this month that the nuclear weapons states and, in particular, the US, which is most strongly advocating international adherence to the protocol, are not compelled to have IAEA safeguards on their nuclear activities and that, in the view of Hanoi officials, the Additional Protocol is likewise 'not universal' in its scope and application."[13]

During the end of the Clinton administration, close US allies pressed for universalization of the AP. As Hibbs recounted at the time, "Sensing that the effort to implement the IAEA's bold post-Iraq plan for 'enhanced safeguards' was losing steam internationally, last April a handful of states, led by Australia, Canada, and the Netherlands, pressed at the 2000 NPT Review Conference in New York to make the AP binding on all NPT parties. The move was opposed by a majority of NPT states."[14] A US official familiar with this period explained that the United States supported this effort by its allies at the Review Conference but was not involved in part because promotion of the AP would be more effective coming from states that had already concluded the new agreement.[15]

Nuclear nonproliferation became a top priority of the George W. Bush administration in the aftermath of the September 11 attacks. According to officials who served in the administration at this time, promoting nuclear nonproliferation was a White House–led effort, and the AP became one of the key areas of focus.[16] In May 2002, President Bush sent the AP to the Senate for its advice and consent to ratification. In his letter of transmittal, President Bush stated that "universal adoption" of the AP was "a central goal of nonproliferation policy."[17]

Once the United States sought ratification, the US campaign for AP universalization began in earnest. In this effort, the United States employed its tools of influence, especially low-cost diplomacy and inducements.

In late 2003, members of the Bush national security staff came up with a list of near-term steps to promote nuclear nonproliferation, including a major speech on the topic. In February 2004, President Bush delivered this speech at the National Defense University (NDU) in Washington, DC. He announced a new inducement to persuade states to conclude an AP—linking the supply of US nuclear technology to adoption of the AP, similar to the way the Carter administration had linked supply to full-scope safeguards and NPT accession in the 1970s. Bush stated:

> It is the charge of the International Atomic Energy Agency to uncover banned nuclear activity around the world and report those violations to the U.N. Security Council. We must ensure that the IAEA has all the tools it needs to fulfill its essential mandate. America and other nations support what is called the Additional Protocol, which requires states to declare a broad range of nuclear activities and facilities and allows the IAEA to inspect those facilities. As a fifth step, I propose that by next year, only states that have signed the Additional Protocol be allowed to import equipment for their civilian nuclear programs. Nations that are serious about fighting proliferation will approve and implement the Additional Protocol.[18]

As a traditional, albeit waning, supplier of civilian nuclear assistance, the United States declaring that it would only supply states if they concluded an AP agreement would likely have an impact on the decision calculus of many states. This inducement was especially useful for nonproliferation because of the increased interest in nuclear power around the world during this period in the early 2000s—the so-called nuclear renaissance. But for this inducement to be truly effective, other suppliers needed to adopt this policy. The United States sought to globalize its new domestic nuclear supply policy by convincing members of the Nuclear Suppliers Group to condition their supply of civilian technology on the conclusion of an AP.[19] During the Bush administration and continuing with the Obama administration, the United States pressed members of the Nuclear Suppliers Group to make this change, finally finding partial success in 2011, with a new rule establishing that states must have concluded an AP or have a "regional inspection regime" to receive technology for uranium enrichment or plutonium reprocessing.[20] Though the new rule did not cover all nuclear supply, enrichment and reprocessing capabilities allow states to develop the fissile material for nuclear weapons and thus are the most sensitive nuclear technologies.

President Bush sought to push for AP universality through every possible channel available to the United States.[21] Statements within the final documents of international ministerial meetings and conferences—an example of low-cost diplomacy—were one of the means by which the Bush administration promoted the AP multilaterally. A few months after Bush's NDU speech, the United States encouraged the June 2004 G8 meeting to make a statement on nonproliferation that included the AP. The "G8 Action Plan on Nonproliferation" from this meeting reads in part, "We seek universal adherence to IAEA comprehensive safeguards and the Additional Protocol and urge all states to ratify and implement these agreements promptly. We are actively engaged in outreach efforts toward this goal, and ready to offer necessary support. The Additional Protocol must become an essential new standard in the field of nuclear supply arrangements. We will work to strengthen NSG guidelines accordingly. We aim to achieve this by the end of 2005."[22]

Later the same month at the US-EU summit, leaders made a similar declaration on nonproliferation reaffirming the statement made at the G8 summit and again emphasizing the importance of the AP.[23]

Having secured support for the AP in Europe, the Bush administration moved its focus to Asia. According to officials at the time, the Bush administration tried to push the Association of Southeast Asian Nations (ASEAN) and the Asia-Pacific Economic Cooperation (APEC) forum to have a stronger nonproliferation agendum.[24] The Bush administration was successful in securing AP language in the final ministerial document of the 2004 APEC forum.[25] The document set a deadline for states to conclude the AP. It reads: "Ministers also recognized that all APEC economies are implementing, have concluded, or aim to conclude an Additional Protocol with the International Atomic Energy Agency by the end of 2005, reflecting their determination not to allow illicit nuclear activities in our region through their collective commitment to expanded transparency on nuclear-related activities."[26]

After the 2004 APEC meeting, members of the administration followed up with the participants to remind them of their commitment to conclude an AP by the end of 2005. Thailand's signature in September 2005 is attributable to this deadline and related US diplomacy, according to one former US official.[27]

When engaging bilaterally with foreign governments, Bush administration officials made clear that the AP was "something responsible countries did."[28] Foreign governments knew that concluding this agreement was a means to please US officials and thus was advantageous to any state trying to improve relations.

Beyond inducements and low-cost diplomacy, the United States has also sought to help train and educate nuclear authorities in other nations about safeguards. One of the most important US educational outreach efforts has occurred through the National Nuclear Security Administration (NNSA) and its International Nuclear Safeguards and Engagement Program, founded in 2008. The mission of this program is to "collaborate with partners to strengthen domestic and international safeguards at all stages of nuclear development."[29] US experts engage with the technical community in foreign governments to help develop safeguards practices and to teach their officials what is required to fulfill safeguards obligations with the IAEA.

US financial resources have also supported the promotion and execution of international safeguards. The United States has traditionally supplied about one-quarter of the IAEA's regular operating budget, while also contributing significantly to the IAEA's voluntary or extrabudgetary funds. For example, from 2011 to 2015, the United States provided $79–90 million annually in extrabudgetary expenses.[30] These funds went to "high-priority safety, security and health cooperation projects," such as funding for the Fukushima disaster response.[31] In addition, the United States has provided extra funding for safeguards implementation, including the extra efforts in Iran during the implementation of the Joint Comprehensive Plan of Action. In 2017, 2018, and 2019, the amount for extrabudgetary funds provided by the United States increased to $94.8 million annually.[32]

Japan and the Additional Protocol

Japan was engaged in the discussions over the text of the AP throughout the negotiation process in the 1990s. With one of the larger civilian nuclear programs in the world, Japanese leaders were keenly interested in how their nuclear industry would be affected by the new safeguards agreement. Japan joined the group of similarly concerned states described above in bargaining with the United States over the AP text. In general, the United States pushed for a more intrusive agreement while the group of states with large nuclear energy programs was in favor of the new safeguards but wanted to minimize the impact on industry. The United States was largely successful in achieving its goals within the AP negotiations, persuading Japan and the group of like-minded states to agree to its preferred inspection protocol via low-cost and high-cost diplomacy.

In the late 1990s, Japan continued to be highly embedded in the US-led order, albeit with some friction in the economic sphere. Despite disagreements over trade—especially related to the steel industry—the allies reaffirmed their security relationship during the Clinton administration and cooperated on addressing the growing North Korean missile threat. In 1998, the Japanese Foreign Ministry wrote, "The Japan-US relationship provides an indispensable foundation for peace, stability, and prosperity in the Asia-Pacific region," emphasizing the importance of US leadership.[33] During the 1990s, the United States continued to be Japan's top trade partner.[34] The two mature democratic nations continued to be aligned overall when it came to political values. Japan remained a "full democracy" according to its Polity score[35] and was assessed as "free" according to Freedom House.[36] On the UN General Assembly measure of foreign policy concordance, Japan was still significantly above the global average, though on a slight downward trajectory. Based on Japanese embeddedness within the US-led order, Tokyo would be expected to conclude an AP quickly after US diplomatic outreach. With the AP and Japan, much of the persuasive diplomacy occurred during the negotiation process.

Two groups engaged in most of the negotiations over the AP. The United States, France, the United Kingdom, and Australia were considered "the most active" states in the process.[37] The second group, a coalition of nonnuclear weapon states with significant nuclear activities, included Germany, Japan, Belgium, Spain, Canada, Brazil, Argentina, and South Korea.[38] A German diplomat, Reinhard Loesch, became the leader of this second grouping.

Between the first and second Committee 24 meetings, the United States conducted two rounds of bilateral negotiations with Loesch; he represented the concerns of the coalition members. The other states, including Japan, were assumed to prefer this unified method of negotiating with the United States because it kept the US delegation from being able to "divide and conquer" by engaging bilaterally with each state.[39] The US delegation developed a close working relationship with their German counterparts where they were able to come to compromise positions, and then both countries "worked with others in their respective camps to persuade them to accept the products of that work."[40] In this way, German officials would persuade Japanese leaders through low-cost diplomacy to go along with the positions it negotiated with US officials. Thus, Japan was only indirectly negotiating with the United States in this case.

After the second Committee 24 meeting, German officials continued to voice concerns on behalf of the states with significant nuclear infrastructure, which included Japan, about the proposed safeguards agreement. The US delegation lobbied the National Security Council to secure a letter drafted from President Clinton to the German government on the importance of the AP, which was ultimately sent as a cable in the president's name. Following Clinton's cable, an example of high-cost diplomacy, Loesch and his team came to the United States and spent a full Saturday with members of the US team overcoming the remaining hurdles. Loesch was confident he could sell the finalized agreement to other states, including Japan.[41] According to one US official, the United States "got virtually everything [it] wanted" in the final document.[42]

Any challenge for the US government in persuading the Japanese government to support the AP occurred during negotiations over the text. Many of the Japanese inputs during AP negotiations related to making the new safeguards agreement less burdensome to its nuclear industry. For example, Japan proposed that additional short-notice access be limited to "instances of inconsistencies" found by inspectors and that these visits should allow twenty-four-hour advance notice.[43] By working with German officials, the United States was able to persuade Japan and the other states in the grouping to go along with its preferred safeguards text.

Once the text was official, Japan was the first state with significant nuclear infrastructure to conclude an AP.[44] Before signing, Japan requested the IAEA conduct two "trials" of the new safeguards provisions at the two "most complex" nuclear facilities in Japan.[45] In addition, Japan had to amend domestic laws related to inspections.[46] Japan signed in December 1998, six months after the United States did. According to one former Japanese official, there was little opposition once the AP text was finalized.[47] In Japan, discussion of the new agreement was limited to nuclear regulators and those in the nuclear industry.[48] Among this limited community, discussions were largely technical, such as disagreements over how many man-hours the new inspection regime would require.[49] Industry largely supported the AP because it would relax safeguards on nonsensitive locations and focus more attention on sensitive facilities. For most civilian nuclear sites in Japan, the safeguards burden was expected to lessen as a result of adopting the AP.[50] In reality, the civilian nuclear sector did not see this savings in budgets or manpower initially because of the preparations required for more stringent, short-notice safeguards.[51]

There was also a discussion in Tokyo at this time over Japanese nuclear supply to other states, and some in government thought an AP should be a condition of supply. Japan could not set this policy, it was thought, without having concluded an AP itself.[52] After finalizing the necessary domestic legislation, Japan brought the AP into force in December 1999.

Once the AP was established, Japan became a leading promoter of the new safeguards agreement in both its rhetoric and resources. Japanese leaders, for example, have regularly called for universalizing of the AP in international forums.[53] In 2000, at the IAEA Board of Governors meeting, Japan proposed a "Plan of Action" to promote the AP as the universal safeguards standard.[54] The IAEA began a more formalized process of promoting the AP in 2001, aided by US and Japanese extrabudgetary contributions.[55] According to the IAEA, "a number of States are actively involved in efforts to promote wider adherence to the additional protocol. The most vocal proponent is Japan, which was also the first country with a major nuclear cycle to bring into force an additional protocol."[56] Japan has held a number of conferences to help other states learn more about the domestic requirements for being able to conclude an AP. In the early 2000s, Japan launched an informal "Friends of the Additional Protocol," through its mission in Vienna.[57] In 2005, Japan, along with New Zealand and the European Union, called for the AP to be a requirement of any supply of nuclear material and technology.[58]

For a single state, the funds and bureaucratic resources Japan has devoted to the AP are comparable only to the United States. Japan has become a very helpful state in promoting the nonproliferation regime and has taken on an educational and outreach mission for the AP similar to the approach traditionally taken by the hegemon. These efforts benefit both Japan and the United States; AP promotion by a fellow nonnuclear state may be more palatable to some states than outreach from the United States, and the Japanese help promote the extant nuclear order from which they benefit.

As expected by a theory based around US global leadership, Japan—a highly embedded state—quickly concluded an AP and has gone on to support other states in finalizing their own APs. Most of the US persuasion regarding the AP occurred when the text was being hammered out between US and German officials. The Germans represented Japan and other states with significant nuclear infrastructure. To persuade the Germans to go along with its preferred text of the new safeguards agreement, US leaders employed low-cost and high-cost diplomacy. Table 5.1 summarizes the outcomes for

Table 5.1 Assessing observable implications for Japanese adherence to the Additional Protocol

State	*The US and its allies will promote the universalization of the NPT and other regime agreements through the use of their tools of influence*	*Decisions to adhere to (or support) the NPT or other regime agreements will reflect consideration of US policy preferences and persuasive tools*	*Decisions to adhere to (or support) the NPT or other regime elements will reflect embeddedness within the US-led order*
Japan	Yes	Yes	Yes

observable implications related to regime membership in this case. It is followed by a discussion of the alternative explanations.

The security theory finds some relevance in this case in that the nuclear program that threatened Japan the most, North Korea's program, was becoming less of a danger during this period. North Korea had committed to the 1994 Agreed Framework, freezing its plutonium development. It may have been more difficult for Tokyo to conclude an AP in the late 1990s if Japanese officials were more concerned about North Korean proliferation. Japan used the AP to signal its own benign intentions to the rest of the world. One former Japanese official explained that Tokyo ratified the AP so quickly because of its existing enrichment and reprocessing capabilities. Concluding an AP would be a confidence-building measure ensuring that other states would not have second thoughts about Japanese nuclear intentions.[59] Moreover, requiring an AP for its nuclear technology customers would enhance international security by decreasing the likelihood that its exports would be used for weapons proliferation.

There is little evidence from Japan's AP decision-making process that it was focused on nuclear disarmament by the five NPT nuclear weapon states before concluding an AP, but Japan was concerned about fairness in the AP negotiations. Tokyo wanted to ensure that the nuclear weapon states, especially the United States, would conclude an AP as well. In meetings before the AP came into force, Japan repeated that it expected "a certain degree of parallelism" from the nuclear weapon states.[60] The US commitment to conclude an AP likely helped Tokyo in moving forward in concluding the safeguards agreement.

Finally, the domestic political economy theory is consistent with this case in the sense that Japan continued to be an outward-facing state in terms of trade, so it would be expected to support strengthening the regime. While it was the United States that pushed and negotiated for the AP, Japan joined in part to aid its domestic nuclear industry by saving money on safeguards.

Indonesia and the Additional Protocol

Indonesia voted to conclude an AP in September 1999, making it an early adopter of the AP, especially relative to its region. The domestic context for Indonesia's ratification was one of great upheaval. The Asian financial crisis led to economic disaster in 1997 and 1998. The Indonesian economy contracted by 15 percent in 1998, negating many of the gains of President Suharto's thirty-year reign and bringing the economy back to 1970s levels.[61] Suharto resisted the conditions set by a $43 billion International Monetary Fund (IMF) bailout.[62] In an echo of the Carter presidency two decades before, President Clinton sent former vice president Walter Mondale to Jakarta in March 1998 to encourage Suharto to comply with the IMF conditions.[63] Suharto defied political pressure and announced he would run for a seventh term with B. J. Habibie, his minister for research and technology, as his vice president. The economic crisis worsened, with students rioting across the country and calling for Suharto's resignation. Economic panic led to rising prices across the country. With few options, Suharto resigned in May 1998.[64] Following the end of the three-decade Suharto regime, Habibie became president and sought widespread political and economic reforms.[65] It was in this period of reform in which the Indonesian Parliament ratified the AP.

Indonesian embeddedness within the US-led global order reflected the ups and downs of this tumultuous period. The United States remained a top trade partner for Indonesia, but the Asian financial crisis and the IMF's stringent requirements for assistance led to Indonesian opposition to the "Washington Consensus" in 1997 and 1998.[66] As the United States pressured the Suharto regime to comply with IMF terms in the spring of 1998, anti-Americanism was rife in the Indonesian press and among its leaders.[67] After Suharto resigned in 1998 and the reformist era began under President Habibie, relations with the United States improved. Habibie loosened restrictions on the press, freed political prisoners, and announced plans for swift national elections.[68] In other words, Habibie promoted changes consistent with US political values. The United States reengaged with Jakarta as a result of Habibie's democratizing reforms, gaining influence within the state in the process. The Habibie administration undertook US- and IMF-supported political reforms, securing IMF loans for the beleaguered nation.[69] In June 1999, the United States aided parliamentary elections across the island nation by supporting the election commission and funding election monitors. The United States looked favorably on Indonesian reforms, but Washington did restrict aid after the bloodshed in East Timor in 1999 following the East Timorese referendum.[70] Freedom House assessed Indonesia as "not free" through most of the 1990s, changing the assessment to "partially free" in 1998–1999 as a result of Habibie's reforms. According to Polity data, the Indonesian regime moved from autocracy to democracy in 1998 and 1999 (from –7 to 6), a significant change.[71] In terms of the UN General Assembly measure of foreign policy similarity, 1996 was the low point, and then there was an uptick in 1997 and 1998, but Indonesia remained significantly below the global average on this measure. In these two years, Indonesia's foreign policy concordance with the US-led order was similar to that of China, Afghanistan, Egypt, and Oman. Based on all these factors, Indonesia went from moderately embedded and trending toward weakly embedded within the US-led order in the last years of the Suharto regime to being a moderately embedded state under Habibie. Based on this coding, we would expect the United States to use several tools of influence to bring Jakarta on board with the AP. Contrary to expectations of this theory, however, Indonesia swiftly ratified the AP during the new Habibie administration.

After Indonesian parliamentary elections in June 1999, a busy phase followed in the legislature. The People's Consultative Assembly (MRP)—now a much more representative body of seven hundred members—adopted an unprecedented number of constitutional changes and new laws. It was during this period, on September 29, 1999, that Indonesia ratified the AP. The United States and its allies, including Australia, had been pressing states to conclude the safeguards agreement since 1997 when it was formalized by the IAEA. What accounts for the timing of Indonesia's conclusion of the AP? According to one Indonesian diplomat who worked on nuclear nonproliferation issues for Habibie, Indonesia's democratizing led the West, and especially the United States, to perceive an opening to increase pressure on Indonesia to ratify the AP.[72] To date, there is little additional evidence of this pressure. Instead, effective low-cost diplomacy may have originated from a different Western state and US ally, Australia.

As described previously, Australia played an important role in AP negotiations within the IAEA. Indonesia participated in the IAEA's Committee 24 meetings but was not a major player. During these IAEA meetings, the Australian safeguards expert John Carlson became friendly with the chairman of Indonesia's nuclear regulatory agency, Mohamad Ridwan. Ridwan would sometimes come to the meetings as an adviser to members of the Indonesian Foreign Ministry.[73] Ridwan had worked for Habibie when the president had previously served as Indonesia's technology minister. As the chairman of BAPETEN (Badan Pengawas Tenaga Nuklir), a government institution established in 1998 to regulate nuclear energy in Indonesia, Ridwan reported directly to president Habibie, a known nuclear enthusiast (see chapter 3 on Indonesia and the NPT). With Ridwan, Carlson discussed the value of the AP for Indonesia in securing cooperation in the field of nuclear technology.[74] Ridwan then reportedly advocated concluding an AP to President Habibie.[75]

Ridwan likely found a receptive ear in Habibie, who held a PhD in engineering from the Technical University of Aachen in Germany and worked early in his career for a German aerospace firm.[76] Habibie was a long-standing technology promoter within Indonesia and had an interest in civilian nuclear technology. When Indonesia was seeking nuclear energy in the 1980s under President Suharto, Habibie led the proponents of this position as the cabinet minister in charge of research and technology.[77] Habibie again pushed for a civilian nuclear program in the mid-1990s, arguing that eventually the country would require nuclear power for its energy needs.[78] The new president had a close relationship with Ridwan at this time. One former Australian official familiar with this period speculates that it would have been easy for Ridwan to convince President Habibie of the value of the AP as they both shared an interest in advancing nuclear energy in Indonesia.[79]

As the previous chapter recounted, Indonesia's nuclear technology leaders had supported the indefinite extension of the NPT in 1995 because they thought it would be a positive step for securing nuclear supply, but they were overruled by the Indonesian Foreign Ministry. With Habibie as president, the nuclear energy agency was elevated within the government, and it was able to overrule reservations from the Foreign Ministry. Knowing that Western suppliers would want their customers to have stringent safeguards, the Indonesian government was swift to conclude an AP. By this reading of events, US pressure was less relevant to the timing of the Indonesian AP than having encouragement from a neighbor—albeit a strong US ally—and a leader who wanted nuclear technology from the United States and its allies. The fact that the new Indonesian legislature was passing so many bills in a short amount of time during the period of AP ratification and the little available evidence of the legislature's consideration of the AP suggests that Habibie communicated to the legislature that this piece of legislation was a high priority of his, and it caused little debate.

The period in which Indonesia ratified the AP, in the fall of 1999, was a phase of increasing embeddedness with US global leadership, as President Habibie had undertaken US-backed reforms and the United States had funded the first free and fair elections in Indonesia. The United States had been pushing Indonesia to ratify the AP since 1997, which it resisted under the increasingly anti-American leadership of Suharto in the late 1990s. After the government transition, relations improved and the Habibie administration concluded an AP. Consistent with a theory of regime adherence based on US global leadership, a close US ally aided the United States in promoting nuclear nonproliferation policies. In this case, a friendly relationship between an Australian safeguards representative—low-cost diplomacy—and the leader of Indonesia's nuclear agency likely played a role in convincing the nuclear agency that an AP would help facilitate nuclear supply for Indonesia. Habibie, a long-time nuclear energy advocate, was persuaded that supply would be more forthcoming from the United States and other suppliers if the country had an AP in place. Based on the available evidence, it appears that a newly democratic government more favorable to nuclear technology and the role played by Australian safeguards colleagues were the factors that explain Indonesian conclusion of an AP in September 1999. Table 5.2 summarizes the outcomes for observable implications related to regime membership in this case.

The security theory finds little support in this case. Though there were concerns by some during the Suharto regime that Indonesia may have sought a nuclear weapons program eventually, there is little evidence of this, and it is unlikely that Indonesia had been hedging prior to its AP ratification.

Fairness had been an importance aspect to the Indonesian government's position on regime agreements during Suharto's reign. During the lead-up to the NPT extension decision in 1995, Indonesian leaders sought greater concessions on nuclear disarmament from nuclear-weapons-possessing states. That was also the Indonesian position on concluding an AP under the Suharto regime. The United States and the IAEA had been pressing Indonesia, as well as other states in Southeast Asia seeking civilian nuclear programs, to ratify the AP since 1997. Mark Hibbs reports that these states objected based on lack of disarmament progress by the nuclear states, as well as to the AP's import and export requirements and the potential these requirements could have on foreign intelligence collection.[80] Some Indonesian leaders were especially displeased by the outcome of the 1995 NPT Review and Extension Conference, in which the nuclear powers were able to achieve indefinite extension of the treaty while making few meaningful concessions. Thus, the fairness theory appears to find some support initially in this case, but this changed with the incoming Habibie administration.

The key factor is the difference between the Suharto and Habibie regimes. Under Suharto, the Ministry of Foreign Affairs held sway over nuclear nonproliferation policy and connected its nonproliferation commitments to disarmament progress by the nuclear weapon states. Under Habibie, the civilian nuclear regulatory agency appears to have gained influence and perceived the AP to be in its interest in terms of nuclear supply. This is not to argue that these were not real concerns about lack of disarmament progress, but they do not seem to be determinative for Indonesian decision-making in the case of the AP. The United States did not make major arms reductions

Table 5.2 Assessing observable implications for Indonesian adherence to the Additional Protocol

State	*3. The US and its allies will promote the universalization of the NPT and other regime agreements through the use of their tools of influence*	*4. Decisions to adhere to (or support) the NPT or other regime agreements will reflect consideration of US policy preferences and persuasive tools*	*5. Decisions to adhere to (or support) the NPT or other regime elements will reflect embeddedness within the US-led order*
Indonesia	Yes	Yes	No

in this period, and Indonesia concluded an AP—the US Senate was actively considering CTBT ratification when Indonesia ratified the AP, but there is no evidence either way that this mattered. The Senate would go on to reject the CTBT two weeks after Jakarta's AP ratification.[81]

During Habibie's short presidency, the Indonesian government became more outward facing in terms of its economy to receive assistance from international organizations and state donors. The United States was an especially important actor in Habibie's quest to shore up his regime. So while Solingen's domestic political economy theory applies in this case, her theory fails to account for the key role of the United States in setting up the conditions for which leaders are incentivized to become more involved with the global economy.

Egypt and the Additional Protocol

Egypt has not concluded an AP safeguards agreement. It is one of a handful of states with nuclear infrastructure that resists the call for the AP to become the universal safeguards standard for the NPT; its leaders argue the AP should not be a requirement for nuclear supply. In their rhetoric about the AP, Egyptian leaders point to Israel's status outside of the NPT, as well as lack of disarmament progress among the nuclear weapon states.[82] One leader has also said concluding an AP would cause Egypt to be too reliant on other powers for its nuclear power requirements.[83] The United States has engaged with Egypt on this issue but has had little success.

Because Egypt has not yet concluded an AP, the period covered by this case spans from 1997, when the AP was first established, through 2020. During this time, Egypt went from Mubarak's leadership, where Egypt is coded as a moderately embedded state to the lowest point in US-Egyptian relations since the Nasser era. Today Egypt is still best considered a moderately embedded state because of the continued US provision of aid and bilateral trade relations, but all the factors related to political values point to a weakly embedded state. During this period, the Egyptian regime was assessed as an autocracy and a closed anocracy (Polity scores spanning from –6 to 2).[84] The UN General Assembly data show a steady downward trajectory through the period, indicating a widening gap in foreign policy preferences with the US-led order. In fact, by this measure, Egypt has one of the lowest levels of foreign policy concordance with the US-led order in the international system. Public opinion polling provides a window in the growing anti-Americanism in the state. In the ten years that the Pew Research Center has polled Egyptians on favorability toward the United States and its leadership, low favorability measures have become even lower. A high point, in 2006, saw 30 percent of Egyptians saying they were favorable to the United States. In 2014, the last year for which data are available, that number was 10 percent, the lowest measure of all forty-three states in which Pew conducted polling.[85] In this poll, 53 percent of Egyptians said they were "very unfavorable toward the United States."[86] According to one analyst, "Anti-Americanism—always latent in Egyptian society, media, and politics—has exploded beyond its traditional boundaries to become a core feature of political discourse and official propaganda in Egypt."[87] In recent years, the Sisi-led government has becoming increasingly close to the Russian government, another state with pervasive anti-American sentiment.[88] In 2017, Egypt signed an agreement allowing Russian forces to use Egyptian airfields and in 2019 agreed to purchase Russian fighter jets despite significant US reservations.[89]

As a moderately embedded state trending weaker, Egypt is expected to be slow in concluding an AP. To date, Egypt has refused to conclude this safeguards agreement. Unfortunately, there is limited evidence available on particular US efforts to persuade the Egyptians to conclude an AP. The sensitivity of this topic means fewer former and current US officials are willing to discuss negotiations with the Egyptians. Available evidence mainly stems from media reports and statements from Egyptian leaders. Based on these reports, it appears the United States has attempted to employ positive inducements in the form of civilian nuclear technology to secure Egyptian commitment to the AP. It is also possible, however, that the limited evidence of US persuasion may be indicative of US leaders realizing that Cairo is so negatively inclined toward US global leadership that there is little that will sway its government on this issue. Indeed, what little evidence exists is from the Mubarak period, when Egyptian leadership was somewhat more amenable to the United States than it became under the Sisi regime.

A desire for nuclear power was a factor in Egypt's accession to the NPT in 1981, but the proposals for civilian nuclear energy never materialized. The plans for one reactor, at El Dabaa, were abandoned following the Soviet Union's Chernobyl disaster in 1986. Twenty years later, in 2006, Egyptian leaders announced that they were again pursuing a nuclear energy program.[90] Egypt's Foreign Minister Ahmed Aboul Gheit declared in a speech during this period that his country would not conclude an AP. The foreign minister argued, "Egypt will not accept any additional obligations in this matter." He went on to state, "The protocol remains in reality a voluntary instrument that cannot be imposed."[91] Though specific outreach efforts by US leaders at this time are unknown, it appears that the foreign minister's statement was in response to pressure by the United States and other nuclear suppliers for Egypt to conclude the AP and promise not to develop enrichment or reprocessing technologies—the technologies for developing fissile material for nuclear weapons.[92]

In January 2008, a Muslim Brotherhood website reported that Egypt was facing great pressure from the United States and other nuclear technology suppliers to conclude an AP to receive additional civilian nuclear technology. As stated in an article on the Muslim Brotherhood website: "The pressure is being used at a time when Egypt is facing obstacles in the way of its ambitious plan to use nuclear energy for peaceful purposes. It is noteworthy that the United States, Canada, France and other European countries have made their support of Egypt conditional to its signing of the Additional Protocol, which Egypt earlier refused to sign."[93]

According to Mark Hibbs, Egypt is one of the states "the IAEA and some member states have tried at length" to convince to conclude an AP because of its existing nuclear capabilities.[94] Relative to the rest of its region, Egypt has significant nuclear infrastructure. It has no power-generating nuclear reactors, but Egypt possesses two research reactors, facilities for mining, milling, fuel fabrication, waste management, and a limited reprocessing capability.[95] In addition, it has a regulatory agency and universities that can provide training in nuclear research.

Egypt has been able to resist pressure to conclude an AP and still pursue its nuclear energy plans in part because Russia and China have signed nuclear cooperation agreements with Cairo. In November 2007, Egyptian media declared that "Russian Deputy Foreign Minister Sergei Kislyak expressed approval of Egypt's nuclear energy ambitions and pledged to provide Cairo with assistance in reaching them."[96] In March 2008, the two states signed a nuclear deal that allowed Russia to bid on Egypt's first large nuclear reactor.[97]

After the 2008 nuclear deal, Egypt's nuclear energy plans stalled, but they have since moved forward. In May 2015, the Chinese National Nuclear Corporation and the Egyptian Nuclear Power Plant Authority signed a memorandum of understanding allowing China to become one of the key partners in establishing Egypt's nuclear energy program.[98] In November 2015, Cairo penned a similar memorandum with Russia for construction of a nuclear reactor project at El Dabaa.[99] The Egyptian government approved another contract with Russia for support of the El Dabaa nuclear power plant project in December 2018.[100] Russia agreed to provide a $25 billion loan to finance and operate the plant.[101] A few months later, Egypt welcomed a safety team from the IAEA to assess the site of the future nuclear power plant and make recommendations.[102] The site was approved by Egyptian nuclear authorities in March 2019, though the groundbreaking ceremony was delayed due to the COVID-19 pandemic.

As expected by the theory of regime adherence based on US global leadership, the United States and its closest allies have sought to persuade Egypt to conclude an AP using nuclear supply as a positive inducement. Thus far, this gambit has been unsuccessful, mainly because Egypt is securing nuclear cooperation from Russia and China; these states do not appear to require an AP for the supply of nuclear power plants. Moreover, as Egypt has become more and more anti-American in recent years, it is unlikely that Egyptian leaders will agree to conclude an AP when it associates the nonproliferation regime with a US-led global order.

The limited available evidence on Egypt and the AP does not allow for adjudication among competing explanations for Cairo's lack of adherence. It is clear that Egypt is growing increasingly unfavorable toward the US-led order at a time when it is refusing to conclude an AP as well as many other multilateral arms control measures. US efforts to influence Egypt since 2006, when it declared a renewed interest in nuclear energy, have been unsuccessful in garnering Egyptian commitment to the AP. Egypt's partnerships with China and Russia—states that also resist US global leadership—have meant that Egypt need not conclude an AP to import civilian nuclear technology.

In conclusion, there appears to be some limited evidence that the United States and its allies have used tools of persuasion to try to influence the Egyptian government's calculus about AP adherence. This first observable implication of regime membership is consistent with the case. The other two observable implications do not find support in this case. Egyptian considerations do not reflect US policy preferences, and Egypt's refusal to conclude an AP is more consistent with a weakly embedded state or an antagonistic state. It is worth noting, however, that many of Egypt's behaviors and its political values have become more in line with a weakly embedded state over the past decade. Table 5.3 summarizes the outcomes for observable implications related to regime membership in the Egyptian case.

There is limited evidence that Egypt's resistance to concluding an AP stems from a desire to hedge and leave open the possibility of a nuclear weapon program. Mubarak reportedly rejected an offer of nuclear material and technology from a former Soviet operative in the late 1990s.[103] The IAEA has uncovered some concerning activity, but it does not appear to be part of an organized nuclear weapons program. For example, the IAEA discovered that between 2004 and 2006, Egyptian physicists engaged in nuclear material processing activities that should have been reported to the IAEA but were not. The IAEA has said these activities "were permissible" but should have been reported.[104] In addition, IAEA inspectors discovered traces of highly enriched uranium in Egypt in 2009.[105] These revelations were a result of the strengthened implementation of existing IAEA safeguards provisions that occurred after the discovery of the Iraqi

Table 5.3 Assessing observable implications for Egyptian adherence to the Additional Protocol

State	*The US and its allies will promote the universalization of the NPT and other regime agreements through the use of their tools of influence*	*Decisions to adhere to (or support) the NPT or other regime agreements will reflect consideration of US policy preferences and persuasive tools*	*Decisions to adhere to (or support) the NPT or other regime elements will reflect embeddedness within the US-led order*
Egypt	Yes	No	No

nuclear weapons program in the early 1990s. Nonetheless, these discoveries do not appear to indicate a clandestine program.

When Mohamed Morsi was elected in 2012, there was greater reason for concern about Egyptian nuclear weapons intentions due to Morsi's membership in the Muslim Brotherhood. The Muslim Brotherhood used the lack of progress on an Egyptian nuclear energy program as a means to criticize the Mubarak regime.[106] Some leaders within the group also made statements about the desirability of an Egyptian nuclear deterrent. For example, in 2006, a Muslim Brotherhood spokesperson reportedly stated, "We [Egyptians] are ready to starve in order to own a nuclear weapon that will represent a real deterrent and will be decisive in the Arab-Israeli conflict."[107] Muslim Brotherhood leaders also spoke favorably of a potential Iranian nuclear weapons program.[108]

Some analysts suspect that Russia may allow the Sisi government to enrich uranium as part of the nuclear cooperation between the two.[109] If the Egyptians were to receive enrichment technology from Russia—a transaction that would be against the rules of the Nuclear Suppliers Group—and use that path as a means to develop nuclear weapons, Cairo may be less likely to conclude an AP. The IAEA's revelations about Egypt's undeclared plutonium activities in the mid-2000s may mean that Egyptian leaders realize that inspectors would likely discover a clandestine program under a more stringent safeguards agreement. Any discussion of Russia supplying enrichment technology is speculation, however, and there is no evidence today that the current Egyptian government is hedging while a member of the NPT.

Among the three commonly cited reasons Egyptian leaders provide for not adhering to the AP, one is the lack of disarmament progress by nuclear weapon states (including Israel). Cairo has provided this reasoning for not ratifying other international arms control treaties as well, including the Chemical Weapons Convention, the CTBT, and the African Nuclear-Weapons-Free Zone.[110] Egypt has long prioritized nuclear disarmament, and it is possible this does play some role in its decision-making about the nuclear nonproliferation regime. Egypt is a member of a grouping of states known at the New Agenda Coalition, which seeks to promote nonproliferation and disarmament.[111] The disarmament rhetoric is also, however, a way for Egyptian leaders to rally support against Israel and the United States. Israel's status outside of the NPT is one of the reasons Egypt's leaders provide for not joining additional nonproliferation agreements. Egyptian leaders have faced domestic criticism for Egypt's position in the NPT while Israel remains outside of the treaty.[112] According to Jim Walsh, in numerous interviews with Egyptian and Arab leaders, he was told, "Egypt and other MENA countries would refuse to adopt the AP until they saw movement on the question of Israel's nuclear weapons."[113] Based on over twenty years of voicing anger over Israel's status outside of the NPT, it seems likely that the salience

Table 5.4 Summary of chapter 5 evidence

State	*The US and its allies will promote the universalization of the NPT and other regime agreements through the use of their tools of influence*	*Decisions to adhere to (or support) the NPT or other regime agreements will reflect consideration of US policy preferences and persuasive tools*	*Decisions to adhere to (or support) the NPT or other regime elements will reflect embeddedness within the US-led order*
Japan	Yes	Yes	Yes
Indonesia	Yes	Yes	No
Egypt	Yes	No	No

of the Israeli nuclear weapons program continues to affect Egypt's positions on nonproliferation agreements.

Finally, if Solingen's domestic theory were operating, Egypt would have been expected to conclude an AP in the early 2000s when it was engaged in several reforms to become a more outward-facing, market-based economy. That Egypt has consistently refused suggests there is something else at work.

Both the relatively limited amount of time since of the adoption of the AP and the low salience of the safeguards agreement outside of the nuclear nonproliferation community mean there is less available evidence about states' decision-making regarding AP adherence. Key documents remain classified, and US efforts to convince states to conclude APs are often still too sensitive to discuss on the record. As a result, the conclusions herein regarding the APs are tentative.

As expected, based on its high level of embeddedness within the US-led order, Japan was an early adopter of the AP. Through the AP negotiation process, the United States made clear that it prioritized the AP, but the role of Japan's nuclear industry was also important in this case. Indonesia ratified the AP during a period of transition when a leader more favorable to US leadership and to nuclear technology came to power. Evidence indicates the United States had pressured Jakarta to join the AP previously, but it was more likely that it was a US ally, Australia, that persuaded Jakarta to join when it did. As in Japan, those in favor of Indonesia receiving nuclear technology from Western suppliers also likely played an important part in bringing about ratification. Finally, Egypt, as a moderately embedded state trending toward weakly embedded, has resisted concluding an AP for more than twenty years as its leadership has become increasingly anti-American. Whereas fairness concerns about disarmament and more intrusive inspections may have played a role in decision-making during the Mubarak regime, rampant anti-Americanism and the rejection of US global leadership now appears to be sufficient for Egypt's disinterest in joining the AP.

Conclusion

Maintaining the Regime in a Changing Global Order

This book set out to explain adherence to the nuclear nonproliferation regime. Until now, this topic has not been systematically studied by scholars, though it has profound implications for international security. The evidence presented in the previous chapters indicates that adherence to the regime is best explained by the leadership role played by the United States. The logic of this theory is straightforward. Due to their global interests, hegemonic powers like the United States have the greatest strategic interest in preventing the emergence of additional nuclear weapon states. The United States, at times with the help of the Soviet Union, has been the primary instigator of global nuclear nonproliferation treaties and agreements. Once a nonproliferation agreement is finalized, the United States works through diplomatic channels to request that each state in the international system commits to the new set of rules enshrined in the agreement. The United States has sought universal participation in each such agreement, working to secure the adherence of even the most unlikely states in terms of nuclear proliferation risk. By and large, states do not join these agreements until the United States explicitly requests their participation. From there, states engage in a cost-benefit assessment to determine whether they should comply. The states most deeply embedded within the broader US-led global order commit relatively quickly following low-cost US diplomacy because they are supportive of US global leadership. Often these early joiners then work to promote the agreement among states where they have particular influence. Moderately and weakly embedded states are less likely to join these agreements so easily. To secure their commitment, the US government must alter their cost-benefit calculations by engaging in high-cost diplomacy; sometimes the US government resorts to positive inducements and coercion to persuade weakly embedded states. The US government has eventually been able to change the calculation of most moderately and weakly embedded states, while antagonistic states are very difficult to persuade.

The four empirical chapters in this book illustrate support for a theory of regime adherence built around US global leadership. Chapter 2 chronicles the key role of the United States in developing and promoting the elements of the nuclear nonproliferation regime, from establishing the IAEA, NPT, and NSG to more recent developments, including the Model Additional Protocol and the International Convention for the Suppression of Acts of Nuclear Terrorism. While Soviet leaders largely supported earlier efforts, in most cases they allowed the United States to take the lead in developing new institutions, drafting the treaties and statutes, and promoting universalization of these new initiatives. This chapter also demonstrates that when the United States does not prioritize the regime, it weakens.

To examine the connection between embeddedness within the US-led order and states' nonproliferation regime commitments in more detail, chapters 3, 4, and 5 explore decision-making in Japan, Indonesia, Egypt, South Africa, and Cuba. Across the case studies, which include data from US national and presidential archives and over forty elite interviews, there is strong support for the importance of US and allied leadership in explaining regime adherence.

The case of Japan serves to test the theory's expectations for a state that is highly embedded within the US-led order throughout the nuclear era. The examination of Japan began with its lengthy decision to ratify the NPT. Though the choice to ratify the NPT did not come as easily as its embeddedness would anticipate, the United States played a key role in Tokyo's decision to join in 1976. Japan did not ratify the NPT until its safeguards agreement with the IAEA was negotiated and the US government was explicit about its interest in Japanese ratification. In addition, ratification occurred after US leaders and allies highlighted that joining the NPT would facilitate continued US technical cooperation in the nuclear field and after the United States reaffirmed its security commitment to Japan. Two alternative theories of regime commitment find relevance in this case as well: the conflicting desires of a hawkish Diet faction wishing to maintain a nuclear weapon option for Japan's security and disarmament proponents seeking greater disarmament progress before joining the NPT help explain the six-year delay between Tokyo's signature and ratification. The domestic political economic theory is consistent with this case but is unable to explain the particular timing of Japanese ratification.

Twenty years later, as expected due to its continued embeddedness within the US-led regime, Japan joined the United States in calling for indefinite extension of the NPT and promoted this position to other states. Consistent with expectations of the fairness theory, many Japanese leaders took this position reluctantly because they preferred to maintain disarmament leverage over the NPT's five nuclear weapon states through time-bound treaty extensions as an alternative to indefinite extension. But US diplomacy and global concern that Japan's hesitancy over extension meant it was interested

in pursuing nuclear weapons led Japan to support indefinite extension. And then in the late 1990s, as expected, Japan quickly concluded an AP, and has been one of the most significant diplomatic and financial supporters of this agreement. In this way, the Japanese case illustrates another expectation of a theory of regime adherence based on US leadership—the hegemon's allies using their own diplomatic and financial resources to promote elements of the nuclear nonproliferation regime.

In line with expectations, Indonesia, a moderately embedded state in the 1970s, took a relatively long time to join the NPT; it ratified in 1979, after signing the treaty in 1970. Similar to the Japanese case, Indonesia faced little US pressure to join the treaty during the early 1970s when Nixon was president. The United States had means of leverage as a supplier of military and economic aid to Jakarta, but as discussed in chapter 2, the Nixon administration was anomalous among US presidents for its lack of high-level interest in expanding NPT membership. Indonesia's foreign policy concordance with the US-led global order reached its highest level in 1972 (the only period in which Indonesia scored above the global average), further suggesting that the early 1970s was an opportune time for the United States to press Indonesia to ratify the treaty, if the Nixon administration had been so inclined. Indonesia's ratification came after receiving high-cost diplomatic attention from the Carter administration in the late 1970s and during a period in which Jakarta sought global suppliers for its planned civilian nuclear energy program. The United States had recently tightened its standards for the supply of civilian nuclear technology, leaving Indonesian leaders feeling they had no choice but to ratify the NPT if they wanted to develop an indigenous nuclear energy program. In the 1990s, during the debate over NPT extension, Indonesia led a group of nonaligned states in supporting a rolling extension, a position in opposition to US policy preferences. Indonesia was a moderately embedded state trending toward weakly embedded during this period. Despite US engagement and a promise to support a Southeast Asian Nuclear-Weapons-Free Zone—a goal long sought by Jakarta—Washington could do little to sway Indonesia. In the end it was strong US and allied diplomacy that split the nonaligned bloc, making it impossible for Indonesia to succeed in leading an alternative to indefinite extension. When it came to the conclusion of an AP, Jakarta's ratification in 1999 occurred much earlier than expected based on its moderate embeddedness within the US-led order at the time. A new technology-focused president in Jakarta with ties to the nuclear regulatory agency, a motivated legislature, and Australia's diplomatic influence led the Indonesian Parliament to conclude an AP in September 1999.

Egypt's ratification of the NPT occurred in 1981 after the Carter administration brokered the Camp David Accords. Though the NPT was not formally part of the accords, peace with Israel paved the way for Sadat to be more open to NPT ratification. Similar to Indonesia a few years before, it was persistent US diplomacy, Cairo's desire for civilian nuclear technology, and the promise of preferential financing for nuclear technology after ratification that encouraged Cairo's ratification in 1981. The year 1981 was a high point for Egyptian institutional commitment to the nuclear nonproliferation regime, as well as a high point for Egyptian embeddedness within the US-led order. In 1995, a moderately embedded Egypt that was trending toward weakly embedded joined Indonesia in opposing indefinite extension of the NPT and used the conference to highlight Israel's nonmembership, even delaying the extension decision within the conference to push for a resolution on a Middle East Weapons of Mass Destruction-Free Zone. Despite US diplomatic pressure and offers of nuclear technology, Egypt has not concluded an AP. Cairo's stated reasons for rejecting this safeguards agreement include Israel's continued status as a non-NPT member. Egypt has become extremely anti-American in recent years, suggesting that it is unlikely this state will conclude an AP any time soon.

This book also chronicled two brief case studies: Cuba's decision to join the NPT in 2002 and South Africa's decision to support indefinite NPT extension in 1995. Cuba has been an antagonistic state within the US-led global order since its communist revolution in the late 1950s. Consistent with expectations, Cuba long refused to join elements of the nuclear nonproliferation regime. Cuban leaders stated their support for the treaty in theory and practice but pointed to their poor relationship with the hegemonic power to the north in explaining why they could not join. The Soviet Union, Cuba's patron throughout the Cold War, was unable to persuade Cuba to join the NPT and conclude a comprehensive safeguards agreement. Cuba did finally join the NPT and conclude an AP in the run up to the 2003 Iraq War. As the Bush administration was accusing Iraq of having hidden WMD programs, it was also charging Cuba with maintaining a clandestine biological weapons program. Cuba sought to show greater transparency through its commitment to these nuclear nonproliferation regime agreements. It appears as though Cuba is a rare case of a state joining nonproliferation agreements due to a potential military threat.

South Africa was a key state in the achievement of the indefinite extension of the NPT in 1995. As chapter 4 illustrates, South African leaders had to decide whether their position on extension should follow the NAM, of which they were a newly minted member, or that of the United States. At the time of this decision, the United States was promising hundreds of millions of dollars to aid South Africa's transition from apartheid to democracy. Both vice president Gore and president Clinton asked personally for South Africa's support in this matter. South African deputy president Mbeki ultimately made the choice to support indefinite extension if complemented by nonbinding principles about the future of the NPT. As anticipated, it required special efforts by the United States to bring this moderately embedded state on board.

Implications of this Research

The results of this research have important implications for the study of global order making, prospects for US relative decline, and the future of the nuclear order. The balance of this chapter describes those implications before concluding with policy recommendations.

IMPLICATIONS FOR THE STUDY OF GLOBAL ORDER

This book has illustrated the means by which a hegemonic power creates order in the international system. In this particular case, the United States led the process of creating multilateral institutions to stop nuclear proliferation and reduce the dangers of nuclear material. Scholars, most notably G. John Ikenberry, have highlighted the unprecedented level of global institutionalization following World War II.[1] The United States used its unparalleled power after 1945 to create and promote institutions that would support a specific US-favored international order. While it is common today for some to question whether this so-called rules-based liberal order ever really existed, the majority of states in the international system have had some involvement in these US-promoted institutions, to include the nuclear nonproliferation regime. But as the evidence in this book illustrates, the creation of each nonproliferation treaty and agreement was just the beginning of a great deal of work by the US government. Global order making goes beyond the initial creation of institutions; it entails promoting global rules year after year and leading the way when adaptations of the rules are deemed necessary. In countless cables and meetings, US diplomats—and sometimes, presidents and vice presidents—have sought to persuade foreign leaders to join nonproliferation treaties and agreements. For each agreement, the US government pursued universal adherence. This ambitious goal has meant engaging with the smallest states and those with minimal interest in civilian nuclear technology. The United States aimed to influence every last state because it sought to create a truly worldwide regime to establish a strong global norm against nuclear proliferation. US leaders could have instead chosen only to persuade states that had some realistic chance of seeking nuclear weapons, saving significant time and effort. But that alternate order would lack the normative strength of a universal regime.

The efforts of a deep bench of diplomats were supported by other sources of American power. In meetings in which US diplomats tried to persuade states to join particular nonproliferation initiatives, they were often able to mention benefits provided to the states by the United States, such as military or economic aid, foreign military sales, or assistance in helping join a particular international organization. US officials have rarely issued threats or explicitly offered positive inducements in the nonproliferation regime context, but mentioning the existence of hegemon-provided benefits shapes the cost-benefit assessment of foreign governments when considering whether to comply with a US request for commitment. And, of course, in some high-stakes cases, like the 1995 fight over the future of the NPT, some US officials did resort to explicit coercion to ensure the treaty continued in perpetuity. US leaders were able to make these threats because of the aid the United States provided to several states and because the importance of the NPT's extension made the threats credible to the target governments. Order making and order maintaining are thus made easier when the hegemon is providing benefits to a multitude of states. The more the hegemon is involved in the wider world, through aid, military sales, trade, and international and regional organizations, the more tools it has to translate its preferred outcomes into global rules.

In addition, global order making is facilitated when the hegemon has a grouping of states that are highly embedded within its global order. These states, many of them allies, join new global institutions after minimal diplomatic outreach by the hegemon. Having a critical mass of states join an agreement early helps build momentum for a new initiative. Just as significantly, many of these highly embedded states then promote the new agreement to less embedded states, especially those with which they have historical or cultural ties. US allies have been one of the most important force multipliers in the creation of the US-led global order.

IMPLICATIONS OF RELATIVE US DECLINE

If the US continues to decline in relative terms—that is, if other states become increasingly materially powerful, shrinking the gap between themselves and the United States—then the United States will likely lose some of the leverage afforded by its previously dominant position and will have to compete with other powerful states for influence. The United States has been able to sway reluctant adherents to the regime through low-cost diplomacy, high-cost diplomacy, positive inducements, and occasionally through coercion. Though the United States is predicted to remain a powerful state well into the twenty-first century, it will become less economically dominant as other states in the system grow in power. Moreover, as the global system becomes increasingly multipolar, smaller states may be able to play powerful states against one another and secure aid and other benefits from non-US sources with fewer strings attached. If the United States reduces its global commitments in terms of economic and military aid, it will lose opportunities for leverage. The most significant way by which the United States could lose influence and the ability to shape the global order is by weakening or withdrawing from its alliance commitments. Promoting and sustaining global rules would be much more difficult without the cooperation provided by US allies.

IMPLICATIONS FOR THE FUTURE OF THE NUCLEAR ORDER

This research has shown the importance of the US role in creating the nuclear nonproliferation regime and promoting regime adherence. During the 1960s, many states in the international system were concerned with the threat of nuclear proliferation, but it required the United States, in cooperation with the Soviet Union, to establish the NPT and to encourage all other states to join. In this effort, the two superpowers were quite successful, as only five states remain outside of the NPT today. Since the NPT was established, the United States has played the key leadership role in the creation of new elements of the regime, including the Nuclear Suppliers Group, the Model Additional Protocol, the Comprehensive Test Ban Treaty, UN Security Council Resolution 1540, and in the effort to extend the NPT indefinitely in 1995. The many treaties and agreements are an indication that this regime has had to be malleable, adjusting as new proliferation challenges arose. Historically, when the regime has displayed weaknesses, the United States has provided leadership to establish new regime elements to address them.

A primary implication of this research is that the nuclear nonproliferation regime will be affected by changes in the distribution of global power. The regime has survived and thrived under US hegemony in both bipolar and unipolar systems. Potential alternative global power arrangements could adversely affect it. A period without a clear hegemon could endanger the regime, as it would lack a state powerful enough to address regime weaknesses, encourage adherence, and organize the international community to address violations. Thus, the relative decline of the United States would negatively affect the regime if a rising power, such as China, does not take on the role of regime underwriter soon enough. A gap between hegemons could be a dangerous period in terms of global proliferation activities. In a truly multipolar system without a clear dominant power, it may be difficult for great powers to coordinate action within the regime, even if all of the great powers agree on the value of nuclear nonproliferation. In addition, in a multipolar system in which great powers are competing for influence, traditional tools of US persuasion may be less effective. Other great powers may provide aid or nuclear assistance without strings attached, removing major tools in the nuclear nonproliferation tool kit. In sum, the nuclear nonproliferation regime appears to have benefited from the global distribution of power during the nuclear age. In the future, different power configurations, such as multipolarity, may not lend themselves to successful continuation of the regime, thus undermining international security.[2]

Policy Implications

Given the findings of this research, what can US policy makers do to promote the health of the nuclear nonproliferation regime? This section outlines five brief policy recommendations, before offering a lengthier discussion of the way forward on nuclear disarmament. While the fairness theory of regime effectiveness found limited support in the case studies presented herein, there are current trends suggesting that dissatisfaction over the lack of fairness in the treaty could have a larger effect in the future.

RENEW THE US COMMITMENT TO DIPLOMACY AND THE DIPLOMATIC CORPS

Since the end of the Cold War, the United States has reduced its priority on diplomacy. The Department of Defense has taken on greater responsibilities, even as military leaders have advocated for better funding of the State Department. In media accounts during the Trump presidency, the State Department was regularly referred to as being "hollowed out."[3] Several long-serving officials had left the department, and several high-level positions remained unfilled. By one measure of global diplomatic strength, China surpassed the United States in 2019.[4] The Biden administration has committed to rebuilding US diplomacy,[5] but this task will take more than four years. This book has illustrated the importance of US diplomacy in creating international order. It was State Department and ACDA officials who sent cables around the world asking US diplomats to meet with foreign counterparts and seek their states' commitments to nuclear nonproliferation regime agreements. It was Foreign Service officials who sent countless démarches and held numerous meetings explaining to foreign governments the value of nonproliferation agreements and highlighting the importance with which the US considered such agreements. The ability to successfully promote new global nonproliferation rules required a depth of knowledge of nonproliferation and of the countries targeted for commitment.

STRENGTHEN AND MAINTAIN ALLIANCE RELATIONSHIPS

US allies have significantly aided the development of the US-led global ordering project since World War II. Allies help develop rules of order, quickly join new agreements, and promote agreements to other states. This book demonstrated the importance of European allies, as well as Japan and Australia, in promoting specific nonproliferation agreements and the 1995 extension of the NPT. If the United States distances itself from its allies or decides it is no longer willing to provide security guarantees to its allies, US leaders should recognize that the cost savings of these efforts will make other US policy goals, like the promotion of certain global rules, more costly. The US will find it much more difficult to advance global norms and rules as an actor operating alone in the world. In a period of multipolarity, allies will be especially important to US efforts to maintain existing global rules and promote new ones.

LOCK IN THE NUCLEAR NONPROLIFERATION REGIME

Based on the prospect of decreased influence as the world grows increasingly multipolar and fragmented, US leaders should act with urgency in attempting to lock in existing elements of the nonproliferation regime with as many states as possible in the near term. There is power in the near-universal nature of the regime, but not all of the elements have widespread support. The AP safeguards agreement is the most significant agreement missing key members of the international community; Brazil, Argentina, Venezuela, Belarus, Syria, Saudi Arabia, Iran, and Egypt are significant holdouts. Attention at the highest levels of US leadership and novel issue linkages will likely be required to persuade these reluctant states to conclude the safeguards agreement.

WORK MORE CLOSELY WITH CHINA ON NUCLEAR NONPROLIFERATION

The United States must find ways to creatively engage with China on nuclear nonproliferation. Though China is a regional power and a rising global power, thus far it has not taken a significant leadership role in the nuclear nonproliferation regime. This is perhaps not surprising considering its very pressing domestic priorities and its focus on economic growth. Moreover, the United States has prioritized nonproliferation to such an extent that Chinese leaders may assume they can allow the United States to do the work of promoting the regime while China focuses on other goals. This is not to say China has been entirely disinterested in nuclear nonproliferation. Indeed, China has demonstrated a growing concern for nonproliferation and the regime over time, and this trend should be encouraged by US leaders. From the 1950s to the 1980s, China sided with developing nations regarding the NPT, considering it an inherently discriminatory treaty and refusing to join. After the Cold War ended, Beijing's view began to change, and China acceded to the NPT in 1992. Since then, China has joined most nonproliferation agreements. Chinese leaders are rhetorically supportive of the regime,[6] but in practice, US leaders are still trying to get the Chinese to become more deeply engaged. Recent efforts includes the five NPT nuclear weapons states' effort to develop a single glossary of nuclear terms, but more must be done. US diplomats have been making attempts at engagement, but to date, the Chinese are far from being the partners in nonproliferation that the Soviets were during the Cold War.

BOLSTER THE US NUCLEAR INDUSTRY

The NPT's article 4 promises that nonnuclear members of the treaty will have access to peaceful nuclear technology. This book has shown that the promise of peaceful nuclear technology has been an important tool in bringing states deeper into the nuclear nonproliferation regime; peaceful nuclear technology was a factor in Japanese, Indonesian, and Egyptian decisions to join the NPT. The continued global interest in nuclear energy is thus encouraging for nonproliferation efforts if technology suppliers insist their customers join all of the relevant regime treaties and agreements.

The United States was fortunate that periods of global interest in nuclear energy, such as the 1970s or early 2000s, coincided with periods in which US leaders were attempting to promote greater commitments to elements of the nuclear nonproliferation regime. At the time of this writing, the desire for nuclear energy remains strong in many states around the world. Reducing reliance on fossil fuels to combat climate change has added to this interest. The so-called nuclear renaissance has not materialized as anticipated in part due to the enormous costs associated with building nuclear facilities and the relatively low cost of fossil fuels, but approximately thirty states around the world are still planning for new nuclear power programs.[7]

The challenge of using supply as a nonproliferation tool is that the United States and its allies are no longer the most popular or preferred suppliers of nuclear technology. Today Russia and China offer favorable nuclear deals and financing, without the constraints faced by the floundering US nuclear industry. Russia in particular is focused on building its nuclear export business and is building or is slated to build as many as thirty-three reactors globally in a number of countries.[8] Unfortunately, Russia and China do not appear to be pressuring their customers to join nuclear nonproliferation agreements as part of their nuclear deals. Egypt is a key example. Both China and Russia have agreed to participate in Egypt's nuclear reactor project in El Dabaa, but they do not require the conclusion of an AP as part of this process. If nuclear energy expands to new states around the world, and states do not have the most stringent safeguards agreements with the IAEA, the inherent dual-use nature of civilian nuclear technology means some states may lose faith in the nuclear nonproliferation regime. These states will no longer be able to assume that their neighbors are not going to proliferate or that their neighbors will get caught and punished if they do. Lack of trust in the constraining power of the regime may cause some governments to reconsider their nonnuclear status.

In terms of policy, the United States should look for ways to improve its domestic nuclear industry so it will be a sought-after supplier and thus will have leverage in promoting nonproliferation agreements to its customers. Moreover, being a supplier means the United States has more insight into states' nuclear programs, providing opportunities to better assess whether a program is secretly being used for nonpeaceful purposes. If other states have better technology than the United States and do not hold the importing states to high nonproliferation standards, the nuclear nonproliferation regime will be weakened. The US nuclear industry has stagnated for a number of reasons, including cheaper fossil fuels, high operating costs, and the persistent problem of waste disposal. Though the United States has more nuclear power plants than any other country in the world, the reactor fleet is aging, and there are few new plants in the pipeline. A stagnating domestic industry hurts innovation in the long term and could undermine US nonproliferation efforts.

FIND A WAY FORWARD ON NUCLEAR DISARMAMENT

Based on the findings of this book, there appears to be limited evidence for a connection between the five NPT nuclear-weapons-possessing states pursuing disarmament and the timing of NPT states' commitments to the regime. In other words, the case studies found limited evidence for the fairness theory when it comes to regime adherence. Nonetheless, many practitioners and nonproliferation advocates posit that this link between disarmament progress and nonproliferation cooperation exists.[9] It is a logical extension of the NPT conceptualized as a bargain in which nuclear weapon states gain the security of limited proliferation and in return non-nuclear weapon states are promised access to peaceful nuclear technology and eventual disarmament. And yet the evidence from this project provides little direct support for the fairness theory to date. Many foreign leaders complain about disarmament progress in speeches, and then many of those same leaders take on additional regime commitments without related disarmament progress. But it may be the case that over time, as disarmament progress is deemed too slow or nonexistent, the regime will be affected by this perceived unfairness. In other words, the NPT and the broader regime may appear less fair over time.

In the course of researching the connection between disarmament and nonproliferation, I was provided with examples by many former US officials with backgrounds in arms control and nonproliferation concerning how disarmament progress or lack of progress affected nonproliferation decision-making. One often-cited example was the US promise, in the lead-up to the decision on indefinite extension of the NPT, to conclude CTBT negotiations by 1996. This was the "price" of extension according to one official.[10] And yet it is hard to find examples of where this CTBT promise influenced specific states to support indefinite extension. It should be noted, however, that this is a difficult causal relationship to uncover, as many weakly embedded states sought multiple concessions from the nuclear weapon states in the lead-up to the NPT Review and Extension Conference. States could have "pocketed" the CTBT agreement and asked for more without publicly acknowledging that their increased willingness to support indefinite extension was a result of the CTBT promise. As a second example, a number of those interviewed suggested President Obama's 2009 Prague speech and his stated commitment to a world free of nuclear weapons had a salutatory effect on the nuclear nonproliferation regime. For example, the 2010 NPT

Review Conference had improved "atmospherics" over the 2005 conference.[11] In a third example, one former official stated that President Obama was able to garner global cooperation on sanctioning the Iranian government over its suspected nuclear weapons program because of his perceived commitment to nuclear disarmament. This former official suggested it would have been almost impossible for President George W. Bush to so successfully corral states in pressuring Iran in the way Obama did.[12]

The interpretations of these former officials may be accurate, but for the cases examined within this book, it was embeddedness in the US-led global order, not US nuclear disarmament efforts, that best explains nuclear nonproliferation regime adherence. Indeed, if a theory of regime adherence based on US global leadership is accurate, many nonproliferation regime decisions are not going to be related to the regime's disarmament-nonproliferation bargain but to US diplomatic influence and sometimes US coercion. Even when a state is dissatisfied with disarmament progress, there are likely going to be ways by which the United States can shape the interests of the state to bring about commitment using its tool kit. But that may not always be the case.

When the United States and the Soviet Union agreed to include NPT article 6 in the draft text, it was in part because the disarmament commitment lacked specificity—there was no timeframe for disarmament or any specific disarmament steps required. Nonetheless, the non-nuclear states expected possession to be temporary and so there was an inherent sense of fairness in the treaty.[13] The nuclear weapon states and nonnuclear weapon states both had rights and responsibilities. Over time, and especially since the end of the Cold War, nonnuclear weapon states and nuclear disarmament advocates have called for the five official nuclear weapon states to fulfill their NPT article 6 disarmament commitment. After fifty years, the treaty no longer seems as fair to many of its members. The United States has focused on nonproliferation more than the other parts of the treaty, peaceful uses of nuclear technology and nuclear disarmament. The treaty's text thus has led to dynamics the creators perhaps did not fully anticipate. In their writing on international law, Laura Ford Savarese and John Fabian Witt argue that the United States has often used international law to its strategic benefit, only to find that its commitments to law often have constrained US actions at a later point in time. In other words, international agreements, like the NPT, can have downstream effects, or entailments, that the originators did not plan for and that sometimes cause strategic challenges down the road.[14] Arguably, this is what is occurring today over the NPT's article 6. A vague commitment to disarmament was necessary for the strategically useful treaty to be adopted, but the United States is now under great pressure to show progress on this commitment. If US leaders behave as if they are not constrained by article 6, they undermine the NPT and the broader regime.

Division over disarmament threatens the widespread support for the NPT, support that the United States has worked hard to achieve. States that are dissatisfied regarding disarmament may not support additional efforts to strengthen the rules of the regime or cooperate as much when the United States seeks to address cases of regime violation. Disappointment over disarmament progress by the five official nuclear weapon states in the NPT is epitomized by the Treaty on the Prohibition of Nuclear Weapons (TPNW), a treaty banning nuclear weapons and all activities associated with nuclear weapons, such as assisting in their creation, possessing them, or threatening their use.[15] The treaty's backers aim to stigmatize nuclear weapons and create a global norm against their possession.[16] No nuclear-weapons-possessing states or states protected by extended nuclear deterrence voted in favor of adopting the treaty—the vast majority of these states did not participate in negotiations.

The TPNW was one outcome of a humanitarian movement against nuclear weapons that began in the early 2010s. This campaign argued that the use of nuclear weapons—accidental or intentional—is inconsistent with humanitarian principles and thus would most likely violate international humanitarian law. In three international conferences in 2013 and 2014, they brought together experts and survivors of the attacks in Japan as well as from nuclear testing sites to talk about how these weapons affect bodies, communities, food supply chains, the environment, and the planet. The campaign argues that all people have a right to speak out on nuclear weapons issues because all people could be affected by their use.[17] Leaders from states that seek protection from nuclear deterrence have criticized the TPNW at length, arguing that it will achieve nothing other than damaging the NPT and broader nuclear nonproliferation regime.[18]

Advocates of the TPNW do not see the treaty as inconsistent with the NPT, but the treaty is unique from most elements of the nonproliferation regime because it was not created with support from nuclear-weapons-possessing states or promoted by the United States or another superpower. It is not part of the US-led order—US leaders in both parties have actively campaigned against it. The NPT was in the strategic interest of the United States, and though a treaty stigmatizing nuclear weapons has nonproliferation benefits, the new treaty also seeks to create a norm against any nuclear possession, including the weapons possessed by the United States. Thus, US leaders see this new treaty as threatening to US security and the US-led order by undermining nuclear deterrence and its alliance relationships. The new treaty entered into force on January 22, 2021, with treaty proponents arguing that nuclear weapons have been made illegal under international law.[19]

For most of the NPT's history, the United States has overcome states' resistance to joining new regime elements stemming from their disarmament frustrations because its hegemonic status afforded it several tools to influence states' decisions. In other words, the United States has been able to change the cost-benefit calculations of foreign decision-makers, so their interest in participating in the regime outweighs their frustrations over disarmament.

As US relative power wanes in the coming years, the United States will have fewer of these levers of influence, making it less able to mitigate frustrations with the regime. It is not that states will necessarily leave the NPT en masse, but they will likely be less supportive of the treaty and will be reluctant to support future adaptations to the treaty. In sum, the ban treaty will be a test of whether the United States can hold the regime together in a context in which it is not as powerful as it was in earlier periods of the regime. The longer the treaty lasts without the five nuclear weapon states taking more significant disarmament measures, the more the treaty will be perceived as unfair or unjust.

In the early nuclear age, it was anticipated that all technologically capable nuclear states would develop nuclear weapons. President Kennedy famously warned of a future world in which fifteen, twenty, or even twenty-five states possessed nuclear weapons. The nuclear nonproliferation regime has been successful when considering that twenty-seven nations have sought nuclear weapons programs and only nine states possess nuclear weapons today. But the success of the regime cannot just be measured in the small number of nuclear weapon states but also in the ways in which the regime creates a focal point for states to come together to address regime cheaters and other problems related to nuclear security. The multilateral effort to address the Iranian nuclear problem is a good example of how the regime promotes coordination and cooperation among states. This book has illustrated how US leadership has been one of the most important factors in championing regime adherence. But there are many reasons to question whether this record will continue into the future. US relative decline, the diffusion of power around the globe, and the weakening of US alliance relationships mean the regime faces a difficult future. US leaders should anticipate these challenges now and do what they can to shore up the regime by working with allies and rising powers to lock in the nonproliferation regime for an increasingly uncertain future.

Notes

Introduction

1. John F. Kennedy, "Press Conference 52" (speech, Washington, DC, March 21, 1963), John F. Kennedy Library, https://www.jfklibrary.org/Research/Research-Aids/Ready-Reference/Press-Conferences/News-Conference-52.aspx.

2. Some scholars do not present the nonproliferation regime as a success, in part because it enshrines a system of nuclear weapon "haves" and "have-nots." For a rich and detailed history of US nuclear nonproliferation policy that makes this point, see Shane J. Maddock, *Nuclear Apartheid: The Quest for American Atomic Supremacy from World War II to the Present* (Chapel Hill: University of North Carolina Press, 2010). As the current book illustrates, however, without the special status afforded to the most powerful nuclear-weapon-possessing states, there would not be a nuclear nonproliferation regime to reduce proliferation pressures among most states in the international system. Nonetheless, as described in the concluding chapter, many NPT members perceive that the regime has become less fair over time as the five nuclear weapon states have not fulfilled their article 6 commitment to pursue disarmament.

3. France and China were named as nuclear weapon states in the 1968 treaty text, but they did not join the NPT until the early 1990s.

4. For a detailed narrative of the development of the NPT, see Mohamed I. Shaker, *The Nuclear Non-Proliferation Treaty, Origin and Implementation 1959–1979*, 3 vols. (New York: Oceana, 1980). See also Matthew Harries, "The Role of Article VI in Debates about the Non-Proliferation Treaty" (Ph.D. diss., King's College, 2014).

5. Hedley Bull, "Rethinking Non-Proliferation," *International Affairs* 51, no. 2 (1975): 175, https://doi.org/10.2307/2617231.

6. "Eight Years Later: New 'Threshold States,'" Central Intelligence Agency, Directorate of Intelligence, Office of Political Research, Research Study, "Managing Nuclear Proliferation: The Politics of Limited Choice: December 1975," secret, excised copy, CREST, National Archives Library, College Park, MD, National Security Archive, https://nsarchive2.gwu.edu/NSAEBB/NSAEBB155/index.htm.

7. Ashok Kapur, "Nth Powers of the Future," *Annals of the American Academy of Political and Social Science* 430, no. 1 (1977): 84–95, https://doi.org/10.1177/000271627743000110.

8. The five states are India, Pakistan, Israel, North Korea, and South Sudan.

9. For scholarship emphasizing coercion, see Andrew J. Coe and Jane Vaynman, "Collusion and the Nuclear Nonproliferation Regime," *Journal of Politics* 77, no. 4 (2015): 983–997, https://doi.org/10.1086/682080; and Nicholas L. Miller, *Stopping the Bomb* (Ithaca, NY: Cornell University Press, 2020). Scholarship emphasizing norms includes Maria Rost Rublee, *Nonproliferation Norms: Why States Choose Nuclear Restraint* (Athens: University of Georgia Press, 2009).

10. On this definition, see Daniel H. Nexon and G. John Ikenberry, "Hegemony Studies 3.0: The Dynamics of Hegemonic Orders," *Security Studies* 28, no. 3 (2019): 17, https://doi.org/10.1080/09636412.2019.1604981. Nexon and Ikenberry cite Alexander D. Barder, *Empire Within: International Hierarchy and Its Imperial Laboratories of Governance* (New York: Routledge, 2015). In recent years, some scholars have criticized the often sloppy and undefined use of the term *hegemon*. See, for example, Meghan McConaughey, Paul Musgrave, and Daniel H. Nexon, "Beyond Anarchy: Logics of Political Organization, Hierarchy, and International Structure," *International Theory* 10, no. 2 (2018): 181–218, https://doi.org/10.1017/S1752971918000040; and Janice Bially Mattern and Ayse Zarakol, "Hierarchies in World Politics," *International Organization* 70, no. 3 (2016): 623–654, https://doi.org/10.1017/S0020818316000126. For an alternative conception of nuclear hegemony, see Nick Ritchie, "A Hegemonic Nuclear Order: Understanding the Ban Treaty and the Power Politics of Nuclear Weapons," *Contemporary Security Policy* 40, no. 4, (2019): 409–434, https://doi.org/10.1080/13523260.2019.1571852.

11. G. John Ikenberry, *After Victory: Institutions, Strategic Restraint, and the Rebuilding of Order after Major Wars*, new ed. (Princeton, NJ: Princeton University Press, 2001), 163.

12. Miles Kahler, "Multilateralism with Small and Large Numbers," *International Organization* 46, no. 3 (1992): 681–708, https://doi.org/10.1017/S0020818300027867; Ikenberry, *After Victory*, chap. 6.

13. Kahler, "Multilateralism," 681.

14. Carla Norrlof, *America's Global Advantage: US Hegemony and International Cooperation* (Cambridge: Cambridge University Press, 2010).

15. The "liberal" in *liberal order* refers to an international system based around promoting (1) the rule of law and respect for state sovereignty, (2) democracy, and (3) human rights, as well as a system of free trade.

16. Michael J. Mazarr, Miranda Priebe, Andrew Radin, and Astrid Stuth Cevallos, *Understanding the Current International Order* (Santa Monica, CA: RAND, 2016), https://www.rand.org/pubs/research_reports/RR1598.html.

17. On the ways in which the United States and the Soviet Union both cooperated and competed in the nuclear nonproliferation realm, see Jeffrey D. Colgan and Nicholas L. Miller, "Rival Hierarchies and the Origins of Nuclear Technology Sharing," *International Studies Quarterly* 63, no. 2 (2019): 310–321, https://doi.org/10.1093/isq/sqz002.

18. On the changing patterns of nuclear supply over the nuclear age and its effects on proliferation, see Eliza Gheorghe, "Proliferation and the Logic of the Nuclear Market," *International Security* 43, no. 4 (2019): 88–127, https://doi.org/10.1162/isec_a_00344.

19. Document 02, State Department telegram GADEL 35 to U.S. Delegation to the United Nations, October 5, 1958, confidential, National Security Archive, https://nsarchive.gwu.edu/dc.html?doc=5017511-Document-02-State-Department-telegram-GADEL-35.

20. Treaty on the Non-Proliferation of Nuclear Weapons (NPT), 1970, https://www.un.org/disarmament/wmd/nuclear/npt/text/.

21. Coe and Vaynman, "Collusion," 989. Other scholars who argue that great powers perceive nuclear nonproliferation to be in their strategic interest include Daniel Verdier, "Multilateralism, Bilateralism, and Exclusion in the Nuclear Proliferation Regime," *International Organization* 62, no. 3 (2008): 439–476, https://doi.org/10.1017/S0020818308080156; Colgan and Miller, "Rival Hierarchies"; Matthew Kroenig, "Exporting the Bomb: Why States Provide Sensitive Nuclear Assistance," *American Political Science Review* 103, no. 1 (2009): 113–133, https://doi.org/10.1017/S0003055409090017; Michael C. Horowitz, *The Diffusion of Military Power: Causes and Consequences for International Politics* (Princeton, NJ: Princeton University Press, 2010), 106. Scholars who have argued that established nuclear states care about nuclear nonproliferation more than nonnuclear states include Joseph F. Pilat, "The French, Germans, and Japanese and

the Future of the Nuclear Supply Regime," in *The Nuclear Suppliers and Nonproliferation: International Policy Choices*, ed. Rodney W. Jones et al. (Lexington, MA: Lexington Books, 1985), 81–92; William C. Potter, "The Soviet Union and Nuclear Proliferation," *Slavic Review* 44, no. 3 (1985): 468–488, https://doi.org/10.2307/2498015; George Quester, "The Statistical 'N' of the 'Nth' Nuclear Weapon States," *Journal of Conflict Resolution* 27, no. 1 (1983): 161–179, https://doi.org/10.1177/0022002783027001006; Miller, *Stopping the Bomb.*

22. Coe and Vaynman, "Collusion," 989.

23. Coe and Vaynman, "Collusion," 989.

24. Executive Secretary George S. Springsteen to Secretary of State Kissinger, "Analytical Staff Meeting," July 11, 1974, enclosing "Discussion Paper on U.S. Nuclear Nonproliferation Policy," secret, Record Group 59, Records of the Department of State (RG59), Executive Secretariat Records, Memorandums of the Executive Secretariat, 1964–1975, box 12, S/S Staff Meeting, National Security Archive, https://nsarchive2.gwu.edu/nukevault/ebb467/.

25. "Roland Timerbaev: The Nuclear Nonproliferation Treaty Has Largely Achieved Its Goals," interview by Anton V. Khlopkov, Arms Control Association, September 2017, https://www.armscontrol.org/act/2017-09/interviews/roland-timerbaev-nuclear-nonproliferation-treaty-largely-achieved-its-goals. See also Roland Popp, "Introduction: Global Order, Cooperation between the Superpowers, and Alliance Politics in the Making of the Nuclear Non-Proliferation Regime," *International History Review* 36, no. 2 (2014): 195–209, http://dx.doi.org/10.1080/07075332.2014.899263.

26. Avner Cohen, "Israel and the Evolution of U.S. Nonproliferation Policy: The Critical Decade (1958–1968)," *Nonproliferation Review* 5, no. 2 (1998): 7.

27. Cohen, "Israel and the Evolution," 7.

28. This assumption is presented in "'As Explosive as a Nuclear Weapon': The Gilpatric Report on Nuclear Proliferation," January 1965, Freedom of Information Act request to State Department, https://nsarchive2.gwu.edu//NSAEBB/NSAEBB1/docs/doc07.pdf. For more on the US assumptions of nuclear domino theory, see Nicholas L. Miller, "Nuclear Dominoes: A Self-Defeating Prophecy?," *Security Studies* 23, no. 1 (2014): 33–73, https://doi.org/10.1080/09636412.2014.874189; and Miller, *Stopping the Bomb.*

29. Executive Secretary George S. Springsteen to Secretary of State Kissinger, "Analytical Staff Meeting," July 11, 1974.

30. Kroenig, "Exporting the Bomb."

31. Kroenig, "Exporting the Bomb," 116.

32. Robert Jervis, "Unipolarity: A Structural Perspective," *World Politics* 61, no. 1 (2009): 212, https://www.jstor.org/stable/40060225.

33. Maddock, *Nuclear Apartheid*, 2.

34. Ariel E. Levite, "Never Say Never Again: Nuclear Reversal Revisited," *International Security* 27, no. 3 (2002–2003): 59, https://www.jstor.org/stable/3092114.

35. Francis J. Gavin, "Strategies of Inhibition," *International Security* 40, no. 1 (2015): 9–46, https://doi.org/10.1162/ISEC_a_00205 10-11.

36. Jonathan R. Hunt, *The Nuclear Club: How America and the World Policed the Atom from Hiroshima to Vietnam* (manuscript, forthcoming 2022), 469.

37. Hunt, *The Nuclear Club*, 17.

38. See, for example, *Foreign Relations of the United States*, 1977–1980, vol. 26, "Arms Control and Nonproliferation," ed. Chris Tudda (Washington, DC: US Government Printing Office, 2015), doc. 332; *Foreign Relations of the United States*, 1969–1976, volume E-14, part 2, "Documents on Arms Control And Nonproliferation, 1973–1976," ed. Kristin L. Ahlberg, Bonnie Sue Kim, and Chris Tudda (Washington, DC: US Government Printing Office, 2015), doc. 95.

39. Cited in Rebecca Davis Gibbons and Stephen Herzog, "Durable Institution Under Fire? The NPT Confronts Emerging Multipolarity," *Contemporary Security Policy*, (2021): 10, https://doi.org/10.1080/13523260.2021.1998294.

40. The NPT's article 5 states that "potential benefits from any peaceful applications of nuclear explosions will be made available to non-nuclear-weapon States Party to the Treaty on a non-discriminatory basis," but because the explosive devices for peaceful uses are no different from devices used in a weapon, India's explosion raised proliferation concerns.

41. Jeffrey M. Kaplow, "State Compliance and the Track Record of International Security Institutions: Evidence from the Nuclear Nonproliferation Regime," *Journal of Global Security Studies* (2021): 1–19, https://doi.org/10.1093/jogss/ogab027.

42. Charles Kindleberger, *The World in Depression, 1929–1939* (Berkeley: University of California Press, 1973).

43. Stephen D. Krasner, "State Power and the Structure of International Trade," *World Politics* 28, no. 3 (1976): 322–323, https://doi.org/10.2307/2009974.

44. Susan Strange, "The Persistent Myth of Lost Hegemony," *International Organization* 41, no. 4 (1987): 551–574, https://www.jstor.org/stable/2706758; Robert Gilpin, *War and Change in World Politics* (Cambridge: Cambridge University Press, 1981); Krasner, "State Power"; Carla Norloff, "Hegemony, Hierarchy, and Unipolarity: Theoretical and Empirical Foundations of Hegemonic Order Studies," *Oxford Research Encyclopedia of Politics*, July 27, 2017, 2, https://doi.org/10.1093/acrefore/9780190228637.013.552.

45. Isabelle Grunberg, "Exploring the 'Myth' of Hegemonic Stability," *International Organization* 44, no. 4 (1990): 431–477, https://doi.org/10.1017/S0020818300035372.

46. Timothy J. McKeown, "Hegemonic Stability Theory and 19th Century Tariff Levels in Europe," *International Organization* 37, no. 1 (1983): 73–91, https://www.jstor.org/stable/2706486; Duncan Snidal, "The Limits of Hegemonic Stability Theory," *International Organization* 39, no. 4 (1985): 579–614, https://doi.org/10.1017/S002081830002703X.

47. Robert O. Keohane, *After Hegemony* (Princeton, NJ: Princeton University Press, 1984).

48. Norrlof makes this point in "Hegemony, Hierarchy, and Unipolarity."

49. Carla Norrlof, *America's Global Advantage: US Hegemony and International Cooperation* (New York: Cambridge University Press, 2010).

50. See, for example, Miller, "Nuclear Dominoes."

51. Stephen D. Krasner, "Structural Causes and Regime Consequences: Regimes as Intervening Variables," *International Organization* 36, no. 2 (1982): 185, https://www.jstor.org/stable/2706520.

52. Matthew Fuhrmann and Yonatan Lupu, "Do Arms Control Treaties Work? Assessing the Effectiveness of the Nuclear Nonproliferation Treaty," *International Studies Quarterly* 60, no. 3 (2016): 537, https://doi.org/10.1093/isq/sqw013.

53. Harald Müller and Andreas Schmidt, "The Little Known Story of De-proliferation: Why States Give Up Nuclear Weapon Activities," in *Forecasting Nuclear Proliferation in the 21st Century: The Role of Theory, Volume 1*, ed. William C. Potter and Gaukhar Mukhatzhanova (Stanford, CA: Stanford University Press, 2010), 158.

54. Rublee, *Nonproliferation Norms*, Chap. 2.

55. Scott D. Sagan, "Why Do States Build Nuclear Weapons? Three Models in Search of a Bomb," *International Security* 21, no. 3 (1996–1997): 73–82, https://doi.org/10.1162/isec.21.3.54.

56. On the process of socialization, see Alastair Iain Johnston, *Social States: China in International Institutions 1980–2000* (Princeton, NJ: Princeton University Press, 2007).

57. Fuhrmann and Lupu, "Do Arms Control Treaties," 531–532.

58. Nicholas L. Miller, "Why Nuclear Energy Programs Rarely Lead to Proliferation," *International Security* 42, no. 2 (2017): 40–77, https://doi.org/10.1162/ISEC_a_00293; Rebecca Davis Gibbons, "Supply to Deny: The Benefits of Nuclear Assistance for Nuclear Nonproliferation," *Journal of Global Security Studies* 5, no. 2 (2020): 282–298, https://doi.org/10.1093/jogss/ogz059.

59. Allison Carnegie and Austin Carson, "The Disclosure Dilemma: Nuclear Intelligence and International Organizations," *American Journal of Political Science* 63, no. 2 (2019): 282, https://doi.org/10.1111/ajps.12426.

60. Jana von Stein, "Do Treaties Constrain or Screen? Selection Bias and Treaty Compliance," *American Political Science Review* 99, no. 4 (2005): 611–622, https://doi.org/10.1111/ajps.12426; Beth A. Simmons and Daniel Hopkins, "The Constraining Power of International Treaties: Theory and Methods," *American Political Science Review* 99, no. 4 (2005): 623–631, https://doi.org/10.1017/S0003055405051920.

61. Qualitative literature includes Joseph S. Nye, "Maintaining a Nonproliferation Regime," *International Organization* 35, no. 1 (1981): 15–38, https://www.jstor.org/stable/2706554;

Mitchell Reiss, *Bridled Ambition: Why Countries Constrain Their Nuclear Capabilities* (Washington, DC: Woodrow Wilson Center Press with Johns Hopkins University Press, 1995); Sagan, "Why Do States Build"; Etel Solingen, "The Political Economy of Nuclear Restraint," *International Security* 19, no. 2 (1994): 126–159, https://doi.org/10.2307/2539198; Etel Solingen, *Nuclear Logics: Contrasting Paths in East Asia and the Middle East* (Princeton, NJ: Princeton University Press, 2007); Rublee, *Nonproliferation Norms*; Harald Müller, "Between Power and Justice: Current Problems and Perspectives of the NPT Regime," *Strategic Analysis* 34, no. 2 (2010): 189–201, https://doi.org/10.1080/09700160903542740; Müller and Schmidt, "Little Known Story"; Mariana Budjeryn, "The Power of the NPT: International Norms and Ukraine's Nuclear Disarmament," *Nonproliferation Review* 22, no. 2 (2015): 203–237, https://doi.org/10.1080/10736700.2015.1119968; and Coe and Vaynman, "Collusion." Quantitative literature linking the treaty with decreased levels of proliferation include Dong-Joon Jo and Erik Gartzke, "Determinants of Nuclear Weapons Proliferation," *Journal of Conflict Resolution* 51, no. 1 (2007): 167–194, https://doi.org/10.1177/0022002706296158; Matthew Fuhrmann, "Spreading Temptation: Proliferation and Peaceful Nuclear Cooperation Agreements," *International Security* 34, no. 1 (2009): 7–41, https://doi.org/10.1162/isec.2009.34.1.7; Matthew Kroenig, "Importing the Bomb: Sensitive Nuclear Assistance and Nuclear Proliferation," *Journal of Conflict Resolution* 53, no. 2 (2009): 161–180, https://www.jstor.org/stable/20684580; Fuhrmann and Lupu, "Do Arms Control Treaties."

62. Fuhrmann and Lupu, "Do Arms Control Treaties," 537.

63. For example, see Kindleberger, *The World in Depression;* Gilpin, *War and Change*; Keohane, *After Hegemony*; Ikenberry, *After Victory*.

64. Ikenberry and Nexon, "Hegemony Studies 3.0," 4.

65. On the ways in which domestic political trends can undermine the hegemon's global order, see Paul Musgrave, "International Hegemony Meets Domestic Politics: Why Liberals Can Be Pessimists," *Security Studies* 28, no. 3 (2019): 451–478, https://doi.org/10.1080/09636412.2019.1604983.

1. Explaining Adherence to the Nuclear Nonproliferation Regime

1. See the introduction, note 62.

2. Kal Raustiala and Ann-Marie Slaughter, "International Law, International Relations and Compliance," in *Handbook of International Relations,* ed. Walter Carlsnaes, Thomas Risse, and Beth A. Simmons (Oxford: Oxford University Press, 2002), 538.

3. For example, see Målfrid Braut-Hegghammer, *Unclear Physics: Why Iraq and Libya Failed to Build Nuclear Weapons* (Ithaca, NY: Cornell University Press, 2016); Jacques Hymans, *The Psychology of Nuclear Proliferation: Identity, Emotions and Foreign Policy* (Cambridge: Cambridge University Press, 2006); Kurt M. Campbell, Robert J. Einhorn, and Mitchell B. Reiss, *The Nuclear Tipping Point: Why States Reconsider Their Nuclear Choices* (Washington, DC: Brookings Institution, 2004).

4. In the case of the NPT extension in Chapter 4, adherence will be defined as supporting indefinite extension of the treaty, as this was the means to make the treaty permanent.

5. Many states join international agreements, including those in the nuclear nonproliferation regime, in a two-step process of signing and then ratifying. For a detailed theoretical explanation of the differences in states' motivations for these two steps, see Stephen Herzog, "After the Negotiations: Understanding Multilateral Nuclear Arms Control," (PhD diss., Yale University, 2021).

6. John Simpson and Darryl Howlett, "The NPT Renewal Conference: Stumbling toward 1995," *International Security* 19, no. 1 (1994): 41, https://doi.org/10.2307/2539148.

7. Martha Finnemore and Kathryn Sikkink, "International Norm Dynamics and Political Change," *International Organization* 52, no. 4 (1998): 887–917, https://www.jstor.org/stable/2601361.

8. On the use of the US State Department's démarches and cables, see "5 FAH-1 H-613 DEMARCHES," in the Department's *Foreign Affairs Manual,* July 2, 2019, https://fam.state.gov/fam/05fah01/05fah010610.html#H613.

9. US State Department, "Good Offices and Démarches" (unclassified), *Foreign Affairs Manual*, undated, https://fam.state.gov/fam/07fam/07fam0030.html.

10. Charles Stuart Kennedy, "Moments in US Diplomatic History: The NPT and the Aftermath of India's Nuclear Test—May 1974," Association for Diplomatic Studies and Training, https://adst.org/2015/05/the-npt-and-the-aftermath-of-indias-nuclear-test-may-1974/.

11. Jonathan L. Freedman and Scott C. Fraser, "Compliance without Pressure: The Foot-in-the-Door Technique," *Journal of Personality and Social Psychology* 4 (1966): 195–202, https://doi.org/10.1037/h0023552.

12. "Joint Statement—One Community, Our Future," 2004 APEC Ministerial Meeting, Santiago, Chile, November 17–18, 2004, http://www.apec.org/Meeting-Papers/Ministerial-Statements/Annual/2004/2004_amm.aspx.

13. Jeffrey Checkel, "Why Comply? Social Learning and European Identity Change," *International Organization* 55, no. 3 (2001): 553–588, https://doi.org/10.1162/00208180152507551.

14. Alastair Iain Johnston, "Treating International Institutions as Social Environments," *International Studies Quarterly* 45, no. 4 (2001): 496, https://www.jstor.org/stable/3096058.

15. "NPT Adherence: Trinidad and Tobago," Cable from Secretary of State to American Embassy Spain, AAD, NARA, 1979STATE208433, August 10, 1979.

16. Robert B. Cialdini, "The Science of Persuasion," *Scientific American* 284, no. 2 (2001): 76–81, https://www.jstor.org/stable/26059056.

17. Daniel W. Drezner, "The Trouble with Carrots: Transaction Costs, Conflict Expectations, and Economic Inducements," *Security Studies* 9, no. 1–2 (1999): 189, https://doi.org/10.1080/09636419908429399. See also Miroslav Nincic, "Getting What You Want: Positive Inducements in International Relations," *International Security* 35, no. 1 (2010): 138–183, https://www.jstor.org/stable/40784650.

18. *Foreign Relations of the United States*, 1977–80, vol. 26, *Arms Control and Nonproliferation*, ed. Chris Tudda (Washington, DC: US Government Printing Office, 2015), doc. 364.

19. "Background Briefing by Senior Administration Officials," March 4, 1994, file Ukraine, Philip "PJ" Crowley's Files, ca. 1998–ca. 2001, Records of the National Security Council Office of Press and Communications (Clinton Administration), ca. 1993–ca. 2001; https://catalog.archives.gov/id/34395786. Also see Rebecca Davis Gibbons, "Supply to Deny: The Benefits of Nuclear Assistance for Nuclear Nonproliferation," *Journal of Global Security Studies* 5, no. 2 (2020): 282–298, https://doi.org/10.1093/jogss/ogz059.

20. Military threats and sanctions are rarely employed in cases when states do not join agreements.

21. Author discussion with State Department official, Atlanta, GA, July 22, 2014.

22. Susan B. Welsh, "Delegate Perspectives on the 1995 NPT Review and Extension Conference," *Nonproliferation Review* 2, no. 3 (1995): 1–24, https://doi.org/10.1080/10736709508436589.

23. Concordance of foreign policy preferences is assessed using Erik Voeten, Anton Strezhnev, and Michael Bailey, "United Nations General Assembly Voting Data," 2009, Harvard Dataverse, V27, https://doi.org/10.7910/DVN/LEJUQZ. In their article using these data, the authors argue the ideal point "estimates consistently capture the position of states vis-a-vis a US-led liberal order." Michael Bailey, Anton Strezhnev, and Erik Voeten, "Estimating Dynamic State Preferences from United Nations Voting Data," *Journal of Conflict Resolution* 61, no. 2 (2017): 2, https://doi.org/10.1177/0022002715595700.

24. David A. Lake, "Escape from the State of Nature: Authority and Hierarchy in World Politics," *International Security* 32, no. 1 (2007): 50, https://www.jstor.org/stable/30129801.

25. Author interview with official from a NATO state, Washington, DC, August 1, 2017.

26. Ramesh Thakur, Carlyle A. Thayer, G. J. Gill, and Amin Saikal, *The Soviet Union as an Asian-Pacific Power: Implications of Gorbachev's 1986 Vladivostok Initiative* (Boulder, CO: Westview, 1987).

27. "Non-Papers and Démarches: U.S. and British Combined to Delay Pakistani Nuclear Weapons Program in 1978–1981," National Security Archive Electronic Briefing Book no. 352, ed. William Burr (Washington, DC: National Security Archive and Nuclear Proliferation International History Project, 2011), https://nsarchive2.gwu.edu//nukevault/ebb352/index.htm#notes.

28. See Reagan's warnings, for example, in "The United States and the Pakistani Bomb, 1984–1985: President Reagan, General Zia, Nazir Ahmed Vaid, and Seymour Hersh," National Security Archive Electronic Briefing Book no. 531, ed. William Burr (Washington, DC: National Security Archive and Nuclear Proliferation International History Project, 2015), https://nsarchive2.gwu.edu/nukevault/ebb531-U.S.-Pakistan-Nuclear-Relations,-1984-1985/.

29. See, for example, Or Rabinowitz and Nicholas L. Miller, "Keeping the Bombs in the Basement: U.S. Nonproliferation Policy toward Israel, South Africa, and Pakistan," *International Security* 40, no. 1 (2015): 47–86, https://doi.org/10.1162/ISEC_a_00207.

30. Avner Cohen and William Burr, "Israel Crosses the Nuclear Threshold," *Bulletin of the Atomic Scientists* 62, no. 3 (2006): 22–30, https://thebulletin.org/2006/05/israel-crosses-the-threshold/.

31. Tristan A. Volpe, "Atomic Leverage: Compellence with Nuclear Latency," *Security Studies* 26, no. 3 (2017): 526–527, https://doi.org/10.1080/09636412.2017.1306398.

32. Robert Jervis, "Cooperation under the Security Dilemma," *World Politics* 30, no. 2 (January 1978): 167–214, https://doi.org/10.2307/2009958.

33. Kenneth N. Waltz, *Theory of International Politics* (Reading, MA: Addison-Wesley Publishing Company, 1979).

34. Målfrid Braut-Hegghammer, "Revisiting Osirak: Preventive Attacks and Nuclear Proliferation Risks," *International Security* 36, no. 1 (2011): 101–132, https://www.jstor.org/stable/41289690.

35. United Nations, "The United Nations and Disarmament: 1945–1970," Disarmament Affairs Division, June 1970, https://www.un.org/disarmament/publications/yearbook/volume-1945-1970/.

36. George Bunn and Roland M. Timerbaev, "Security Assurances to Non-Nuclear-Weapon States," *Nonproliferation Review* 1, no. 1 (1993): 11–20, https://www.nonproliferation.org/wp-content/uploads/npr/buntim11.pdf.

37. Eric Neumayer, "Do International Human Rights Treaties Improve Respect for Human Rights?," *Journal of Conflict Resolution* 49, no. 6 (2005): 928, https://www.jstor.org/stable/30045143.

38. Cecilia Albin, *Justice and Fairness in International Negotiation* (New York: Cambridge University Press, 2001), 229.

39. Albin, *Justice and Fairness*, 229.

40. "Reinforcing the Global Nuclear Order for Peace and Prosperity: The Role of the IAEA to 2020 and Beyond," report prepared by an Independent Commission at the Request of the Director General of the International Atomic Energy Agency, May 2008, 4.

41. Elizabeth N. Saunders, "The Domestic Politics of Nuclear Choices: A Review Essay," *International Security* 44, no. 2 (2019): 164, https://doi.org/10.1162/isec_a_00361.

42. Solingen, *Nuclear Logics*.

2. How the United States Promotes the Nuclear Nonproliferation Regime

1. For more on areas of US-Soviet/Russian cooperation in the realm of nuclear nonproliferation, see William C. Potter and Sarah Bidgood, eds., *Once and Future Partners: The United States, Russia and Nuclear Non-Proliferation* (London: International Institute for Strategic Security, 2018).

2. James E. Goodby, *At the Borderline of Armageddon: How American Presidents Managed the Atom Bomb* (Lanham, MD: Rowman & Littlefield, 2006), 5.

3. Richard Rhodes, *The Making of the Atomic Bomb* (New York: Simon and Shuster, 1986), 528–537.

4. "Project CANDOR: To Inform the Public of the Realities of the 'Age of Peril,'" secret, July 22, 1953, Atoms for Peace, binder 17, Dwight D. Eisenhower Library, Abilene, KS, http://www.eisenhower.archives.gov/research/online_documents/atoms_for_peace/Binder17.pdf.

5. Shane Maddock, "The Fourth Country Problem: Eisenhower's Nuclear Nonproliferation Policy," *Presidential Studies Quarterly* 28, no. 3 (1998): 553–572, https://www.jstor.org/stable/27551901.

6. Maddock, "Fourth Country Problem," 554.

7. Martha Smith-Norris, "The Eisenhower Administration and the Nuclear Test Ban Talks, 1958–1960: Another Challenge to 'Revisionism,'" *Diplomatic History* 27, no. 4 (2003): 509, https://www.jstor.org/stable/24914294.

8. George Bunn, *Arms Control by Committee: Managing Negotiations with the Russians* (Stanford, CA: Stanford University Press, 1992), 20.

9. Smith-Norris, "Eisenhower Administration," 515.

10. Bunn, *Arms Control by Committee*, 26.

11. Benjamin P. Greene, *Eisenhower, Science Advice, and the Nuclear Test-Ban Debate, 1945–1963* (Stanford, CA: Stanford University Press, 2007), 3.

12. Keith W. Baum, "Treating the Allies Properly: The Eisenhower Administration, NATO, and the Multilateral Force," *Presidential Studies Quarterly* 83, no. 1 (1983): 86, https://www.jstor.org/stable/27547890.

13. Avner Cohen, "Israel and the Evolution of the US Nonproliferation Policy: The Critical Decade (1958–1968)," *Nonproliferation Review* 5, no. 2 (1998): 5, https://www.nonproliferation.org/wp-content/uploads/npr/cohen52.pdf.

14. Avner Cohen, "Israeli Nuclear History: The Untold Kennedy–Eshkol Dimona Correspondence," *Journal of Israeli History* 16, no. 2 (1995): 176, https://doi.org/10.1080/13531049508576058.

15. Cohen, "Israel and the Evolution," 2.

16. Joseph Nye, "US-Soviet Cooperation in a Nonproliferation Regime," in *US-Soviet Security Cooperation: Achievements, Failures, Lessons*, ed. Alexander L. George, Philip J. Farley, and Alexander Dallin (New York: Oxford University Press, 1988), 341.

17. Quoted in Bunn, *Arms Control by Committee*, 40.

18. Francis J. Gavin, "Blasts from the Past: Proliferation Lessons from the 1960s," *International Security* 29, no. 1 (2004–2005): 104, https://doi.org/10.1162/0162288043467504.

19. Cohen, "Israel and the Evolution," 5.

20. Gavin, "Blasts from the Past," 102.

21. Andrew Preston, *The War Council: McGeorge Bundy, the NSC, and Vietnam* (Cambridge, MA: Harvard University Press, 2010), 58.

22. Author interview with former US official, Washington, DC, July 13, 2015.

23. "Negotiations on the Nuclear Non-proliferation Treaty (Secret/Exdis)," September 1968, p. 1, DEF 18–6, Nuclear Non-proliferation Treaty, 1968–1972, Multilateral Political Relations, Multilateral Subject Files, 1948–1976, LEG 7 Congressional Delegations, 1971–1973, DEF 1808 Underground Nuclear Tests and Venting, 1965–1973, box 1, Bureau of European Affairs, Office of Soviet Union Affairs, RG 59 General Records of the Department of State, National Archives, College Park, MD.

24. In 1960, the Ten Nation Committee on Disarmament (TNCD) was founded. It was expanded to eighteen members the following year. The eighteen members included Canada, France, United Kingdom, Italy, United States, Bulgaria, Czechoslovakia, Poland, Romania, Soviet Union, Brazil, Burma, Ethiopia, India, Mexico, Nigeria, Sweden, and United Arab Republic.

25. "Negotiations on the Nuclear Non-proliferation Treaty (Secret/Exdis)," 2.

26. Cited in Gavin, "Blasts from the Past," 105.

27. "A Report to the President by the Committee on Nuclear Nonproliferation" (Gilpatric Report), January 21, 1965, National Security Archive, http://nsarchive.gwu.edu/NSAEBB/NSAEBB1/nhch7_1.htm.

28. Gavin, "Blasts from the Past," 113–114.

29. Gavin, "Blasts from the Past," 130.

30. Gavin, "Blasts from the Past," 100–135.

31. For more on the negotiation process, see Bunn, *Arms Control by Committee*, chaps. 5 and 6.

32. Lyndon Baines Johnson, *The Vantage Point: Perspectives of the Presidency, 1963–1969* (New York: Holt, Rinehart and Winston, 1971), 479.

33. "Draft Treaty on the Non-Proliferation of Nuclear Weapons," Conference of the Eighteen-Nation Committee on Disarmament, August 24, 1967. See also Thomas Graham Jr., *Disarmament Sketches: Three Decades of Arms Control and International Law* (Seattle: University of Washington Press, 2002), 258.

34. Johnson, *Vantage Point*, 479.

35. "Eyes Only for the Secretary," letter from ACDA Director William C. Foster to Secretary of State Dean Rusk, secret, RG 383, August 29, 1967, p. 2, Conference on the ENCD files, Geneva, Switzerland, National Archives, College Park, MD.

36. "Chronology of Principle Development Relations to Arms Control and Disarmament," RG 383, January 19, 1968, p. 5, ACDA files, General Counsel Disarmament Documents 383-84–005 (box 1 of 5), NND 968151, National Archives, College Park, MD.

37. Glenn T. Seaborg, *Stemming the Tide: Arms Control in the Johnson Years* (Lexington, MA: Lexington Books, 1987), 379.

38. Seaborg, *Stemming the Tide*, 379.

39. Seaborg, *Stemming the Tide*, 379–380. Also discussed in Johnson, *Vantage Point*, 490.

40. *Foreign Relations of the United States*, 1964–1968, vol. 7, Vietnam, September 1968–January 1969, ed. Kent Sieg (Washington, DC: Government Printing Office, 2003), doc. 252, https://history.state.gov/historicaldocuments/frus1964-68v07/d252.

41. Gavin, "Blasts from the Past," 119.

42. Gavin, "Blasts from the Past," 117–119.

43. Thank you to William Tobey for pointing this out.

44. "Chronology of Principle Development Relating to Arms Control and Disarmament, September–October 1968," p. 2, NARA, ACDA archives, box 383-84–005 (box 1 of 5).

45. "Chronology of Principle Development Relating to Arms Control and Disarmament, September–October 1968," 2.

46. *Foreign Relations of the United States*, 1969–1976, vol. E-2, Documents on Arms Control and Nonproliferation, 1969–1972, ed. David I. Goldman and David C. Humphrey (Washington, DC: Government Printing Office, 2010), doc. 4, https://history.state.gov/historicaldocuments/frus1969-76ve02.

47. *Foreign Relations of the United States*, 1969–1976, vol. E-2, Documents on Arms Control and Nonproliferation, 1969–1972, doc. 4.

48. Author interview with former US official, Washington, DC, July 13, 2015.

49. Author interview with former US official, Washington, DC, July 13, 2015.

50. *Foreign Relations of the United States*, 1969–1976, vol. E-2, Documents on Arms Control and Nonproliferation, 1969–1972, doc. 4.

51. National Security Council Decision Memorandum 6, "Presidential Decision to Ratify Non-Proliferation Treaty," February 5, 1969.

52. George H. Quester, "Can Proliferation Now Be Stopped?," *Foreign Affairs* 53, no. 1 (1974): 84, https://doi.org/10.2307/20039493.

53. *Foreign Relations of the United States*, 1969–1976, vol. E-2, Documents on Arms Control and Nonproliferation, 1969–1972, doc. 51.

54. Walton L. Brown, "Presidential Leadership and US Nonproliferation Policy," *Presidential Studies Quarterly* 24, no. 3 (1994): 563–575, https://www.jstor.org/stable/27551284.

55. Brown, "Presidential Leadership," 564.

56. Brown, "Presidential Leadership," 564.

57. Brown, "Presidential Leadership," 564.

58. *Foreign Relations of the United States*, 1969–1976, vol. E-2, Documents on Arms Control and Nonproliferation, 1969–1972, doc. 58.

59. *Foreign Relations of the United States*, 1969–1976, vol. E-2, Documents on Arms Control and Nonproliferation, 1969–1972, doc. 22.

60. *Foreign Relations of the United States*, 1969–1976, vol. E-2, Documents on Arms Control and Nonproliferation, 1969–1972, doc. 22.

61. *Foreign Relations of the United States*, 1969–1976, vol. E-2, Documents on Arms Control and Nonproliferation, 1969–1972, doc. 42.

62. *Foreign Relations of the United States*, 1969–1976, vol. E-2, Documents on Arms Control and Nonproliferation, 1969–1972, doc. 44.

63. Parker T. Hart to Secretary Dean Rusk, "Issues to Be Considered in Connection with Negotiations with Israel for F-4 Phantom Aircraft," October 15, 1968, top secret/nodis, note 2, sensitive, source SN 67–69, Def 12–5 Isr, National Security Archive, http://nsarchive.gwu.edu/NSAEBB/NSAEBB189/IN-02.pdf.

64. See, for example, "Israel Crosses the Threshold II: The Nixon Administration Debates the Emergence of the Israeli Nuclear Program," National Security Archive Electronic Briefing Book No. 485, ed. William Burr and Avner Cohen (Washington, DC: National Security Archive and Nuclear Proliferation International History Project, 2014), https://nsarchive2.gwu.edu/nukevault/ebb485/.

65. Special National Intelligence Estimate 4-1-74, "Prospects for Further Proliferation of Nuclear Weapons," August 23, 1974, top secret, excised copy, http://www2.gwu.edu/~nsarchiv/NSAEBB/NSAEBB187/index.htm.

66. Special National Intelligence Estimate 4-1-74, "Prospects for Further Proliferation of Nuclear Weapons."

67. Jayita Sarkar, "The Making of a Non-Aligned Nuclear Power: India's Proliferation Drift, 1964–8," *International History Review* 37, no. 5 (2015): 937, https://doi.org/10.1080/07075332.2015.1078393.

68. Sarkar, "Non-Aligned Nuclear Power," 941.

69. Sarkar, "Non-Aligned Nuclear Power," 941. See also Nicholas L. Miller, "Nuclear Dominoes: A Self-Defeating Prophecy?," *Security Studies* 23, no. 1 (2014): 42–51, https://doi.org/10.1080/09636412.2014.874189.

70. *Foreign Relations of the United States*, 1969–1976, vol. E–7, Documents on South Asia, 1969–1972, eds. Louis J. Smith and Edward C. Keefer (Washington, DC: Government Printing Office, 2005), doc. 300.

71. Bernard Gwertzman, "U.S. Cuts Economic Aid to Indians," *New York Times*, December 7, 1971, A1, https://www.nytimes.com/1971/12/07/archives/us-cuts-economic-aid-to-indians-calling-india-aggressor-washington.html.

72. "National Security Study Memorandum (NSSM) 202 on Nuclear Proliferation," May 23, 1974, History and Public Policy Program Digital Archive, Nixon Presidential Library, National Security Council Institutional Files, Study Memorandums (1969–1974), box H-205, obtained by Fundação Getúlio Vargas, http://digitalarchive.wilsoncenter.org/document/115172.

73. Transcript, Under Secretary Sisco's Principals' and Regionals' Staff Meeting, June 21, 1974, 3:00 p.m., June 26, 1974, secret, excerpts, RG 59, Transcripts of Secretary of State Henry A. Kissinger Staff Meetings, 1973–1977, box 4, http://www2.gwu.edu/~nsarchiv/nukevault/ebb467/docs/doc%203%20Sisco.pdf.

74. Executive Secretary George S. Springsteen to Secretary of State Kissinger, Analytical Staff Meeting, enclosing "Discussion Paper on US Nuclear Nonproliferation Policy," July 11, 1974, p. 2, History and Public Policy Program Digital Archive, RG 59, Executive Secretariat Records, Memorandums of the Executive Secretariat, 1964–1975, box 12, S/S Staff Meeting, http://digitalarchive.wilsoncenter.org/document/119775.

75. "Executive Secretary George S. Springsteen to Secretary of State Kissinger," 2.

76. "Executive Secretary George S. Springsteen to Secretary of State Kissinger," 5.

77. "Executive Secretary George S. Springsteen to Secretary of State Kissinger," 10.

78. "Executive Secretary George S. Springsteen to Secretary of State Kissinger," 6.

79. Nye, "US-Soviet Cooperation," 344.

80. Department of State Memo, "President's 1972 Annual Review of Foreign Policy" (to EUR/SOV Mr. Oken, from PM/ISO Capt ED. R. Day), October 1, 1971, p. 2, POL 1 Annual Foreign Policy Reviews, 1971–1972, POL 1 Annual Foreign Policy Reviews, 1971–1972 to POL 1–2 US-Soviet Relations, 1970–1975, Bureau of European Affairs, Office of Soviet Union Affairs, Multilateral Political Relations, Multilateral Subject Files, 1948–1976, RG 59 General Records of the Department of States, Box 2, National Archives, College Park, MD.

81. Francis J. Gavin, *Nuclear Statecraft: History and Strategy in America's Atomic Age* (Ithaca, NY: Cornell University Press, 2012): 105.

82. James Cameron and Or Rabinowitz, "Eight Lost Years? Nixon, Ford, Kissinger and the Non-Proliferation Regime, 1969–1977," *Journal of Strategic Studies* 40, no. 6 (2017): 10, https://doi.org/10.1080/01402390.2015.1101682.

83. In a memo that Kissinger considered "first rate," Nixon appointee Winston Lord asked if Japan going nuclear might be in the US interest. "Paper Prepared in the National Security Council Staff," National Archives, RG 59, Policy Planning Staff Files, lot 77 D 112, Director's Files, Selected Lord Memos, confidential. The paper was sent to Kissinger on January 23 under a covering memorandum from Winston Lord of the NSC staff, http://2001-2009.state.gov/r/pa/ho/frus/nixon/i/20703.htm.

84. Interview with former senior US official, Washington, DC, May 28, 2014.

85. Gavin, "Blasts from the Past," 111.

86. Gavin, "Blasts from the Past," 111.

87. Gavin, "Blasts from the Past," 113.

88. Scott D. Sagan and Jeremi Suri. "The Madman Nuclear Alert: Secrecy, Signaling, and Safety in October 1969," *International Security* 27, no. 4 (2003): 150–183, https://www.jstor.org/stable/4137607. Also Gavin, "Blasts from the Past," 112.

89. Sagan and Suri, "Madman Nuclear Alert," 150–183.

90. Gavin, "Blasts from the Past," 114.

91. Brown, "Presidential Leadership," 565.

92. *Foreign Relations of the United States*, 1969–1976, vol. E–12, Documents on East and Southeast Asia, 1973–1976, ed. Bradley Lynn Coleman, David Goldman, and David Nickles (Washington, DC: Government Printing Office, 2011), doc. 274.

93. Gerald R. Ford, "Statement on Nuclear Policy," October 28, 1976, online by Gerhard Peters and John T. Woolley, American Presidency Project, http://www.presidency.ucsb.edu/ws/?pid=6561.

94. David Binder, "15 Nuclear Nations Will Discuss Ways to Curb Spread of the Ability to Make Atomic Arms," *New York Times*, November 9, 1976, 7, https://www.nytimes.com/1976/11/09/archives/15-major-nuclear-nations-will-discuss-ways-to-curb-spread-of-the.html.

95. Department of State background paper "Non-Proliferation/Nuclear Suppliers Conference," November 1974, p. 1, POL 7 Ford-Brezhnev Meeting in Vladivostok, 1974 (folder), POL 2 Trends Reports, 1974–1975 to POL 33-8, Law of the Sea, 1970–1974, Multilateral Subject Files, 1948–1976, Bureau of European Affairs, Office of Soviet Union Affairs, Multilateral Political Relations (box 5), Multilateral Subject Files, 1948–1976, RG 59 General Records of the Department of State, National Archives, College Park, MD.

96. State Department Telegram 228213 to US Embassy Moscow, "Nuclear Safeguards Consultations," October 17, 1974, National Archives Access to Archival Databases Online Collections, State Department Telegrams for 1974 and Other Years, cited in National Security Archive Electronic Briefing Book no. 467, April 21, 2014.

97. William Burr, "A Scheme of 'Control': The United States and the Origins of the Nuclear Suppliers' Group, 1974–1976," *International History Review* 36, no. 2 (2014): 255, https://doi.org/10.1080/07075332.2013.864690.

98. Burr, "Scheme of 'Control,'" 255.

99. Treaty on the Non-Proliferation of Nuclear Weapons (NPT), United Nations Office of Disarmament, https://www.un.org/disarmament/wmd/nuclear/npt/text/.

100. Treaty on the Non-Proliferation of Nuclear Weapons (NPT), United Nations Office of Disarmament.

101. Kristine Werdelin Bergan, "Roles and Rationales in the Negotiations of the First Review Conference of the Treaty of Non-Proliferation of Nuclear Weapons, 1973–1975," (MA thesis, University of Bergen, 2011), 48.

102. Bergan, "Roles and Rationales," 71.

103. "NPT RevCon: Analysis of First Week," Cable from US Embassy Geneva to the Secretary of State, May 12, 1975, AAD, NARA, 1975GENEVA03427.

104. Quoted in Potter, "Soviet Union," 471.

105. David Binder, "Ford Plans to Issue Nuclear Guidelines," *New York Times*, September 14, 1976, 11, https://www.nytimes.com/1976/09/14/archives/ford-plans-to-issue-nuclear-guidelines-officials-link-policy.html.

106. Gerald R. Ford, "Statement on Nuclear Policy," October 28, 1976, online by Gerhard Peters and John T. Woolley, American Presidency Project, http://www.presidency.ucsb.edu/ws/?pid=6561.

107. Ford, "Statement on Nuclear Policy."

108. Ford, "Statement on Nuclear Policy."

109. "Presidential Actions—a Brief History," *Frontline*, accessed October 15, 2021, http://www.pbs.org/wgbh/pages/frontline/shows/reaction/readings/rossin1.html.

110. Burton I. Kaufman and Scott Kaufman, *The Presidency of James Earl Carter, Jr.* (Lawrence: University Press of Kansas, 2006), 5.

111. President Carter's inaugural address, Washington, DC, January 20, 1977, http://www.jimmycarterlibrary.gov/documents/speeches/inaugadd.phtml.

112. Kaufman and Kaufman, *Presidency of James Earl Carter, Jr.*, 59.

113. Jimmy Carter, "Nuclear Power Policy Statement on Decisions Reached Following a Review," April 7, 1977, online by Gerhard Peters and John T. Woolley, American Presidency Project, http://www.presidency.ucsb.edu/ws/?pid=7316.

114. Jimmy Carter, "Nuclear Non-Proliferation—Message to the Congress," April 27, 1977, online by Gerhard Peters and John T. Woolley, American Presidency Project, http://www.presidency.ucsb.edu/ws/?pid=7408.

115. Gerard Smith and George Rathjens, "Reassessing Nuclear Nonproliferation Policy," *Foreign Affairs* 59, no. 4 (1981): 878, https://www.foreignaffairs.com/articles/1981-03-01/reassessing-nuclear-nonproliferation-policy.

116. *Foreign Relations of the United States*, 1977–1980, vol. 16, Southern Africa, ed. Myra F. Burton and Adam M. Howard (Washington, DC: US Government Printing Office, 2016), doc. 288.

117. Rabinowitz and Miller, "Keeping the Bombs."

118. Martha S. van Wyk, "Ally or Critic? The United States' Response to South African Nuclear Development, 1949–1980," *Cold War History* 7, no. 2 (2007): 195–225, https://doi.org/10.1080/14682740701284124; cited in Rabinowitz and Miller, "Keeping the Bombs," 64.

119. See, for example, *Foreign Relations of the United States*, 1977–1980, vol. 16, Southern Africa, doc. 344.

120. The Comptroller General, Report to the Congress of the United States, "Evaluation of US Efforts to Promote Nuclear Non-Proliferation Treaty," 21.

121. The Comptroller General, Report to the Congress of the United States, "Evaluation of US Efforts," July 31, 1980, https://www.gao.gov/assets/id-80-41.pdf, 21.

122. Gloria Duffy, "Soviet Nuclear Export," *International Security* 3, no. 1 (1978): 90, https://doi.org/10.2307/2626645.

123. Kaufman and Kaufman, *Presidency of James Earl Carter, Jr.*, 199.

124. Memorandum for the President from Zbigniew Brzezinski, secret, Daily Report, January 3, 1980, National Archives.

125. Rebecca K. C. Hersman and Robert Peters, "Nuclear U-Turns," *Nonproliferation Review* 13, no. 3 (2006): 544, https://doi.org/10.1080/10736700601071629.

126. Quoted in Daniel Southerland, "Nonproliferation Debate: Carter Hit Hard, but Did Reagan Miss Opportunity?," *Christian Science Monitor*, October 30, 1980, https://www.csmonitor.com/1980/1030/103044.html.

127. Quoted in Martin Anderson and Annelise Anderson, *Reagan's Secret War: The Untold Story of His Fight to Save the World from Nuclear Disaster* (New York: Crown, 2010), 62.

128. Anderson and Anderson, *Reagan's Secret War*, 94.

129. Anderson and Anderson, *Reagan's Secret War*, 94.

130. Ronald Reagan, "Statement on United States Nuclear Nonproliferation Policy," July 16, 1981, online by Gerhard Peters and John T. Woolley, American Presidency Project, http://www.presidency.ucsb.edu/ws/?pid=44092.

131. Brown, "Presidential Leadership," 567.

132. Brown, "Presidential Leadership," 522.
133. Brown, "Presidential Leadership," 522.
134. Brown, "Presidential Leadership," 523.
135. Memo to the Secretary of State from S/NP Robert T Kennedy, "Non-Proliferation Accomplishments of the Administration to Date," June 10, 1983.
136. Quoted in Brown, "Presidential Leadership," 567.
137. Brown, "Presidential Leadership," 569.
138. Brown, "Presidential Leadership," 567.
139. Quoted in Anderson and Anderson, *Reagan's Secret War*, 167.
140. Richard Rhodes, *The Twilight of the Bombs* (New York: Vintage Books, 2010), 150–176; Amy F. Woolf, "Nonproliferation and Threat Reduction Assistance: US Programs in the Former Soviet Union," Congressional Research Service, RL31957, March 6, 2012, https://digital.library.unt.edu/ark:/67531/metadc85445/m1/1/high_res_d/RL31957_2012Mar06.pdf; Steven Pifer, *The Trilateral Process: The United States, Ukraine, Russia and Nuclear Weapons*, Arms Control Series Paper 6 (Washington, DC: Brookings, May 2011), https://www.brookings.edu/research/the-trilateral-process-the-united-states-ukraine-russia-and-nuclear-weapons/.
141. Shai Feldman, "The Bombing of Osiraq—Revisited," *International Security* 7, no. 2 (1982): 114–142, https://www.jstor.org/stable/2538435.
142. Dan Reiter, "Preventive Attacks against Nuclear Programs and the 'Success' at Osiraq," *Nonproliferation Review* 12, no. 2 (2005): 362–363, https://www.diplomatie.gouv.fr/IMG/pdf/Osirak.pdf.
143. Brown, "Presidential Leadership," 569.
144. David Kay, "Denial and Deception Practices of WMD Proliferators: Iraq and Beyond," *Washington Quarterly* 18, no. 1 (2005): 85–105, https://www.tandfonline.com/doi/abs/10.1080/01636609509550134?journalCode=rwaq20.
145. "Model Protocol Additional to the Agreements(s) between State(s) and the International Atomic Energy Agency for the Application of Safeguards (INFCIRC/540)," https://www.iaea.org/sites/default/files/infcirc540.pdf.
146. Evan S. Medeiros, *Reluctant Restraint: The Evolution of China's Nonproliferation Policies and Practice, 1980–2004* (Stanford, CA: Stanford University Press, 2007), 72–73; "Meeting between the President and Chinese Ambassador Zhu Qizhen," August 3, 1992, Presidential Meetings, Memorandum of Conversations 7/9/92–12/22/92, Presidential Memcons, Presidential Correspondence, Brent Scowcroft Files, Bush Presidential Records, George H. W. Bush Presidential Library, College Station, TX.
147. William J. Long and Suzette R. Grillot, "Ideas, Beliefs, and Nuclear Policies: The Cases of South Africa and Ukraine," *Nonproliferation Review* 7, no. 1 (2000): 24, https://doi.org/10.1080/10736700008436792.
148. "Joint Declaration on the Denuclearization of the Korean Peninsula," January 20, 1992, http://www.mofa.go.kr/eng/brd/m_5476/view.do?seq=305870&srchFr=&srchTo=&srchWord=&srchTp=&multi_itm_seq=0&itm_seq_1=0&itm_seq_2=0&company_cd=&company_nm=&page=6&titleNm=.
149. Susan J. Koch, *The Presidential Nuclear Initiatives of 1991–1992*, Center for the Study of Weapons of Mass Destruction Case Study 5 (Washington DC: National Defense University Press, 2012), https://ndupress.ndu.edu/Portals/68/Documents/casestudies/CSWMD_CaseStudy-5.pdf.
150. William J. Clinton: "Excerpts of the President-Elect's News Conference in Little Rock," November 12, 1992, online by Gerhard Peters and John T. Woolley, American Presidency Project, http://www.presidency.ucsb.edu/ws/?pid=85225.
151. On Ukraine's decisions regarding its nuclear arsenal, see Mariana Budjeryn, "The Power of the NPT: International Norms and Ukraine's Nuclear Disarmament," *Nonproliferation Review* 22, no. 2 (2016): 203–237, https://doi.org/10.1080/10736700.2015.1119968.
152. Steven Erlanger, "Concessions on Arms Pact Made by US," *New York Times*, January 3, 1993, 8, https://www.nytimes.com/1993/01/03/world/concessions-on-arms-pact-made-by-us.html.

153. Jack Nelson, "Ukraine Agrees to Give Up Its Nuclear Arsenal, Clinton Says," *Los Angeles Times*, January 11, 1994, https://www.latimes.com/archives/la-xpm-1994-01-11-mn-10675-story.html.

154. Steven Greenhouse, "Ukraine Votes to Become a Nuclear-Free Country," *New York Times*, November 17, 1994, A10, https://www.nytimes.com/1994/11/17/world/ukraine-votes-to-become-a-nuclear-free-country.html.

155. David Sanger, "North Korea, Fighting Inspection, Renounces Nuclear Arms Treaty," *New York Times*, March 12, 1993, A1, https://www.nytimes.com/1993/03/12/world/north-korea-fighting-inspection-renounces-nuclear-arms-treaty.html; Michael R. Gordon, "Korea Speeds Nuclear Fuel Removal, Impeding Inspection," *New York Times*, May 28, 1994, 3, https://www.nytimes.com/1994/05/28/world/korea-speeds-nuclear-fuel-removal-impeding-inspection.html.

156. "Agreed Framework of 21 October 1994 between the United States of America and the Democratic People's Republic of Korea," International Atomic Energy Agency Information Circular, November 2, 1994, https://www.iaea.org/sites/default/files/publications/documents/infcircs/1994/infcirc457.pdf.

157. Karen Tumulty and John-Thor Dahlburg, "Clinton Adds 15 Months to Ban on Nuclear Tests," *Los Angeles Times*, July 4, 1993, https://www.latimes.com/archives/la-xpm-1993-07-04-mn-9961-story.html.

158. Rebecca Johnson, "Viewpoint: The CTBT and the 1997 NPT PrepCom," *Nonproliferation Review* 3, no. 3 (1996/1997): 55–56, https://doi.org/10.1080/10736709608436638.

159. Alison Mitchell, "Clinton, at U.N., Signs Treaty Banning All Nuclear Testing," *New York Times*, September 24, 1996, 1, https://www.nytimes.com/1996/09/25/world/clinton-at-un-signs-treaty-banning-all-nuclear-testing.html.

160. Graham, *Disarmament Sketches*, 259.

161. John F. Burns, "Nuclear Anxiety: The Overview; Pakistan, Answering India, Carries Out Nuclear Tests; Clinton's Appeal Rejected," *New York Times*, May 29, 1998, A1, https://www.nytimes.com/1998/05/29/world/nuclear-anxiety-overview-pakistan-answering-india-carries-nuclear-tests-clinton.html.

162. Helen Dewar, "Senate Rejects Test Ban Treaty," *Washington Post*, October 14, 1999, 1A, https://www.washingtonpost.com/wp-srv/politics/daily/oct99/senate14.htm.

163. NSPD-17/HSPD 4 [unclassified version], National Strategy to Combat Weapons of Mass Destruction, December 2002, http://fas.org/irp/offdocs/nspd/nspd-17.html.

164. NSPD-17 / HSPD 4 [unclassified version].

165. David E. Sanger, "Threats and Responses: White House; Bush Warns Foes Not to Use Weapons of Mass Destruction on U.S. Troops," *New York Times*, December 11, 2002, A20, https://www.nytimes.com/2002/12/11/world/threats-responses-white-house-bush-warns-foes-not-use-weapons-mass-destruction.html.

166. "Libya to Give Up WMD," *BBC News*, December 20, 2003, http://news.bbc.co.uk/2/hi/3335965.stm; William Tobey, "A Message from Tripoli: How Libya Gave Up Its WMD," *Bulletin of the Atomic Scientists*, December 3, 2014, https://thebulletin.org/2014/12/a-message-from-tripoli-how-libya-gave-up-its-wmd/.

167. Chaim Braun and Christopher Chyba, "Proliferation Rings: New Challenges to the Nuclear Nonproliferation Regime," *International Security* 29, no. 2 (2004): 5–49, https://doi.org/10.1162/0162288042879959. In "The Secret Treachery of A. Q. Khan," Joshua Pollack argues that India was the fourth customer of A. Q. Khan (*Playboy*, January/February 2012, http://carnegieendowment.org/files/the_secret%20treachery%20of%20aq%20khan.pdf).

168. George W. Bush, State of the Union Address, January 29, 2002, American Presidency Project, http://www.presidency.ucsb.edu/ws/index.php?pid=29645.

169. Shreeya Sinha and Susan Campbell Beachy, "Timeline on Iran's Nuclear Program," *New York Times*, April 2, 2015, https://www.nytimes.com/interactive/2014/11/20/world/middleeast/Iran-nuclear-timeline.html.

170. David E. Sanger, "North Korea Says It Has a Program on Nuclear Arms," *New York Times*, October 17, 2002, A1, https://www.nytimes.com/2002/10/17/world/north-korea-says-it-has-a-program-on-nuclear-arms.html.

171. In fact, the DPRK has not completed the NPT withdrawal paperwork, but for all practical purposes, the state is outside of the treaty.

172. US Department of State, "About the Proliferation Security Initiative," March 19, 2019, accessed January 9, 2022, https://www.state.gov/about-the-proliferation-security-initiative/.

173. Samuel E. Logan, "The Proliferation Security Initiative: Navigating the Legal Challenges," *Journal of Transnational Law and Policy* 14, no. 2 (2005): 256, https://heinonline.org/HOL/LandingPage?handle=hein.journals/jtrnlwp14&div=14&id=&page=.

174. Douglas M. Stinnett, Bryan R. Early, Cale Horne, and Johannes Karreth, "Complying by Denying: Explaining Why States Develop Non-Proliferation Export Controls," *International Studies Perspectives* 12, no. 3 (2011): 308–326, https://www.jstor.org/stable/44218666.

175. Aaron Arnold, "UN Security Council Resolution 1540," WMD Insights, August 2008, http://www.nuclearfiles.org/menu/key-issues/nuclear-weapons/issues/governance/international-coop/res-1540.htm.

176. Stephen E. Miller, *Nuclear Collisions: Discord, Reform & the Nuclear Nonproliferation Regime* (Washington, DC: American Academy of Arts and Sciences, 2012), 13–14, http://www.amacad.org/sites/default/files/academy/pdfs/nonproliferation.pdf.

177. George W. Bush, "President Announces New Measures to Counter the Threat of WMD," (speech, Fort Lesley J. McNair, National Defense University, Washington, DC, February 11, 2004), http://2001-2009.state.gov/t/isn/rls/rm/29290.htm.

178. For an example of these critiques, see Steve Pifer, "SORT vs. New START: Why the Administration Is Leery of a Treaty," Brookings, March 15, 2013, https://www.brookings.edu/blog/up-front/2013/03/15/sort-vs-new-start-why-the-administration-is-leery-of-a-treaty/.

179. Douglas Jehl, "The Struggle for Iraq: Weapons; US Certain that Iraq Had Illicit Arms, Reportedly Ignored Contrary Reports," *New York Times*, March 6, 2004, A6, https://www.nytimes.com/2004/03/06/world/struggle-for-iraq-weapons-us-certain-that-iraq-had-illicit-arms-reportedly.html.

180. Barack Obama (speech, Hradcany Square, Prague, Czech Republic, April 5, 2009), https://obamawhitehouse.archives.gov/the-press-office/remarks-president-barack-obama-prague-delivered.

181. Final Documents of the 2010 NPT Review Conference, http://www.un.org/en/conf/npt/2010/.

182. "United States Information Pertaining to the Treaty on the Non-Proliferation of Nuclear Weapons," State Department, 2010, http://www.state.gov/documents/organization/141928.pdf.

183. Barack Obama (speech, University of Purdue, West Lafayette, Indiana, July 16, 2008), http://www.cfr.org/elections/barack-obamas-speech-university-purdue/p16807.

184. Michael R. Gordon, "Pentagon to Press Russia on Arms Pact Violation" *New York Times*, December 10, 2014, A14, https://www.nytimes.com/2014/12/11/us/politics/pentagon-to-press-russia-on-arms-pact-violation.html.

185. See the full text of the Iran deal: http://apps.washingtonpost.com/g/documents/world/full-text-of-the-iran-nuclear-deal/1651/.

186. Edith M. Lederer, "U.S. Urges Countries to Withdraw from U.N. Treaty that Would Ban Nuclear Weapons," *PBS News Hour*, October 21, 2020, https://www.pbs.org/newshour/world/u-s-urges-countries-to-withdraw-from-u-n-treaty-that-would-ban-nuclear-weapons.

187. Susan B. Epstein and Paul K. Kerr, "IAEA Budget and US Contributions: In Brief," Congressional Research Service, Report R44384 (Washington, DC, February 17, 2016), 2.

188. Author interview with US official, Washington, DC, July 17, 2015.

189. Author interview with former US official, Arlington, VA, April 14, 2015.

3. Slow but Successful US Promotion of the NPT

1. Draft Treaty: State Department Instructions CA-1545 to Diplomatic Posts, "Aide-Memoire on the Draft Non-Proliferation Treaty (NPT)," August 24, 1967, secret, National Security Archive, https://nsarchive2.gwu.edu/nukevault/ebb253/index.htm.

2. Document 29a: State Department Cable 194569 to All Diplomatic Posts, July 1, 1968, limited official use, National Security Archive, https://nsarchive2.gwu.edu/nukevault/ebb253/index.htm.

3. Several European allies were in favor of the NPT, but as members of the European Atomic Energy Community (EURATOM), they did not join the treaty until EURATOM had finalized safeguards negotiations with the IAEA in 1975.

4. "Bilateral Security Treaty between the United States of America and Japan," September 8, 1951, https://avalon.law.yale.edu/20th_century/japan001.asp.

5. "Treaty of Mutual Cooperation and Security between Japan and the United States of America," Ministry of Foreign Affairs of Japan, January 19, 1960, http://www.mofa.go.jp/region/n-america/us/q&a/ref/1.html.

6. "Joint Statement of Japanese Prime Minister and US President Johnson," Washington, DC, January 13, 1965, http://www.ioc.u-tokyo.ac.jp/~worldjpn/documents/texts/JPUS/19650113.D1E.html; "Joint Statement of Japanese Prime Minister Satō and US President Johnson," Washington, DC, November 15, 1967, http://www.ioc.u-tokyo.ac.jp/~worldjpn/documents/texts/JPUS/19671115.D1E.html.

7. Laura Stone, "Whither Trade and Security: A Historical Perspective," in *The US-Japan Alliance: Past, Present and Future*, ed. Michael J. Green and Patrick M. Cronin (New York: Council on Foreign Relations, 1999), 250.

8. Stone, "Whither Trade and Security," 251.

9. Makoto Iokibe and Takuya Sasaki, "The 1960s: Japan's Economic Rise and the Maturing of the Partnership," in *The History of US-Japan Relations: From Perry to the Present*, ed. Makoto Iokibe (Singapore: Palgrave Macmillan, 2017), 149–169.

10. Stone, "Whither Trade and Security," 255.

11. Aaron Forsberg, *America and the Japanese Miracle: The Cold War Context of Japan's Postwar Economic Revival, 1950–1960* (Chapel Hill: University of North Carolina Press, 2000), 199.

12. U.S. Agency for International Development (USAID), "Foreign Aid Explorer: The Official Record of U.S. Foreign Aid," accessed October 16, 2021, https://explorer.usaid.gov/.

13. Monty G. Marshall, Ted Robert Gurr, and Keith Jaggers, "Polity IV Project: Political Regime Characteristics and Transitions, 1800–2009," Center for Systemic Peace, 2010.

14. Freedom House, *Freedom in the World*, "Comparative and Historical Data," "Country and Territory Ratings and Statuses, 1973–2019," accessed October 17, 2021, https://freedomhouse.org/report/freedom-world.

15. Japan's average on Bailey et al.'s UN General Assembly voting measure during these years was 1.12. For comparison, the global average was 0.10. Bailey et al. argue the measure "can be interpreted as states' positions towards the US-led liberal order." Erik Voeten, Anton Strezhnev, and Michael Bailey 2009, "United Nations General Assembly Voting Data," https://doi.org/10.7910/DVN/LEJUQZ, Harvard Dataverse, V27.

16. See, for example, "NPT," confidential, Department of State Telegram, October 16, 1967, NPT Japan 1966 & 1967 (folder), Director's Office NPT Files (383/77/043), box 4 of 9, National Archives, College Park, MD.

17. See, for example, NPT Japan 1966 & 1967 (folder), Director's Office NPT Files (383/77/043), box 4 of 9, National Archives, College Park, MD.

18. ACDA Memorandum to the Acting Director and All Bureau Heads from Samuel De Palma (ACDA/IR), "NPT: Japanese Attitudes; Points they May Raise; Initiatives They May Support," secret, September 5, 1967, NPT Japan 1966 & 1967 (folder), Director's Office NPT Files (383/77/043), box 4 of 9, National Archives, College Park, MD.

19. Department of State Telegram from Secretary of State Dean Rusk to Tokyo Ambassador, "NPT Security Assurances—Draft UN Res," secret, November 15, 1967, NPT Japan 1966 & 1967 (folder), Director's Office NPT Files (383/77/043), box 4 of 9, National Archives, College Park, MD.

20. Maria Rost Rublee, *Nonproliferation Norms: Why States Choose Nuclear Restraint* (Athens: Georgia University Press, 2009), 65.

21. "Joint Statement of Japanese Prime Minister Satō and US President Johnson."

22. "Chronology of Principal Developments Relating to Arms Control and Disarmament, September—October 1968," 3, ACDA Files, box 383-84-005, box 1 of 5, National Archives, College Park, MD.

23. State Department, Memorandum of Conversation between Takeo Miki, Foreign Minister of Japan and the Secretary of State, "Non-proliferation Treaty" (part 2 of 2), secret, September 16, 1967, p. 2, NPT Japan 1966 & 1967 (folder), Director's Office NPT Files (383/77/043), box 4 of 9, National Archives, College Park, MD.

24. Department of State Telegram from Ambassador to Japan to Secretary of State Dean Rusk, "US-Japan NPT Experts Meeting," secret, November 4, 1967, NPT Japan 1966 & 1967 (folder), Director's Office NPT Files (383/77/043), box 4 of 9, National Archives, College Park, MD.

25. Department of State Telegram from Ambassador to Japan to Secretary of State Dean Rusk, "US-Japan NPT Experts Meeting."

26. George H. Quester, "Japan and the Nuclear Non-Proliferation Treaty," *Asian Survey* 10, no. 9 (1970): 766, https://doi.org/10.2307/2643028.

27. *Foreign Relations of the United States*, 1969–1976, vol. E-2, Documents on Arms Control and Nonproliferation, 1969–1972, ed. David I. Goldman and David C. Humphrey (Washington, DC: US Government Printing Office, 2007), doc. 44.

28. John E. Endicott, "The 1975–76 Debate Over Ratification of the NPT in Japan," *Asian Survey* 17, no. 3 (1977): 277, https://doi.org/10.2307/2643501.

29. *Foreign Relations of the United States*, 1969–1976, vol. E-2, doc. 55.

30. *Foreign Relations of the United States*, 1969–1976, vol. E-2, doc. 57.

31. For example, see Bernard Gwertzman, "Kissinger Tells Asian Allies US Stands by Them," *New York Times*, June 19, 1975, A1, https://www.nytimes.com/1975/06/19/archives/kissinger-tells-asian-allies-us-stands-by-them-warns-states-on.html; Tillman Durdin, "Kissinger Begins Japanese Talks," *New York Times*, June 11, 1972, 11, https://www.nytimes.com/1972/06/11/archives/kissinger-begins-japanese-talks-he-reassures-leaders-in-3day-tokyo.html.

32. *Foreign Relations of the United States*, 1969–1976, vol. E-2, doc. 58.

33. *Foreign Relations of the United States*, 1969–1976, vol. E-2, doc. 58.

34. *Foreign Relations of the United States*, 1969–1976, vol. E-2, doc. 58.

35. *Foreign Relations of the United States*, 1969–1976, vol. E-12, Documents on East and Southeast Asia, 1973–1976, ed. Bradley Lynn Coleman, David Goldman and David Nickles (Washington, DC: US Government Printing Office, 2010), doc. 179.

36. *Foreign Relations of the United States*, 1969–1976, vol. E-2, doc. 30.

37. For example, see "IEA/Japan Safeguards Negotiations: 2. GOJ Contribution to IAEA Study," Cable from US Embassy Tokyo to the Secretary of State, AAD, NARA, 1976TOKYO 01718, January 8, 1976.

38. See the following U.S. cables: 1975TOKYO01200, 1975IAEAV00711, 1975TOKYO00296, 1975STATE011137.

39. T. Haginoya, "The National System of Safeguards: Experience in Japan," *IAEA Bulletin*, Summer 1985, https://www.iaea.org/sites/default/files/27203491922.pdf.

40. "December 12 EA Press Summary," Cable from the Secretary of State to Asia-Pacific Diplomatic Posts, AAD, NARA, 1973STATE243571, December 13, 1973.

41. Quester, "Japan and the Nuclear," 776.

42. *Foreign Relations of the United States*, 1969–1976, vol. E-12, doc. 189.

43. *Foreign Relations of the United States*, 1969–1976, vol. E-12, doc. 192.

44. Fred C. Ikle and Winston Lord to Secretary Kissinger, July 31, 1974, "Analytical Staff Meeting on Non-proliferation Strategy," secret, RG 383; Tab A, "Non-Proliferation: Strategy and Action Program," secret, 10; ACDA Non-Proliferation Strategy and Action Program, Arms Control and Foreign Policy Seminar, January–August 1974; Office of Administration (Formerly Executive Director Office) Subject Files Pertaining to ACDA Nonproliferation Strategy and Nuclear Safeguards, 1974–1976 (box 383/98/0085), US Arms Control and Disarmament Agency, National Archives, College Park, MD.

45. Fred C. Ikle and Winston Lord to Secretary Kissinger, July 31, 1974, "Analytical Staff Meeting on Non-Proliferation Strategy."

46. "Memorandum for S—the Secretary, Analytical Staff Meeting," secret, July 11, 1973, pp. 2–3, https://www.fordlibrarymuseum.gov/library/document/0353/1555879.pdf.

47. The White House, "Press Conference of Henry A. Kissinger, Secretary of State and Assistant to the President for National Security Affairs," Hotel Okura, November 20, 1974, http://www.fordlibrarymuseum.gov/library/document/0248/whpr19741120-005.pdf.

48. "Joint Communique Following Discussions with Prime Minister Tanaka of Japan," November 20, 1974, American Presidency Project, https://www.presidency.ucsb.edu/documents/joint-communique-following-discussions-with-prime-minister-tanaka-japan.

49. Action Memorandum: Japan's NPT Ratification Process as Crucial Stage," Cable from the Secretary of State, Washington DC, to American Consulate, Jerusalem, February 14, 1975, AAD, NARA, 1975STATE034232.

50. "Japan and NPT," Cable from US Mission Vienna to the Secretary of State, Washington, DC, February 19, 1975, AAD, NARA, 1975TOKYO02142.

51. "US. Approach to GOJ on NPT," secret RG 59, Action Memorandum, February 20, 1975, Japan and the US, 1960–1976, JU01921, Records of the Department of State, Records of the Policy Planning Staff, Director's Files (Winston Lord), 1969–1977, Winston Lord Sensitive Non-China, 1975, National Archives, College Park, MD.

52. "US. Approach to GOJ on NPT."

53. "Japan and NPT," Cable from the Secretary of State to the US Embassy Tokyo (immediate), February 25, 1975, AAD, NARA, 1975STATE041780.

54. See, for example, "Japan-IAEA Safeguards Agreement," Cable from US Mission Vienna to the Secretary of State (Immediate), AAD, NARA, 1975IAEAV01928, March 5, 1975.

55. "Japan and NPT," Telegram from the Secretary of State to Embassy in Tokyo, February 25, 1975, NARA, AAD, 1975STATE041780; cited in Joseph O'Mahoney, "When Breaking the Norm Strengthens the Norm: India's 1974 Nuclear Explosion and the Nuclear Nonproliferation Treaty," presented at the American Political Science Association Annual Meeting, Boston, MA, September 2018.

56. Endicott, "1975–76 Debate," 293.

57. "Miki Visit Paper: NPT," Telegram from US Embassy Tokyo to the Secretary of State, July 11, 1975, NARA, ADD, 1975TOKYO09291.

58. "Japanese NPT Ratification," Telegram from Secretary of State to US Embassy Tokyo, September 13, 1975, NARA, AAD, 1975STATE218169; cited in O'Mahoney, "When Breaking the Norm."

59. Endicott, "1975–76 Debate," 289.

60. "Subject: Japanese Upper House Ratifies NPT," Cable from US Embassy Tokyo to the Secretary of State, AAD, NARA, 1976TOKYO07638, May 24, 1976.

61. "Foreign Minister on NPT," Cable from US Embassy Tokyo to the Secretary of State, March 22, 1975, Washington, DC, AAD, NARA, 1975TOKYO03711.

62. Quoted in Endicott, "1975–76 Debate," 282.

63. "Fonoff Scenario for NPT Ratification," Cable from US Embassy Tokyo to the Secretary of State, April 8, 1975, NARA, AAD, 1975TOKYO04577.

64. "Miyazawa Visit: Agenda Topic Two—Security Relations," Cable from US Embassy Tokyo to the Secretary of State, AAD, NARA, 1975TOKYO04507, April 7, 1975.

65. Memorandum to the President (Nixon) from Henry A. Kissinger, "Call of Japanese Foreign Minister Kiichi Miyazawa," secret, April 4, 1975, POL 5–2, p. 2, Foreign Minister (FonMin) Miyazawa (folder), Office of the Country Director for Japan, Records Relating to Japanese Political Affairs, 1960–1975 (Inspections, 1975 to Agreements, 1975), RG 59 General Records of the Department of State, National Archives, College Park, MD.

66. *Foreign Relations of the United States*, 1969–1976 vol. E-12, doc. 203.

67. Quoted in Endicott, "1975–76 Debate," 282.

68. "Lower House Expected to Ratify NPT April 28," Cable from US Embassy Tokyo to the Secretary of State, April 27, 1976, AAD, NARA, 1976TOKYO06192.

69. "GOJ/LDP Shelve NPT," Cable from US Embassy Tokyo to Secretary of State, June 20, 1975, NARA, AAD, 1975TOKYO08288.

70. "Rightest Attacks Prime Minister," Cable from US Embassy Tokyo to Secretary of State, AAD, NARA, 1975TOKYO08079, June 17, 1975.

71. "Prime Minister Miki—President Ford Meeting Discussion Outline," July 25, 1975, History and Public Policy Program Digital Archive, Diplomatic Archives of the Ministry of Foreign Affairs of Japan. Obtained for NKIDP by Kyungwon Choi (Kyushu University) and translated for NKIDP by Ryo C. Kato, http://digitalarchive.wilsoncenter.org/document/118654.

72. "Japan-US. Joint Announcement to the Press (by Prime Minister Takeo Miki and President Gerald R. Ford)," Washington, DC, August 6, 1975, *A Documentary History of US-Japanese Relations, 1945–1997,* 901–903, *Public Papers of the Presidents: Gerald Ford, 1975,* vol. 2, pp. 1112–1117; The World and Japan Database Project, Database of Japanese Politics and International Relations, Institute of Oriental Culture, University of Tokyo, http://www.ioc.u-tokyo.ac.jp/~worldjpn/documents/texts/JPUS/19750806.O1E.html.

73. "Japan-US. Joint Announcement to the Press (by Prime Minister Takeo Miki and President Gerald R. Ford)."

74. Endicott, "1975–76 Debate," 289.

75. "Japan, 8 Years Late, Ratifies Treaty to Halt Nuclear Spread," *New York Times,* May 25, 1976, 2, https://www.nytimes.com/1976/05/25/archives/japan-8-years-late-ratifies-treaty-to-halt-nuclear-spread.html; see also, "'Unequal Treaty,'" Cable from US Embassy Tokyo to the Secretary of State, May 12, 1976, AAD, NARA, 1976TOKYO06988.

76. "Subject: Japanese Upper House Ratifies NPT," Cable from US Embassy Tokyo to the Secretary of State, May 24, 1976, AAD, NARA, 1976TOKYO07638.

77. Rublee, *Nonproliferation Norms,* 68.

78. Memorandum of Conversation, "Ford-Miki Luncheon Conversation," State Dining Room, White House, Washington, DC, June 30, 1976, http://www.fordlibrarymuseum.gov/library/document/0314/1553489.pdf.

79. Rublee, *Nonproliferation Norms,* 63–64.

80. "Action Memorandum: Japan's NPT Ratification Process as Crucial Stage."

81. "Japan: NPT Ratification," Cable from US Embassy Tokyo to Secretary of State, March 17, 1975, AAD, NARA, 1975TOKYO03451.

82. "Japan: NPT Ratification."

83. "GOJ/LDP Shelve NPT," Cable from US Embassy Tokyo to Secretary of State, June 20, 1975, AAD, NARA, 1975TOKYO08288.

84. "Japan, 8 Years Late, Ratifies Treaty to Halt Nuclear Spread."

85. NPT Treaty Text, https://www.un.org/en/conf/npt/2005/npttreaty.html.

86. "GOJ NPT Ratification Plans," Cable to the Secretary of State from US Embassy Tokyo, March 12, 1975, AAD, NARA, 1975TOKYO03241.

87. Prime Minister Satō laid out the three nuclear principles in a speech in December 1967, and they were adopted by the Diet in 1971.The three principles include not possessing nuclear weapons, not manufacturing nuclear weapons, and not introducing these weapons to Japanese territory.

88. "Lower House Expected to Ratify NPT April 2," Cable from US Embassy Tokyo to Secretary of State, April 27, 1976, AAD, NARA, 1976TOKYO06192.

89. Solingen, *Nuclear Logics,* 69.

90. Paul F. Gardner, *Shared Hopes, Separate Fears: Fifty Years of US-Indonesian Relations,* (Philadelphia: University of Pennsylvania Press, 1997), 265.

91. Department of State, SECRET Memorandum from Henry Kissinger for the President, Subject: Your Meeting with President Suharto of Indonesia, May 26, 1970, Richard M. Nixon Papers, Subject Numeric Files, 1970–1973, box 2272, National Security Archive, http://nsarchive.gwu.edu/NSAEBB/NSAEBB242/19700526_memo.pdf.

92. USAID, "Foreign Aid Explorer: The Official Record of U.S. Foreign Aid."

93. Memorandum of Conversation, President Suharto of Indonesia, The President, Dr. Kissinger, May 26, 1970, Richard M. Nixon Papers, Subject Numeric Files, 1970–1973, box 2272, National Security Archive, http://nsarchive.gwu.edu/NSAEBB/NSAEBB242/19700526_memcon.pdf.

94. Joe Renouard, *Human Rights in American Foreign Policy: From the 1960s to the Soviet Collapse* (Philadelphia: University of Pennsylvania Press, 2015), 137–138.

95. Marshall, Gurr, and Jaggers, "Polity IV Project."

96. CIA NIE 55–67, "Prospects for Indonesia," February 15, 1967, p. 14, Central Intelligence Agency's Freedom of Information Act Electronic Reading Room, http://www.foia.cia.gov/sites/default/files/document_conversions/89801/DOC_0000208831.pdf.

97. CIA NIE 55–67, "Prospects for Indonesia," 17.

98. "Indonesians Accept Nuclear Controls," *New York Times*, October 28, 1965, B5, https://www.nytimes.com/2011/03/18/business/global/18atomic.html.

99. *Preventing Nuclear Dangers in Southeast Asia and Australasia* (London: International Institute for Strategic Studies, 2009), 62–63.

100. "Indonesia: Ratification of Treaty on the Non-Proliferation of Nuclear Weapons (NPT)," United Nations Office for Disarmament Affairs, January 9, 2022, http://disarmament.un.org/treaties/a/npt/indonesia/rat/washington.

101. "Developments Regarding NPT Ratification," Cable from US Mission Vienna to the Secretary of State, October 19, 1973, AAD, NARA, 1973IAEAV08666.

102. *Foreign Relations of the United States*, 1969–1976, vol. E-2, doc. 13.

103. "Indonesia and NPT," Cable from American Embassy Jakarta to the Secretary of State, September 5, 1975, NARA, ADD, 1975JAKART10938.

104. "Indonesia and NPT."

105. "Annual Australian-Indonesian Discussions," Cable from American Embassy Jakarta to the Secretary of State, November 1, 1974, AAD, NARA, 1974JAKART13374.

106. "Indonesia and Non-Proliferation Treaty," Cable from American Embassy Jakarta to the Secretary of State, March 4, 1975, AAD, NARA, 1975JAKART02686.

107. "Whitlam-Suharto Talks in Townsville," Cable from American Embassy Canberra to the Secretary of State, April 8, 1975, NARA, AAD, 1975CANBER02154.

108. "Indonesia and NPT," Cable from the US Mission to the IAEA Vienna to American Embassy Jakarta and Secretary of State, September 3, 1975, AAD, NARA, 1975IAEAV07512.

109. "Indonesia and NPT," Cable from American Embassy Jakarta to the Secretary of State, September 5, 1975, NARA, ADD, 1975JAKART10938.

110. "Ivdonesian [*sic*] Interest in Assistance in Nuclear Energy Field," Cable from American Embassy Jakarta to the Secretary of State, April 25, 1975, NARA, AAD, 1975JAKART04912.

111. "IAEA Board of Governors—Research Reactor Projects for Indonesia and Thailand," Cable from US Mission Vienna to the Secretary of State, May 31, 1974, AAD, NARA, 1974IAEAV04882.

112. "Subject: IAEA 19th General Conference: Afternoon September 26 (Closing)," Cable from US Mission to the IAEA to the Secretary of State, October 1, 1975, NARA, AAD, 975IAEAV08380.

113. Jakarta Domestic Service—1974-07-04 "Indonesia Plans to Develop Nuclear Industry," Daily Report, Asia & Pacific, FBIS-APA-74-131 on 1974-07-08, p. N1.

114. Daniel Poneman, "Nuclear Policies in Developing Countries," *International Affairs* 57, no. 4 (1981): 568–584. IAEA study: International Atomic Energy Agency, *Nuclear Power Planning Study for Indonesia* (Vienna: IAEA, 1976).

115. Poneman, "Nuclear Policies," 577–578.

116. "The Annual Report for 1976," International Atomic Energy Agency, July 1977, p. 21, https://inis.iaea.org/collection/NCLCollectionStore/_Public/40/091/40091121.pdf.

117. "Annual Report for 1976."

118. "Indonesia and NPT," Cable from US Embassy Jakarta to the Secretary of States, January 11, 1977, NARA, ADD, 1977JAKART00459.

119. "Indonesia and NPT," Cable from the Secretary of State to US Embassy Jakarta, January 12, 1977, NARA, AAD, 1977STATE006736.

120. "Indonesia and NPT," Cable from the Secretary of State to US Embassy Jakarta, January 12, 1977, NARA, AAD, 1977STATE006736.

121. "Indoensian [*sic*] and NPT," Cable from American Embassy Tokyo to the Secretary of State (Immediate), January 14, 1977, NARA, AAD, 1977TOKYO00641.

122. "Indonesia and NPT," Cable from American Embassy London to the Secretary of State, January 14, 1977, NARA, AAD, 1977LONDON00710.

123. "Call by Ambassador Rusmin Nuryadin on Deputy Secretary," Cable from the Secretary of State to US Embassy Jakarta, February 23, 1977, NARA, AAD, 1977STATE040549.

124. "Indonesia and NPT," Cable from American Embassy Jakarta to the Secretary of State, March 3, 1977, NARA, AAD, 1977JAKART02722.

125. "Message to Suharto," Cable from the Secretary of State to US Embassy Jakarta, March 5, 1977, NARA, AAD, 1977STATE049686.

126. "GOI Reportedly Fears US Embargo on Sale of Nuclear Materials," Cable from Secretary of State to US Embassy Jakarta, April 20, 1977, NARA, AAD, 1977STATE088510.

127. "Formal Indonesian Decision to Ratify the Non-Proliferation Treaty," Cable from US Embassy Jakarta to the Secretary of State, May 11, 1977, NARA, AAD, 1977JAKART06071.

128. "USUN Daily Unclassified Summary No. 32 Nov. 2, 1977," Cable from the US Mission to the UN to the Secretary of State (Immediate), November 3, 1977, AAD, NARA, 1977USUNN04301.

129. "GOI Request for List of Signatories of Treaties on Bacteriological and Nuclear Weapons," Cable from US Embassy Jakarta to Secretary of State, January 30, 1978, AAD, NARA, 1978JAKART01284.

130. "Indonesian Non-Proliferation Treaty (NPT) Ratification," Cable from Secretary of State to US Embassy Jakarta, March 31, 1978, AAD, NARA, 1978STATE083078.

131. "Negotiation of Agreements for Peaceful Unclear [*sic*] Cooperation," Cable from US Embassy Vienna to Secretary of State, April 21, 1978, AAD, NARA, 1978JAKART05209.

132. "Negotiation of Agreements for Peaceful Unclear [*sic*] Cooperation."

133. "Indonesian Non-Proliferation Treaty (NPT) Ratification," Cable from US Embassy Jakarta to the Secretary of State, April 29, 1978, AAD, NARA, 1978JAKART05584.

134. Memorandum for the President from the Vice President, "Visit to the Pacific," April 26, 1978, NSA Staff Materials, Far East Files, box 7, Carter Library, Atlanta, GA.

135. Memorandum for Dr. Zbigniew Brzezinski, "Status of Actions from the Vice President's Asian Trip," January 31, 1979, NSA Staff Materials, Far East Files, box 7, Carter Library, Atlanta, GA.

136. "Indonesian Parliament Takes Up NPT Ratification," Cable from US Embassy Jakarta to the Secretary of State, August 21, 1978, AAD, NARA, 1978JAKART11355.

137. "Government Faces Ratification of the Nuclear Non-proliferation Treaty," Daily Report Jakarta, August 19, 1978, p. N1, FBIS: Asia & Pacific.

138. Jakarta ANTARA—1978-11-16 Minister Says Larger Nuclear Reactor Needed for Research, Daily Report, Asia & Pacific, FBIS-APA-78-223 on 1978-11-17, under the heading(s): Indonesia, p. N2.

139. "33rd UNGA: Negative Security Assurances (Nuclear Non-Use), NPT," Cable from US Embassy Jakarta to Secretary of State, October 19, 1978, AAD, NARA, 1978JAKART14276.

140. "33rd UNGA: Negative Security Assurances (Nuclear Non-Use), NPT."

141. "NPT Adherence: Indonesia," Cable from the Secretary of State to the US Embassy Jakarta, October 25, 1978, AAD, NARA, 1978STATE271435.

142. "Indonesian Ratification of NPT," Cable from US Embassy Jakarta to the Secretary of State, November 27, 1978, AAD, NARA, 1978JAKART16236.

143. "Indonesia: Ratification of Treaty on the Non-Proliferation of Nuclear Weapons (NPT)," United Nations Office of Disarmament Affairs, accessed October 16, 2021, http://disarmament.un.org/treaties/a/npt/indonesia/rat/washington.

144. "The Text of the Agreement of 14 July 1980 Between Indonesia and the Agency for the Applications of Safeguards in Connections with the Treaty on the Non-Proliferation of Nuclear Weapons," July 14, 1980, http://www.iaea.org/Publications/Documents/Infcircs/Others/infcirc283.pdf.

145. Jakarta Domestic Service—1980-04-02 Nuclear Energy Cooperation Agreement Signed with France, Daily Report, Asia & Pacific, FBIS-APA-80-066 on 1980-04-03, Indonesia, p. N1; Jakarta Domestic Service—1980-10-09, Italy Agrees to Nuclear Energy Cooperation Arrangement, Daily Report, Asia & Pacific, FBIS-APA-80-199 on 1980-10-10, under the heading(s): Indonesia, p. N1.

146. "Four Countries Said to Offer Help to Indonesia for Nuclear Plants," *New York Times*, January 7, 1981, A13, https://www.nytimes.com/1981/01/07/world/four-countries-said-to-offer-help-to-indonesia-for-nuclear-plants.html; Jakarta Antara—1982-06-12 BATAN, FRG'S INTERATOM Sign Reactor Contract, Daily Report, Asia & Pacific, FBIS-APA-82-116 on 1982-06-16, Indonesia, p. N3.

147. The Comptroller General, Report to the Congress of the United States, "Evaluation of US Efforts to Promote Nuclear Non-Proliferation Treaty," 21.

148. Memorandum for Dr. Zbigrew Brzezinski, "Status of Actions from the Vice President's Asian Trip," 1.

149. Memorandum for Dr. Zbigrew Brzezinski, "Status of Actions from the Vice President's Asian Trip," 1.

150. Memorandum for Dr. Zbigrew Brzezinski, "Status of Actions from the Vice President's Asian Trip," 1.

151. "Indonesian and NPT," Cable from American Embassy Jakarta to the Secretary of State, July 30, 1974, AAD, NARA, 1974JAKART09390.

152. "GOI Statements on Development of Nuclear Power," Cable from American Embassy Jakarta to the Secretary of State, August 6, 1974, AAD, NARA, 1974JAKART09660.

153. "GOI Statements on Development of Nuclear Power."

154. "Southeast Asian Nuclear-Weapon-Free-Zone (SEANWFZ) Treaty (Bangkok Treaty)," Nuclear Threat Initiative, (undated) accessed October 16, 2021, https://www.nti.org/learn/treaties-and-regimes/southeast-asian-nuclear-weapon-free-zone-seanwfz-treaty-bangkok-treaty/.

155. USAID, "Foreign Aid Explorer."

156. Rublee, *Nonproliferation Norms*, 110–115.

157. Rublee, *Nonproliferation Norms*, 110–115.

158. Jimmy Carter, "Remarks on the Arrival of the Egyptian President" (speech, Washington, DC, February 3, 1979), http://sadat.umd.edu/archives/speeches/AABS%20Sadat%20Visit%202.3.78.pdf.

159. Anwar Sadat, "Welcoming Remarks on the Arrival of President Carter to Cairo" (Cairo, Egypt, March 8, 1979), http://sadat.umd.edu/archives/speeches/AACO%20Sadat-Carter%20in%20Cairo%203.8.79.pdf.

160. International Trade Administration, "Bilateral Investment Treaties: Egypt," accessed October 16, 2021, https://www.trade.gov/bilateral-investment-treaties.

161. Freedom House, *Freedom in the World*, "Comparative and Historical Data," "Country and Territory Ratings and Statuses, 1973–2019," accessed October 17, 2021, https://freedomhouse.org/report/freedom-world.

162. Marshall, Gurr, and Jaggers, "Polity IV Project."

163. Rublee, *Nonproliferation Norms*, 115. George H. Quester states, "Egypt signed the Treaty under obvious Russian pressure." Quester, "Paris, Pretoria, Peking . . . Proliferation?," *Bulletin of the Atomic Scientists* 26 (1970): 14; Rublee, *Nonproliferation Norms*, 110.

164. Shai Feldman, *Nuclear Weapons and Arms Control in the Middle East* (Cambridge, MA: MIT Press, 1997), 59.

165. Feldman, *Nuclear Weapons*, 59.

166. Feldman, *Nuclear Weapons*, 59. Also see Gawdat Bahgat, "The Proliferation of Weapons of Mass Destruction: Egypt," *Arab Studies Quarterly* 21, no. 2 (Spring 2007): 1–15, https://www.jstor.org/stable/41859024.

167. *Foreign Relations of the United States*, 1969–1976, vol. 25, Arab-Israeli Crisis and War, 1973, ed. Nina Howland and Craig Daigle (Washington, DC: US Government Printing Office, 2011), doc. 63.

168. William B. Quandt, *Camp David: Peacemaking and Politics* (Washington, DC: Brookings Institution, 2015).

169. Quoted in Rublee, *Nonproliferation Norms*, 117.

170. *Foreign Relations of the United States*, 1977–1980, vol. 9, Arab-Israeli Dispute, August 1978–December 1980, ed. Alexander R. Wieland and Adam M. Howard (Washington, DC: US Government Printing Office 2014), doc. 38.

171. *Foreign Relations of the United States,* 1977–1980, vol. 9, doc. 44.
172. *Foreign Relations of the United States,* 1977–1980, vol. 9, doc. 139.
173. *Foreign Relations of the United States,* 1977–1980, vol. 9, doc. 139.
174. Avner Cohen, *Israel and the Bomb* (New York: Columbia University Press, 1998).
175. "Interview with Dean Rust," Association for Diplomatic Studies and Training Foreign Affairs Oral History Project, Association for Diplomatic Studies and Training, Arlington, VA, 2007, 51, http://lcweb2.loc.gov/service/mss/mfdip/2007/2007rus02/2007rus02.pdf.
176. Shai Feldman, "Extending the Nuclear Nonproliferation Treaty: The Middle East Debate," Research Memorandum 28 (Washington, DC: Washington Institute, 1995), 1–14, https://www.washingtoninstitute.org/media/3616.
177. The Comptroller General, Report to the Congress of the United States, "Evaluation of US Efforts to Promote Nuclear Non-Proliferation Treaty," 20.
178. "Revised Draft US-Egypt and US-Israel Peaceful Nuclear Cooperation Agreements," Cable from the Secretary of State to US Embassy Cairo, May 17, 1979, AAD, NARA, 1979STATE125951.
179. "NPT Adherence," Cable from US Embassy Cairo to the Secretary of State, October 18, 1979, AAD, NARA, 1979CAIRO21514.
180. "U.S.-Egyptian Peaceful Nuclear Cooperation Agreement," Cable from the Secretary of State to US Embassy Cairo, December 22, 1979, AAD, NARA, 1979STATE330062.
181. "US-Egyptian Peaceful Nuclear Cooperation Agreement," Cable from the Secretary of State to US Embassy Cairo, December 26, 1979, AAD, NARA, 1979STATE331387.
182. Jim Walsh, "Bombs Unbuilt: Power, Ideas and Institutions in International Politics" (PhD diss., MIT, 2001), 182.
183. Shai Feldman, *Israeli Nuclear Deterrence: A Strategy for the 1980s* (New York: Columbia University Press, 1982), 72.
184. Quoted in Philipp Bleek, "Does Proliferation Beget Proliferation? Why Nuclear Dominoes Rarely Fall" (PhD diss., Georgetown University, 2010), 121. Originally cited in Walsh, "Bombs Unbuilt," 146.
185. Bleek, "Does Proliferation Beget Proliferation?," 121.
186. Quoted in Bleek, "Does Proliferation Beget Proliferation?," 129. Originally found in Rublee, *Nonproliferation Norms,* 109.
187. Barbara M. Gregory, "Egypt's Nuclear Program: Assessing Supplier-Based and Other Developmental Constraints," *Nonproliferation Review* 3, no. 1 (1995): 23, https://www.nonproliferation.org/wp-content/uploads/npr/gregor31.pdf.
188. When exactly the Egyptians knew about the Israeli nuclear weapon program is unclear, but there were rumors and reports on the topics through the 1950s and 1960s. Bleek concludes that there was near consensus among Egyptian leaders by the late 1960s, though they continued to promote ambiguity about the Israeli program in public to avoid the domestic pressure that certainty would create. Bleek, "Does Proliferation Beget Proliferation?," 117–118.
189. Bahgat, "The Proliferation of Weapons of Mass Destruction: Egypt," 5.
190. Bahgat, "Egypt and Weapons of Mass Destruction," 5.
191. Bleek, "Does Proliferation Beget Proliferation?," 124.
192. Walsh, "Bombs Unbuilt," 172.
193. Walsh, "Bombs Unbuilt," 202.
194. Bahgat, "Proliferation of Weapons."
195. "Egypt: Ratification of Treaty on the Non-Proliferation of Nuclear Weapons (NPT)," United Nations Office of Disarmament Affairs, accessed October 16, 2021, http://disarmament.un.org/treaties/a/npt/egypt/rat/london.
196. Polity IV, "Authority Trends, 1946–2013: Cuba, 2014," https://www.systemicpeace.org/polity/cub2.htm. See Marshall, Gurr, and Jaggers, "Polity IV Project."
197. Freedom House, *Freedom in the World,* "Comparative and Historical Data," "Country and Territory Ratings and Statuses, 1973–2019," accessed October 17, 2021, https://freedomhouse.org/report/freedom-world.

198. From 1960 to 2002, the year before it joined the NPT, the average measure for Cuba was –1.60, significantly lower than average. For comparison, Libya's average during the same period is –0.99.

199. USAID, "Foreign Aid Explorer: The Official Record of U.S. Foreign Aid."

200. USAID, "Foreign Aid Explorer: The Official Record of U.S. Foreign Aid."

201. For example, "Cuba to Reject US Aid," *BBC News*, September 11, 1999, http://news.bbc.co.uk/2/hi/americas/168987.stm; "Cuba Rejects Relief Aid from US," *The Guardian*, September 16, 2008, https://www.theguardian.com/world/2008/sep/16/usa.cuba.

202. UN General Assembly, "Non-Proliferation of Nuclear Weapons (2028(XX))," November 19, 1965, http://daccess-dds-ny.un.org/doc/RESOLUTION/GEN/NR0/217/91/IMG/NR021791.pdf.

203. "Timeline of the Nuclear Nonproliferation Treaty (NPT)," *Arms Control Association*, March 2020, https://www.armscontrol.org/factsheets/Timeline-of-the-Treaty-on-the-Non-Proliferation-of-Nuclear-Weapons-NPT.

204. "US-UK Consultations on NPT and Review Conference," Cable from the Secretary of State to US Mission Vienna, September 12, 1978, AAD, NARA, 1978STATE230401.

205. *Foreign Relations of the United States*, 1969–1976, vol. E-2, doc. 355.

206. *Foreign Relations of the United States*, 1964–1968, vol. 11, Arms Control and Disarmament, ed. Evans Gerakas, David S. Patterson, and Carolyn B. Yee (Washington, DC: US Government Printing Office, 1997), doc. 198.

207. *Foreign Relations of the United States*, 1964–1968, vol. 11, doc. 198.

208. As secretary of state, Henry Kissinger had previously engaged in back-channel discussions with Cuban officials in an attempt to improve US-Cuban relations, but these conversations ultimately failed over Cuba sending troops to Angola in 1975. See Frances Robles, "Kissinger Drew Up Plans to Attack Cuba, Records Show," *New York Times*, September 30, 2014, A12, https://www.nytimes.com/2014/10/01/world/americas/kissinger-drew-up-plans-to-attack-cuba-records-show.html.

209. See, for example, "Last Travel Curbs Removed by Carter," *New York Times*, March 10, 1977, 11, https://www.nytimes.com/1977/03/10/archives/last-travel-curbs-removed-by-carter-americans-may-go-to-cuba.html.

210. *Foreign Relations of the United States*, 1977–1980, vol. 23, Mexico, Cuba, and the Caribbean, ed. Alexander O. Poster (Washington, DC: US Government Printing Office, 2007), doc. 18.

211. *Foreign Relations of the United States*, 1977–1980, vol. 26, Arms Control and Nonproliferation, ed. Chris Tudda (Washington, DC: US Government Printing Office, 2015), doc. 418.

212. "Cuba and the Treaty of Tlatelolco," Cable from the Secretary of State to US Interest Section Havana, October 19, 1977, AAD, NARA, 1977STATE251232.

213. *Foreign Relations of the United States*, 1977–1980, vol. 26, doc. 421.

214. *Foreign Relations of the United States*, 1977–1980, vol. 26, doc. 421.

215. "Cuba and the Treaty of Tlatelolco."

216. Hedrick Smith, "US. Sees Cuba's African Buildup Blocking Efforts to Improve Ties," *New York Times*, November 17, 1977, 49, https://www.nytimes.com/1977/11/17/archives/new-jersey-pages-us-sees-cubas-african-buildup-blocking-efforts-to.html.

217. "Castro Meeting with Codel Reuss," Cable from US Interest Section Havana to Secretary of State, January 4, 1978, AAD, NARA, 1978HAVANA00010.

218. "Castro Meeting with Codel Reuss."

219. Bernard Weinraub, "Church Says Soviet Tests US Resolve on Troops in Cuba," *New York Times*, September 10, 1979, A1, https://www.nytimes.com/1979/09/10/archives/church-says-soviet-tests-us-resolve-on-troops-in-cuba-asks.html.

220. A. O. Sulzberger Jr., "1,800 Marines Land at Guantánamo in Show of US Might," *New York Times*, October 18, 1979, A2, https://www.nytimes.com/1979/10/18/archives/1800-marines-land-at-guantanamo-in-show-of-us-might-were-invading.html.

221. For the full text of the act, see Cuban Democracy Act ("CDA"), United States Code Title 22, Foreign Relations and Intercourse, chap. 69, 1992, https://www.treasury.gov/resource-center/sanctions/Documents/cda.pdf.

222. "Japan Urges Cuba to Join the NPT," *Japan Economic Newswire*, January 26, 1995 (Lexus-Nexus).

223. "S. HRG. 107–736, Cuba's Pursuit of Biological Weapons: Fact or Fiction?," Hearing before the US Senate Subcommittee on Western Hemisphere, Peace Corps and Narcotics Affairs, Committee on Foreign Relations, June 5, 2002, https://fas.org/nuke/guide/cuba/sfrc060502.pdf.

224. Ken Alibeck, *Biohazard: The Chilling True Story of the Largest Covert Biological Weapons Program in the World* New York: Random House, 2000), 273–277.

225. "Cuba Dismisses Biological Weapons Report as Ridiculous and Fanciful," *BBC Summary of Broadcasts*, June 26, 1999.

226. "Restrictions on Travel to Cuba, Hearing before a Subcommittee of the Committee on Appropriations," US Senate, 107th Cong., 2nd session, Special Hearing, February 11, 2002, Washington, DC, https://www.govinfo.gov/content/pkg/CHRG-107shrg78446/pdf/CHRG-107shrg78446.pdf.

227. "Beyond the Axis of Evil: Additional Threats from Weapons of Mass Destruction," Heritage Center, Washington, DC, May 6, 2002, https://www.heritage.org/defense/report/beyond-the-axis-evil-additional-threats-weapons-mass-destruction-0.

228. "Chronology of Libya's Disarmament and Relations with the United States," Arms Control Association Fact Sheets and Briefs, March 2021, https://www.armscontrol.org/factsheets/LibyaChronology.

229. "Cuba Accuses United States of Lying about Cuba Preparing Biological Weapons, Urges World to Impede 'Hegemonic Power,'" United Nations press release, May 30, 2002, https://www.un.org/press/en/2002/dcf416.doc.htm.

230. Jonathan Benjamin-Alvarado, "Cuba and the Nonproliferation Regime: A Small State Response to Global Instability," *Nonproliferation Review* 10, no. 3 (2004): 24, https://www.nonproliferation.org/wp-content/uploads/npr/103alva.pdf.

231. Author correspondence with former IAEA official, April 25, 2019.

232. "Cuba Gets Set to Sign Up to Anti-Nuclear Treaty," *Morning Star*, September 16, 2002 (Lexus-Nexus).

233. "Cuba to Sign Nuclear Treaty," *The Advertiser*, September 16, 2002 (Lexus-Nexus).

234. Benjamin-Alvarado, "Cuba and the Nonproliferation Regime," 29.

4. The Hard-Fought Battle for NPT Extension

1. For the full text of the NPT, see "The Treaty on the Non-Proliferation of Nuclear Weapons (NPT)," UN.org, accessed October 16, 2021, http://www.un.org/en/conf/npt/2005/npttreaty.html.

2. Thomas Graham Jr., *Disarmament Sketches: Three Decades of Arms Control and International Law* (Seattle: University of Washington Press, 2002), 258.

3. See, for example, "Final Communiqué," Nuclear Planning Group (Gleneagles, Scotland, October 21, 1992), https://www.nato.int/docu/comm/49-95/c921021a.htm.

4. "Providing US Views on NPT Prepcom Issues," Cable from US Mission Vienna to Secretary of State, M-2008-02837, March 12, 1993, Department of State, FOIA Reading Room, https://foia.state.gov/Search/Results.aspx?searchText=%22wider%20Western%20group%22%20AND%20NPT&beginDate=&endDate=&publishedBeginDate=&publishedEndDate=&caseNumber=.

5. Holum offered the job to Graham on July 2, 1993. He was confirmed in July 1994. Graham, *Disarmament Sketches*, 228.

6. Graham, *Disarmament Sketches*, 228.

7. David B. Ottoway and Steve Coll, "A Hard Sell for Treaty Renewal," *Washington Post*, April 14, 1995, 1A, https://www.washingtonpost.com/archive/politics/1995/04/14/a-hard-sell-for-treaty-renewal/51a544fc-5f73-43e5-af69-90d3e7280a9a/.

8. Barbara Opall, "US Turns Up Diplomatic Heat for NPT Votes," *Defense News*, February 6–12, 1995.

9. "The head of the Venezuela negotiating team . . . resigned in protest after his Government suddenly dropped its opposition to the signing at the last minute, under massive pressure from Washington." Sarang Shidore, "Only Big Nuclear Powers Gain from Nonproliferation Treaty" (letter to the editor), *New York Times*, May 19, 1995, A30, https://www.nytimes.com/1995/05/19/opinion/l-only-big-nuclear-powers-gain-from-nonproliferation-treaty-582695.html.

10. Shidore, "Only Big Nuclear Powers."

11. Author interview with former US official, Washington DC, July 22, 2014; author interview with former US official, Arlington, VA, April 14, 2015.

12. Ottoway and Coll, "Hard Sell for Treaty."

13. William Potter and Gaukhar Mukhatzhanova, *Nuclear Politics and the Non-Aligned Movement*, vol. 427 of Adelphi Papers (London: Routledge, for International Institute for Strategic Studies, 2011).

14. Author interview with non-US former official, New York, May 5, 2015.

15. "Interview with Dean Rust," Association for Diplomatic Studies and Training Foreign Affairs Oral History Project, Association for Diplomatic Studies and Training, Arlington, VA, 2007, 63, http://lcweb2.loc.gov/service/mss/mfdip/2007/2007rus02/2007rus02.pdf.

16. Author interview with former US official, Washington, DC, November 8–9, 2018.

17. For a detailed account of the diplomacy involved in achieving this outcome, see Michal Onderčo, *Networked Nonproliferation: Making the NPT Permanent* (Stanford, CA: Stanford University Press, 2021).

18. For example, see Yoshitomo Takana, "Statement by H.E. Mr. Yoshitomo Takana, Representative of Japan" (speech, First Committee of the Forty-Ninth Session of the General Assembly, United Nations, New York, October 18, 1994), http://www.disarm.emb-japan.go.jp/Statements/UN941018.htm.

19. See, for example, William J. Clinton, "Remarks and a Question-and-Answer Session" (speech, Waseda University, Tokyo, Japan, July 7, 1993), American Presidency Project, https://www.presidency.ucsb.edu/documents/remarks-and-question-and-answer-session-waseda-university-tokyo; The Council of Economic Advisers and US Treasury Department, "US Trade Policy with Japan: Assessing the Record, An Update," April 12, 1996, https://clintonwhitehouse4.archives.gov/textonly/WH/EOP/CEA/html/trade-update.html.

20. Monty G. Marshall, Ted Robert Gurr, and Keith Jaggers, "Polity IV Project: Political Regime Characteristics and Transitions, 1800–2009," Center for Systemic Peace, 2010; Freedom House, *Freedom in the World*, "Comparative and Historical Data," "Country and Territory Ratings and Statuses, 1973–2019," accessed October 17, 2021, https://freedomhouse.org/report/freedom-world.

21. Concordance of foreign policy preferences is assessed using Voeten, Strezhnev, and Bailey 2009, "United Nations General Assembly Voting Data," https://doi.org/10.7910/DVN/LEJUQZ, Harvard Dataverse, V27. Michael A. Bailey, Anton Strezhnev, and Erik Voeten, "Estimating Dynamic State Preferences from United Nations Voting Data," *Journal of Conflict Resolution*, 61 no. 2 (2017): 430–456.

22. "Japan–United States Relations, 1945–1997," Ministry of Foreign Affairs of Japan, accessed October 16, 2021, http://www.mofa.go.jp/region/n-america/us/relation.html.

23. Graham, *Disarmament Sketches*, 259.

24. "Political Declaration: Shaping the New Partnership," G-7 Summit, Munich, July 7, 1992, http://www.g8.utoronto.ca/summit/1992munich/political.html. See also FBIS, "Political Declaration Criticized" OW1207050193 Tokyo NIHON KEIZAI SHIMBUN in Japanese, July 9, 1993, Morning Edition, 2—"For Official Use Only."

25. Mitsuru Kurosawa, "Beyond the 1995 NPT Conference: A Japanese View," *Osaka University Law Review* 43 (1996): 11–22, https://ir.library.osaka-u.ac.jp/repo/ouka/all/11822/oulr043-011.pdf.

26. FBIS, "Spokesman: Tokyo Not Preserving Nuclear Option" OW1307114993 Tokyo KYODO in English, 1120 GMT July 13, 1993.

27. Maria Rost Rublee, "The Future of Japanese Nuclear Policy," *Strategic Insights* 8 (2009): 1–11, http://edocs.nps.edu/npspubs/institutional/newsletters/strategic%20insight/2009/rubleeApr09.pdf.

28. FBIS, "Tokyo to Support Indefinite NPT Extension," OW1707120393 Tokyo YOMIURI SHIMBUN in Japanese, July 17, 1993, Morning Edition, 1, For Official Use Only.

29. Interview with former Japanese official, Cambridge, MA, May 23, 2019.

30. Masanori Kikuta, "US: Positive Step Forward," OW2807093393 Tokyo KYODO in English, 0900 GMT, July 28, 1993 (FBIS).

31. Kikuta, "US: Positive Step Forward."

32. "Muto's NPT Remarks Made without 'Permission'" OW2907051393 Tokyo KYODO in English, 0505 GMT, July 29, 1993 (FBIS).

33. "Saito: US Ties Still 'Axis' of Foreign Policy," OW0208114093 Tokyo KYODO in English, 1127 GMT, August 2, 1993 (FBIS).

34. Hosokawa Morihiro, "Address to Diet" (speech, 127th Session of the National Diet, Tokyo, Japan, August 23, 1993), http://japan.kantei.go.jp/127.html.

35. FBIS, "Japan: Reportage on Hosokawa's Activities at U N Session," Text on UN address, OW2709223993 Tokyo KYODO in English, 2202 GMT, September 27, 1993.

36. For example, see Yoshitomo Tanaka, "Statesmen at the United Nations" (speech, First Committee of the Forty-Ninth Session of the General Assembly, United Nations, New York, October 18, 1994).

37. Jacquelyn S. Porth, "In Meetings, Christopher Urges Indefinite NPT Extension," *USIA*, April 18, 1995, https://fas.org/nuke/control/npt/news/950418-387721.htm.

38. Elaine Sciolino, "US. Political Strategy at Tokyo Talks," *New York Times*, June 30, 1993, A8, https://www.nytimes.com/1993/06/30/world/us-political-strategy-at-tokyo-talks.html.

39. Sciolino, "US. Political Strategy."

40. FBIS, "Deputy Director Okamura: NPT 'Unequal,'" PM1307102593 Paris LIBERATION in French, July 9, 1992, 12.

41. "Tokyo Summit Political Declaration: Striving for a More Secure and Humane World," Tokyo, Japan, July 8, 1993, G7 Research Group, http://www.g8.utoronto.ca/summit/1993tokyo/political.html.

42. FBIS, "Political Declaration Criticized," OW1207050193 Tokyo NIHON KEIZAI SHIMBUN in Japanese, July 9, 1993, Morning Edition, 2—"For Official Use Only."

43. FBIS Tokyo KYODO—1993-07-13, "Spokesman: Tokyo Not Preserving Nuclear Option," Daily Report, East Asia, FBIS-EAS-93-132 on 1993-07-13.

44. Rublee, "Future of Japanese Nuclear."

45. Michael J. Green and Katsuhisa Furukawa, "New Ambitions, Old Obstacles: Japan and Its Search for an Arms Control Strategy," *Arms Control Today*, July 1, 2000, https://www.armscontrol.org/act/2000-07/features/new-ambitions-old-obstacles-japan-its-search-arms-control-strategy.

46. Japan Defense Agency, "Concerning the Problem of the Proliferation of Weapons of Mass Destruction (1995)" (unauthorized translation by Masafumi Takubo). The unauthorized translation of this report can be found online: https://s3.amazonaws.com/ucs-documents/nuclear-weapons/Secret+Japanese+Report+on+Nuclear+Options.pdf.

47. Japan Defense Agency, "Concerning the Problem," final page.

48. "Spokesman: Tokyo Not Preserving Nuclear Option," OW1307114993 Tokyo KYODO in English, 1120 GMT, July 13, 1993 (FBIS).

49. "Hiroshima Mayor: Indefinite NPT Hurts Nuclear Ban," OW0608015993 Tokyo KYODO in English, 0150 GMT, August 6, 1993 (FBIS).

50. "Spokesman: Tokyo Not Preserving Nuclear Option."

51. "Spokesman: Tokyo Not Preserving Nuclear Option."

52. "Spokesman: Tokyo Not Preserving Nuclear Option."

53. "Hosokawa Urged Not to Back NPT Extension," OW060909493 Tokyo KYODO in English, 0931 GMT, September 6, 1993 (FBIS).

54. "Oral History Interview with Sir Michael Weston," September 23, 2016, History and Public Policy Program Digital Archive, contributed to NPIHP by Michal Onderčo, http://digitalarchive.wilsoncenter.org/document/177554.

55. See the World Bank's website: "World Integrated Trade Solution, for Indonesia 1990–1999," World Bank, accessed October 16, 2021, https://wits.worldbank.org/CountryProfile/en/Country/IDN.

56. Quoted in Philip Shenon, "Indonesia Seeks to Atone for a Massacre in Timor," *New York Times*, September 17, 1992, A8, https://www.nytimes.com/1992/09/17/world/indonesia-seeks-to-atone-for-a-massacre-in-timor.html.

57. Jessica A. Stanton, *Violence and Restraint in Civil War: Civilian Targeting in the Shadow of International Law* (Cambridge: Cambridge University Press, 2016), 157; for more on US policy regarding Indonesia and East Timor, see "Background on East Timor and US Policy, East Timor Action Network, May 2000," East Timor Action Network, accessed October 16, 2021, http://www.etan.org/timor/BkgMnu.htm#train. Note that some US training of Indonesian military continued after 1992 without congressional knowledge. This activity was cut off in May 1998.

58. Polity IV, "Authority Trends, Indonesia: 1946–2013," accessed October 16, 2021, https://www.systemicpeace.org/polity/ins2.htm; Marshall, Gurr, and Jaggers, "Polity IV Project"; Freedom House, *Freedom in the World*, "Comparative and Historical Data," "Country and Territory Ratings and Statuses, 1973–2019," accessed October 17, 2021, https://freedomhouse.org/report/freedom-world.

59. Concordance of foreign policy preferences is assessed using Voeten, Strezhnev, and Bailey, "United Nations General Assembly"; Bailey, Strezhnev and Voeten, "Estimating Dynamic State Preferences."

60. Author interview with former US official, Arlington, VA, April 14, 2015; author interview with former US official, Washington, DC, February 5, 2014; author interview with non-US former official, United Nations, New York, May 5, 2015.

61. Graham, *Disarmament Sketches*, 301.

62. Graham, *Disarmament Sketches*, 301.

63. Graham, *Disarmament Sketches*, 272.

64. Barbara Crossette, "Nuclear Pact May Continue by Consensus: U.N. Deal to Allow Indefinite Extension," *New York Times*, May 10, 1995, A15, https://www.nytimes.com/1995/05/10/world/nuclear-pact-may-continue-by-consensus.html.

65. Rydell and Dhanapala, *Multilateral Diplomacy*, 9.

66. Graham, *Disarmament Sketches*, 273.

67. Jean Mathieu C. Essis-Essoh, "State Preferences in Multilateral Nuclear Non-Proliferation Policy-Making: An Empirical Analysis of the 1995 N.P.T. Review and Extension Conference," (PhD diss., George Mason University, 1997), 199–200.

68. Susan B. Welsh, "Delegate Perspectives on the 1995 NPT Review and Extension Conference: A Series of Interviews," *Nonproliferation Review* 2, no. 3 (1995): 6, https://www.nonproliferation.org/wp-content/uploads/npr/welsh23.pdf.

69. Welsh, "Delegate Perspectives," 6.

70. Welsh, "Delegate Perspectives," 7.

71. "Letter dated 14 September 1994 from the Head of the Delegation of Indonesia Addressed to the Chairman of the Preparatory Committee for the 1995 Conference of the Parties to the Treaty on the Non-Proliferation of Nuclear Weapons, Transmitting a Document of the Group of Non-Aligned and Other States on Substantive Issues," FAS, accessed October 16, 2021, https://fas.org/nuke/control/npt/docs/211a.htm.

72. Michal Onderčo and Leopoldo Nuti, *Extending the NPT—a Critical Oral History of the 1995 Review and Extension Conference* (Washington, DC: Wilson Center, 2020), 78, https://www.wilsoncenter.org/publication/extending-npt-critical-oral-history-1995-review-and-extension-conference.

73. Miguel Marin-Bosch, "The 1995 NPT Review and Extension Conference," *Irish Studies in International Affairs* 6 (1995): 31, https://www.jstor.org/stable/30001834.

74. National Security Council, Speechwriting Office, and Antony Blinken, "Mandela—Joint Press Conference 10/5/94," Clinton Digital Library, accessed October 16, 2021, https://clinton.presidentiallibraries.us/items/show/9066.

75. Concordance of foreign policy preferences is assessed using Voeten, Strezhnev, and Bailey, "United Nations General Assembly"; Bailey, Strezhnev, and Voeten, "Estimating Dynamic State Preferences."

76. Helen E. Purkitt and Stephen F. Burgess, *South Africa's Weapons of Mass Destruction* (Bloomington: Indiana University Press, 2005), 182.

77. Purkitt and Burgess, *South Africa's Weapons*, 182.

78. Abdul Samad Minty, "Keynote Address," in *The Nuclear Debate: Policy for a Democratic South Africa; Proceedings of a Conference under the Auspices of the ANC Western Cape Science and Technology Group and the Environmental Monitoring Group* (Cape Town: Environmental Monitoring Group: Western Cape, 1994); cited in Michal Onderčo and Anna-Mart Van Wyk, "Birth of a Norm Champion: How South Africa Came to Support the NPT's Indefinite Extension," *Nonproliferation Review* 26, nos. 1–2 (2019): 23–41, https://doi.org/10.1080/10736700.2019.1591771.

79. Graham, *Disarmament Sketches*, 266.

80. "South African Legal Opinion on Article X.2 of the NPT," December 27, 1994, History and Public Policy Program Digital Archive, included in the Document Reader for a Critical Oral History Conference on the 1995 NPT Review and Extension Conference, Rotterdam, The Netherlands, 2018, http://digitalarchive.wilsoncenter.org/document/176509.

81. "South African Legal Opinion on Article X.2 of the NPT."

82. "Oral History Interview with Jean duPreez," April 4, 2018, History and Public Policy Program Digital Archive, contributed to NPIHP by Michal Onderčo, https://digitalarchive.wilsoncenter.org/document/177632.

83. Princeton N. Lyman, *Partner to History: The US Role in South Africa's Transition to Democracy* (Washington, DC: US Institute of Peace, 2002), 238.

84. "Oral History Interview with Jean duPreez."

85. "Oral History Interview with Peter Goosen," June 28, 2017, History and Public Policy Program Digital Archive, contributed to NPIHP by Michal Onderčo, https://digitalarchive.wilsoncenter.org/document/177446.

86. Onderčo, *Networked Nonproliferation*, 75.

87. "Letter, Thabo Mbeki to Al Gore," April 10, 1995, History and Public Policy Program Digital Archive, Archive of the Department of International Relations and Cooperation of South Africa, contributed to NPIHP by Michal Onderčo and Anna-Mart van Wyk, https://digitalarchive.wilsoncenter.org/document/208590.

88. "Letter, Thabo Mbeki to Al Gore."

89. "Letter, Al Gore to Thabo Mbeki," April 13, 1995, History and Public Policy Program Digital Archive, Archive of the Department of International Relations and Cooperation of South Africa, contributed to NPIHP by Michal Onderčo and Anna-Mart van Wyk, https://digitalarchive.wilsoncenter.org/document/208589.

90. Onderčo and Nuti, *Extending the NPT*, 47.

91. Mark Matthews, "Renewal of Nuclear Pact is Uncertain," *Baltimore Sun*, May 16, 1995, https://www.baltimoresun.com/news/bs-xpm-1995-03-16-1995075022-story.html.

92. "Oral History Interview with Princeton Lyman," March 24, 2017, History and Public Policy Program Digital Archive, contributed to NPIHP by Michal Onderčo, https://digitalarchive.wilsoncenter.org/document/177541.

93. "Al Gore: Talk a Lot and Carry a Big Stick," *Newsweek*, October 31, 1994, 30–31, https://www.newsweek.com/al-gore-talk-lot-and-carry-big-stick-189312.

94. Author interview with former US official, Arlington VA, April 14, 2015; author interview with former US official, Washington, DC, February 5, 2014.

95. Jayantha Dhanapala, "The Management of NPT Diplomacy," *Dædalus* 139, no. 1 (2010): 57–67, https://www.jstor.org/stable/i40023480.

96. "Oral History Interview with Princeton Lyman."

97. Graham, *Disarmament Sketches*, 267.

98. R. Jeffrey Smith, "Permanent Nuclear Treaty Extension May Be Approved by Consensus Vote," *Washington Post*, May 8, 1995, A7.

99. "Oral History Interview with Jean duPreez."

100. "Oral History Interview with Jean duPreez."

101. "South Africa," US State Department, archived content, accessed October 16, 2021, https://2009-2017.state.gov/outofdate/bgn/southafrica/130968.htm.

102. "United States of America (USA)," Department of International Relations and Cooperation, Government of South Africa, accessed October 16, 2021, http://www.dirco.gov.za/foreign/bilateral/usa.html.

103. "USA: Clinton Administration Policy and Human Rights in Africa," *Human Rights Watch* 10, no. 1A (March 1, 1998): 18, https://www.refworld.org/docid/3ae6a8504.html.

104. "Message to the Congress on the South Africa–United States Agreement on the Peaceful Use of Nuclear Energy," September 29, 1995, *Public Papers of the Presidents of the United States: William J. Clinton*, book 2 (Washington, DC: US Government Publishing Office, 1995), 1522–1524, https://www.gpo.gov/fdsys/pkg/PPP-1995-book2/html/PPP-1995-book2-doc-pg1522-2.htm.

105. "Message to the Congress on the South Africa-United States Agreement on the Peaceful Use of Nuclear Energy."

106. "US, South Africa Plan to Improve Trade, Fight Crime," *CNN*, February 18, 1999, http://www.cnn.com/WORLD/africa/9902/18/us.sa.talks/.

107. Onderčo, *Networked Nonproliferation*, 81.

108. "Oral History Interview with Jean duPreez."

109. "DFA Director-General Discusses US-SA Relations, Pariah States, DFA Restructuring," Cable from US Embassy Pretoria to the Secretary of State, June 2, 1995, https://foia.state.gov/searchapp/DOCUMENTS/FOIA_Jan2018/F-2016-00610EAN/DOC_0C06026695/C06026695.pdf.

110. "Decision 1: Strengthening the Review Process for the Treaty," NPT/CONF.1995/32 (part 1), Annex, United Nations Digital Library, https://www.un.org/disarmament/wmd/nuclear/npt1995/.

111. "Decision 2: Principles and Objectives for Nuclear Non-Proliferation and Disarmament," NPT/CONF.1995/32 (part 1), Annex, United Nations Digital Library, https://www.un.org/disarmament/wmd/nuclear/npt1995/.

112. See, for example, "Oral History Interview with Tariq Rauf," June 20, 2017, History and Public Policy Program Digital Archive, contributed to NPIHP by Michal Onderčo, http://digitalarchive.wilsoncenter.org/document/177546. John Simpson also recalls that the Canadians were "responsible" for much of the documentation at the NPT Review Conference in 1995. See "Oral History Interview with John Simpson," September 22, 2016, History and Public Policy Program, Digital Archive, contributed to NPIHP by Michal Onderčo, http://digitalarchive.wilsoncenter.org/document/177550.

113. "Oral History Interview with John Simpson."

114. Welsh, "Delegate Perspectives,"11.

115. National Security Council, Speechwriting Office, and Robert Boorstin, "NSC—1995 Goals," Clinton Digital Library, accessed October 16, 2021,https://clinton.presidentiallibraries.us/items/show/10099 (italics in the original).

116. Steven Greenhouse, "Half of Egypt's $20.2 Billion Debt Being Forgiven by US and Allies," *New York Times*, May 27, 1991, A1, https://www.nytimes.com/1991/05/27/business/half-of-egypt-s-20.2-billion-debt-being-forgiven-by-us-and-allies.html.

117. "Perry, in Egypt, Vows US Will Not Cut Aid," *Los Angeles Times*, January 8, 1995, https://www.latimes.com/archives/la-xpm-1995-01-08-mn-17717-story.html.

118. Freedom House, *Freedom in the World*, "Comparative and Historical Data," accessed October 17, 2021, https://freedomhouse.org/report/freedom-world.

119. Polity IV, "Authority Trends: 1946–2013: Egypt," https://www.systemicpeace.org/polity/egy2.htm; Marshall, Gurr, and Keith, "Polity IV Project."

120. Shai Feldman, "Extending the Nuclear Nonproliferation Treaty: The Middle East Debate," Research Memorandum 28 (Washington, DC: Washington Institute, 1995), 4.

121. Graham, *Disarmament Sketches*, 269.

122. "Nonproliferation Pact Raising Tension between US and Egypt," *Washington Post*, January 26, 1995, A22, https://www.washingtonpost.com/archive/politics/1995/01/26/nonproliferation-pact-raising-tension-between-us-and-egypt/5e2a9c0f-9646-420c-a5ba-78fdb5fd0639/.

123. "Nonproliferation Pact Raising Tension between US and Egypt," 21.

124. Graham, *Disarmament Sketches*, 271.

125. Author interview with former US official, Arlington VA, April 14, 2015.

126. Opall, "US Turns Up Diplomatic."

127. Feldman, "Extending the Nuclear Nonproliferation," 12.

128. Gerald M. Steinberg, "Middle East Peace and the NPT Extension Decision," *Nonproliferation Review* 4, no. 1 (1996): 22, https://doi.org/10.1080/10736709608436650.

129. Steinberg, "Middle East Peace," 22.

130. Michael Crowley, "Lobbyists in Striped Pants," *National Journal*, April 1, 1995, 815.

131. Thomas W. Lippman, "Mubarak Reassures Clinton on Nuclear Pact Renewal," *Washington Post*, April 6, 1995, A27, https://www.washingtonpost.com/archive/politics/1995/04/06/mubarak-reassures-clinton-on-nuclear-pact-renewal/57dcece4-8beb-47dd-bb07-c8a51a533bce/.

132. Tariq Rauf and Rebecca Johnson, "After the NPT's Indefinite Extension: The Future of the Global Nonproliferation Regime," *Nonproliferation Review* 3, no. 1 (1995): 30, https://www.nonproliferation.org/wp-content/uploads/npr/raufjo31.pdf; Steinberg, "Middle East Peace," 24.

133. "Resolution on the Middle East," NPT/CONF.1995/32 (part 1), Annex, United Nations Digital Library, https://unoda-web.s3-accelerate.amazonaws.com/wp-content/uploads/assets/WMD/Nuclear/1995-NPT/pdf/Resolution_MiddleEast.pdf.

134. Barbara Crossette, "Gore, at U.N., Says Nuclear Powers Are Fair on Weapons Treaty," *New York Times*, April 20, 1995, A14, https://www.nytimes.com/1995/04/20/world/gore-at-un-says-nuclear-powers-are-fair-on-weapons-treaty.html.

135. Crossette, "Gore, at U.N., Says."

136. Quoted in Crossette, "Gore, at U.N., Says."

137. David Makovsky, "US Urges Positive Israeli Signal on NPT," *Jerusalem Post*, December 15, 1994, 1.

138. Steinberg, "Middle East Peace," 19.

139. David Makovsky, "Peres Plans Meet with Mubarak over NPT Crisis," *Jerusalem Post*, February 20, 1995.

140. Fawaz A. Gerges, "The End of the Islamist Insurgency in Egypt? Costs and Prospects," *Middle East Journal* 54, no. 4 (2000): 592–612, https://www.jstor.org/stable/4329545.

141. Cited in Maria Rost Rublee, *Nonproliferation Norms: Why States Choose Nuclear Restraint* (Athens: Georgia University Press, 2009), 105; Shai Feldman, *Nuclear Weapons and Arms Control in the Middle East* (Cambridge, MA: MIT Press, 1997), 221.

142. Former foreign minister Nabil Fahmy wrote in 2015, "Regrettably, Egypt has shrunk to the periphery of regional relations, exchanging the leadership and vision of Gamal Abdel Nasser and Anwar Sadat for a far less ambitious foreign policy. Though Hosni Mubarak's policies were initially successful in ensuring stability and security and reconciling Egypt with the Arab world, this early proactive phase was followed by a long period of political dormancy and stagnation." "Egypt in the World," *Cairo Review of Global Affairs*, accessed October 16, 2021, https://www.thecairoreview.com/essays/egypt-in-the-world/.

143. Feldman, "Extending the Nuclear Nonproliferation," 7.

144. Feldman, "Extending the Nuclear Nonproliferation," 7.

5. Mixed Success in Promoting a New Safeguards Agreement

1. International Atomic Energy Agency, "Additional Protocol," accessed October 17, 2021, https://www.iaea.org/safeguards/safeguards-legal-framework/additional-protocol.

2. International Atomic Energy Agency, "Additional Protocol."

3. Theodore Hirsch, "The IAEA Additional Protocol: What It Is and Why It Matters," *Nonproliferation Review* 11, no. 3 (2004): 141, https://doi.org/10.1080/10736700408436983.

4. Frank Houck, Michael D. Rosenthal, and Norman A. Wulf, "Creation of the Model Additional Protocol" (paper presented at the Annual Meeting of the Institute of Nuclear Materials Management, Baltimore, MD, July 11–15, 2010), 11.

5. Michael D. Rosenthal, Lisa L. Saum-Manning, Frank Houck, and George Anzelon, *Review of the Negotiation of the Model Protocol Additional to the Agreement(s) between State(s) and the International Atomic Energy Agency for the Application of Safeguards, INFCIRC/540 (Corrected) Volume I, Setting the Stage: 1991–1996* (Upton, NY: Brookhaven National Laboratory, January 2010), 18–19.

6. Phone interview with former US official, December 5, 2014.
7. Phone interview with former US official, December 5, 2014.
8. Author interview with former US official, Arlington, VA, April 14, 2015.
9. Author interview with former US official, Arlington, VA, April 14, 2015.
10. "Conclusions of G8 Foreign Ministers," London, May 9, 1998, Ministry of Foreign Affairs of Japan, accessed October 17, 2021, http://www.mofa.go.jp/policy/economy/summit/1998/g8_min.html.
11. "G8 Okinawa Summit: Documents," Okinawa, Japan, July 21–23, 2000, http://www.g8.utoronto.ca/summit/2000okinawa/.
12. "Conclusions of the meeting of the G8 Foreign Ministers' Meeting," Rome, Italy, July 18–19, 2001, G7 Research Group, accessed October 17, 2021, http://www.library.utoronto.ca/g7/foreign/fm091901_conclusion.html.
13. Mark Hibbs, "Regardless of IAEA, Clinton Visits, Hanoi Questions Safeguards Protocol," *Nuclear Fuel* 25, no. 24 (November 27, 2000): 12.
14. Mark Hibbs, "Safeguards Protocol Losing Steam, IAEA to Press Asia, Middle East," *Nucleonics Week* 42, no. 13 (March 29, 2001): 13.
15. Phone interview with former US official, December 5, 2014.
16. Author interview with former US official, Washington, DC, November 25, 2014; phone interview with former US official, December 5, 2014.
17. "The Protocol to the Agreement of the International Atomic Energy Agency regarding Safeguards in the United States, Message from the President of the United States Transmitting the Protocol Additional to the Agreement between the United States of America and the International Atomic Energy Agency for the Application of Safeguards in the United States of America, with Annexes, Signed at Vienna, June 12, 1998," Senate Treaty Document 107–7, US Government Printing Office, accessed October 17, 2021, http://www.gpo.gov/fdsys/pkg/CDOC-107tdoc7/html/CDOC-107tdoc7.htm.
18. George W. Bush, "President Announces New Measures to Counter the Threat of WMD," (speech, Fort Lesley J. McNair, National Defense University, Washington, DC, February 11, 2004), http://2001-2009.state.gov/t/isn/rls/rm/29290.htm.
19. Mark Hibbs, "Nuclear Suppliers Group and the IAEA Additional Protocol," *Nuclear Energy Brief* (Washington, DC: Carnegie Endowment for International Peace, August 18, 2010), https://carnegieendowment.org/2010/08/18/nuclear-suppliers-group-and-iaea-additional-protocol-pub-41393.
20. The "regional inspection regime" provision was a compromise with Brazil and Argentina—both of which have publicly opposed the AP—to include their unique bilateral nuclear inspection institution, the Brazilian-Argentine Agency for Accounting and Control of Nuclear Materials (ABACC).
21. Author interview with former US official, Washington, DC, August 7, 2014.
22. "G8 Action Plan on Nonproliferation," G8 Summit, Sea Island, Georgia, United States, June 9, 2004, University of Toronto G8 Information Centre, accessed October 17, 2021, http://www.g8.utoronto.ca/summit/2004seaisland/nonproliferation.html.
23. "US-EU Summit: County Clare, Ireland, June 25–26, 2004," (accessed March 3, 2016) .http://dublin.usembassy.gov/ireland/declaration_global.html.
24. Author interview with former US official, Washington, DC, August 7, 2014.
25. Author interview with former US official, Washington, DC, August 7, 2014; author interview with former US official, Washington, DC, November 25, 2014.
26. "Joint Statement—One Community, Our Future," 2004 APEC Ministerial Meeting, Santiago, Chile, November 17–18, 2004, http://www.apec.org/Meeting-Papers/Ministerial-Statements/Annual/2004/2004_amm.aspx.
27. Author interview with former US official, Washington, DC, August 7, 2014.
28. Author interview with former US official, Washington, DC, August 7, 2014.
29. Ron Cain, "DOE Additional Protocol Implementation," Presentation at NGSI Summer Seminar Series, June 29, 2011, http://web.ornl.gov/sci/nsed/outreach/presentation/2011/Cain.pdf.

30. Susan B. Epstein and Paul K. Kerr, "IAEA Budget and US Contributions: In Brief," Congressional Research Service, R44384, February 17, 2016.
31. Epstein and Kerr, "IAEA Budget," 3.
32. Paul K. Kerr, Mary Beth D. Nikitin, and Luisa Blanchfield, "IAEA Budget and U.S. Contributions: In Brief," Congressional Research Services, R44384, April 2, 2021, 4, https://fas.org/sgp/crs/nuke/R44384.pdf.
33. "Significance of the Japan-US. Relationship—President Clinton's Visit to Japan," November 30, 1998, Ministry of Foreign Affairs of Japan, accessed October 17, 2021, http://www.mofa.go.jp/region/n-america/us/visit98/significance.html.
34. Todd Zaun, "A Growing China Becomes Japan's Top Trade Partner," *New York Times*, January 27, 2005, https://www.nytimes.com/2005/01/27/business/worldbusiness/a-growing-china-becomes-japans-top-trade-partner.html.
35. "Polity IV Country Regime Trends 2013: Japan," 2014, https://www.systemicpeace.org/polity/jpn2.htm; Monty G. Marshall, Ted Robert Gurr, and Keith Jaggers, "Polity IV Project: Political Regime Characteristics and Transitions, 1800–2009," Center for Systemic Peace, 2010.
36. Freedom House, *Freedom in the World*, "Comparative and Historical Data," accessed October 17, 2021, https://freedomhouse.org/report/freedom-world.
37. Houck, Rosenthal, and Wulf, "Creation of the Model," 6.
38. Houck, Rosenthal, and Wulf, "Creation of the Model," 6.
39. Author's personal correspondence with former US official, November 13, 2015.
40. Houck, Rosenthal, and Wulf, "Creation of the Model," 7.
41. Phone interview with former US official, December 5, 2014.
42. Phone interview with former US official, December 5, 2014.
43. Michael D. Rosenthal, Lisa L. Saum-Manning, and Frank Houck, "Review of the Negotiation of the Model Protocol Additional to the Agreement(s) between State(s) and the International Atomic Energy Agency for the Application of Safeguards Infcirc/540 (Corrected), Volume II/III: IAEA Committee 24, Major Issues Underlying the Model Additional Protocol (1996–1997)," January 29, 2010, https://www.bnl.gov/isd/documents/71014.pdf; Rosenthal, Saum-Manning, and Houck, "Review of the Negotiation," 65.
44. "Japan's Efforts in the Universalization of the International Atomic Energy Agency (IAEA) Additional Protocol," May 2004, Ministry of Foreign Affairs of Japan, accessed October 17, 2021, http://www.mofa.go.jp/policy/energy/iaea/protocol.html.
45. T. Ogawa, "Implementation of the Additional Protocol in Japan," IAEA-SM-367/6/06, 2001, p. 2, https://www-pub.iaea.org/MTCD/publications/PDF/ss-2001/PDF%20files/Session%206/Paper%206-06.pdf.
46. Ogawa, "Implementation of the Additional."
47. Author interview with former Japanese official, New York, May 6, 2015.
48. Author interview with Japanese nuclear expert, New York, May 7, 2015.
49. Author interview with former Japanese official, New York, May 6, 2015.
50. Author interview with former Japanese official, New York, May 6, 2015.
51. Author interview with former Japanese official, New York, May 6, 2015.
52. Author interview with former Japanese official, New York, May 6, 2015.
53. Masatoshi Shimbo (statement at First Session of the Preparatory Committee for the 2010 NPT Review Conference, Cluster II, Vienna, May 9, 2007), http://www.disarm.emb-japan.go.jp/Statements/070509-2NPT.htm.
54. "Japan's Efforts in the Universalization of the International Atomic Energy Agency (IAEA) Additional Protocol," May 2004, Ministry of Foreign Affairs of Japan, accessed October 17, 2021, http://www.mofa.go.jp/policy/energy/iaea/protocol.html.
55. Houck, Rosenthal, and Wulf, "Creation of the Model," 7.
56. Houck, Rosenthal, and Wulf, "Creation of the Model," 7.
57. "Japan's Efforts in the Universalization of the International Atomic Energy Agency (IAEA) Additional Protocol."
58. "Support Grows for Additional Protocol," *Global Security Newswire*, May 4, 2005.
59. Author interview with former Japanese official, New York, May 6, 2015.

60. Rosenthal, Saum-Manning, and Houck, "Review of the Negotiation," 20.

61. Anthony Smith, "Indonesia's Role in ASEAN: The End of Leadership?," *Contemporary Southeast Asia* 21, no. 2 (1999): 243, https://www.jstor.org/stable/25798455.

62. Paul Blustein, "White House, IMF Launch Joint Effort on Indonesia Crisis," *Washington Post*, January 9, 1998, https://www.washingtonpost.com/wp-srv/inatl/longterm/indonesia/stories/joint010998.htm.

63. "Mondale to Visit Jakarta to Press Suharto on I.M.F. Reform Plan," *New York Times*, February 25, 1998, A6, https://www.nytimes.com/1998/02/25/world/mondale-to-visit-jakarta-to-press-suharto-on-imf-reform-plan.html.

64. Keith B. Richburg, "Suharto Resigns, Names Successor," *Washington Post*, May 21, 1998, A1, https://www.washingtonpost.com/wp-srv/inatl/longterm/indonesia/stories/resignation052198.htm.

65. Keith B. Richburg, "Indonesia Holds Its First Free Elections in 44 Years," *Washington Post*, June 8, 1999, A12, https://www.washingtonpost.com/wp-srv/inatl/longterm/indonesia/stories/voted060899.htm.

66. World Bank, World Integrated Trade Solution (WITS), Indonesia, 1997 and 1998, accessed October 17, 2021, https://wits.worldbank.org/CountryProfile/en/Country/IDN/Year/1998/TradeFlow/EXPIMP/Partner/by-country.

67. David E. Sanger, "U.S. Is Linking Aid to Jakarta to Its Reforms," *New York Times*, March 4, 1998, https://www.nytimes.com/1998/03/04/world/us-is-linking-aid-to-jakarta-to-its-reforms.html.

68. Ikrar Nusa Bhakti, "The Transition to Democracy in Indonesia: Some Outstanding Problems," in *The Asia-Pacific: A Region in Transition*, ed. Jim Rolfe (Honolulu: Asia Pacific Center for Security Studies, 2004), 201.

69. "I.M.F. Approves $460 Million Loan Installment for Indonesia," *New York Times*, March 26, 1999, https://www.nytimes.com/1999/03/26/business/imf-approves-460-million-loan-installment-for-indonesia.html.

70. Steven Mufson and Bradley Graham, "US and IMF Move to Isolate Indonesia," *Washington Post*, September 10, 1999, A1, https://www.washingtonpost.com/wp-srv/inatl/daily/sept99/ustimor10.htm.

71. Polity IV, "Authority Trends, Indonesia: 1946–2013," https://www.systemicpeace.org/polity/ins2.htm; Marshall, Gurr, and Jaggers, "Polity IV Project."

72. Personal correspondence with Indonesian official, Washington DC, March 31, 2014.

73. Author interview with non-US official, Washington DC, March 23, 2015.

74. Author interview with non-US official, Washington DC, March 23, 2015.

75. Author interview with non-US official, Washington DC, March 23, 2015.

76. Richard C. Paddock, "B.J. Habibie Dies at 83; Ushered in Democracy in Indonesia," *New York Times*, September 12, 2019, https://www.nytimes.com/2019/09/12/world/asia/bj-habibie-dead.html.

77. Kenneth L. Whiting, "Oil-Wealthy Indonesia Looks to Nuclear Power to Serve Expanding Energy Needs," *Los Angeles Times*, September 11, 1988, https://www.latimes.com/archives/la-xpm-1988-09-11-mn-2643-story.html.

78. "Safety Concerns Cloud Plans: Does Indonesia Need Nuclear?," *New York Times*, February 3, 1996, https://www.nytimes.com/1996/02/03/business/worldbusiness/IHT-safety-concerns-cloud-plans-does-indonesia-need.html.

79. Personal correspondence with former Australian official, March 10, 2016.

80. Hibbs, "Safeguards Protocol Losing Steam," 13.

81. Helen Dewar, "Senate Rejects Test Ban Treaty," *Washington Post*, October 14, 1999, A1, https://www.washingtonpost.com/wp-srv/politics/daily/oct99/senate14.htm.

82. Maggie Michael, "Egypt Refuses to Sign UN Nuclear Watchdog Protocols for Stricter Inspections," Associated Press News Service, December 12, 2007; Mark Hibbs, "The Unspectacular Future of the IAEA Additional Protocol," *Proliferation Analysis* (Washington, DC: Carnegie Endowment for International Peace, April 26, 2012), http://carnegieendowment.org/2012/04/26/unspectacular-future-of-iaea-additional-protocol#.

83. "Egypt Moves Forward with Nuclear Plans," *Global Security Newswire*, March 31, 2008, http://www.nti.org/gsn/article/egypt-moves-forward-with-nuclear-plans/.

84. Polity IV, "Authority Trends: 1946–2013: Egypt," https://www.systemicpeace.org/polity/egy2.htm; Marshall, Gurr, and Jaggers, "Polity IV Project."

85. Pew Research Center, "Global Opposition to US Surveillance and Drones, But Limited Harm to America's Image," July 14, 2014, 14–16, http://www.pewglobal.org/2014/07/14/chapter-1-the-american-brand/.

86. Pew Research Center, "Global Opposition."

87. Michael Wahid Hanna, "Getting Over Egypt: Time to Rethink Relations," *Foreign Affairs* 94, no. 6 (2015), https://www.foreignaffairs.com/articles/egypt/2015-11-01/getting-over-egypt.

88. Vitaly Naumkin, "Russia and Egypt's 'New Partnership,'" *Al-Monitor*, February 11, 2015, https://www.al-monitor.com/originals/2015/02/moscow-cairo-relations-sisi-putin-egypt-visit.html.

89. David D. Kirkpatrick, "In Snub to U.S., Russia and Egypt Move toward Deal on Air Bases," *New York Times*, November 30, 2017, https://www.nytimes.com/2017/11/30/world/middleeast/russia-egypt-air-bases.html; Hagar Hosny, "Egypt Acquires Russian Fighter Jets Despite US Warning," *Al-Monitor*, August 3, 2020, https://www.al-monitor.com/originals/2020/07/egypt-arms-deal-russia-fighter-jets-united-states-sanctions.html.

90. "Egypt Unveils Nuclear Power Plan," *BBC News*, September 25, 2006, http://news.bbc.co.uk/2/hi/middle_east/5376860.stm.

91. "Egypt Refuses to Sign Nonproliferation Protocol," *Global Security Newswire*, December 12, 2007, https://www.nti.org/gsn/article/egypt-refuses-to-sign-nonproliferation-protocol/.

92. "Egypt Refuses to Sign Nonproliferation Protocol."

93. "Egypt Pressured by USA, France to Sign Additional Nuclear Protocol—Website," *BBC Monitoring Middle East*, January 16, 2008.

94. Hibbs, "Unspectacular Future."

95. For more on Egypt's nuclear infrastructure and plans, see "Nuclear Power in Egypt," World Nuclear Association, May 2021, https://world-nuclear.org/information-library/country-profiles/countries-a-f/egypt.aspx.

96. "Russia to Aid Egyptian Nuclear Plant Construction," *Global Security Newswire*, November 21, 2007, https://www.nti.org/gsn/article/russia-to-aid-egyptian-nuclear-plant-construction/.

97. "Egypt Moves Forward with Nuclear Reactor Plans," *Global Security Newswire*, March 31, 2008, https://www.nti.org/gsn/article/egypt-moves-forward-with-nuclear-plans/.

98. "China, Egypt Agree to Nuclear Cooperation," *World Nuclear News*, March 28, 2015, https://www.world-nuclear-news.org/NP-China-Egypt-agree-to-nuclear-cooperation-2805154.html.

99. "Egypt, Russia Sign Deal to Build a Nuclear Power Plant," *Reuters*, November 19, 2015, https://www.reuters.com/article/us-nuclear-russia-egypt/egypt-russia-sign-deal-to-build-a-nuclear-power-plant-idUSKCN0T81YY20151119.

100. "Egypt Cabinet Approves Renewal of Russian Technical Support for Dabaa Nuclear Power Project," *Ahram Online*, December 27, 2018, https://english.ahram.org.eg/NewsContent/1/64/320817/Egypt/Politics-/Egypt-cabinet-approves-renewal-of-Russian-technica.aspx.

101. "Construction of Dabaa Nuclear Plant to Start Soon," *Egypt Independent*, February 21, 2021, https://egyptindependent.com/construction-of-dabaa-nuclear-plant-to-start-soon/.

102. "An International Atomic Energy Agency (IAEA) Team of Experts Has Concluded an Eight-Day Site and External Events Design (SEED) Review Mission to Egypt," IAEA, February 14, 2019, https://www.iaea.org/newscenter/pressreleases/an-international-atomic-energy-agency-iaea-team-of-experts-has-concluded-an-eight-day-site-and-external-events-design-seed-review-mission-to-egypt.

103. Maria Rost Rublee, *Nonproliferation Norms: Why States Choose Nuclear Restraint* (Athens: Georgia University Press, 2009), 142.

104. "Egypt," Nuclear Threat Initiative, accessed October 17, 2021, http://www.nti.org/country-profiles/egypt/nuclear/.

105. Mark Heinrich, "High-Enriched Uranium Traces Found in Egypt: IAEA," *Reuters*, May 6, 2009, https://www.reuters.com/article/us-nuclear-iaea-egypt/high-enriched-uranium-traces-found-in-egypt-iaea-idUSTRE54543S20090506.

106. Rublee, *Nonproliferation Norms*, 127.

107. Ibrahim Said, "The Bomb and the Beard: The Egyptian MB's Views toward WMD," *Arms Control and Regional Security in the Middle East*, June 11, 2012, n.p., accessed December 4, 2016, https://web.archive.org/web/20120708154415/http://www.middleeast-armscontrol.com/2012/06/11/the-bomb-and-the-beard-the-egyptian-mbs-views-toward-wmd/.

108. Said, "Bomb and the Beard."

109. Sigurd Neubauer and Yoel Guzansky, "A Nuclear Nile: The Politics behind Egypt's Quest for Nuclear Energy," *Foreign Affairs*, December 8, 2015, https://www.foreignaffairs.com/articles/egypt/2015-12-08/nuclear-nile.

110. On Egypt's position regarding the CTBT, see Emily B. Landau, "The Comprehensive Test Ban Treaty (CTBT): Enhancing its Confidence-Building Role," *INSS Insight* no. 796, February 11, 2016, https://www.inss.org.il/publication/the-comprehensive-test-ban-treaty-ctbt-enhancing-its-confidence-building-role/. On linking the Chemical Weapons Convention and the African Nuclear Weapons Free Zone to Israel's NPT status, see "Egypt," Nuclear Threat Initiative.

111. "New Agenda Coalition," Nuclear Threat Initiative, accessed October 17, 2021, http://www.nti.org/learn/treaties-and-regimes/new-agenda-coalition/.

112. Jim Walsh, "The Additional Protocol in the Middle East and North Africa: Explaining Lag in Adoption," in *State Behavior and the Nuclear Nonproliferation Regime*, ed. Jeffrey R. Fields (Athens: University of Georgia Press, 2014), 266.

113. Walsh, "Additional Protocol," 267.

Conclusion

1. G. John Ikenberry, *After Victory: Institutions, Strategic Restraint, and the Rebuilding of Order after Major Wars*, new ed. (Princeton, NJ: Princeton University Press, 2001), 163.

2. For more on how multipolarity could affect the nuclear nonproliferation regime, see Gibbons and Herzog," Durable Institution Under Fire?" Also see Eric Brewer, "Toward a More Proliferated World? The Geopolitical Forces that Will Shape the Spread of Nuclear Weapons," CSIS Project on Nuclear Issues, September 2020, https://www.csis.org/analysis/toward-more-proliferated-world.

3. For example, see Jack Corrigan, "The Hollowing-Out of the State Department Continues," *The Atlantic*, February 11, 2018, https://www.theatlantic.com/author/government-executive/; Gardiner Harris, "Diplomats Sound the Alarm as They Are Pushed Out in Droves," *New York Times*, November 24, 2017, https://www.nytimes.com/2017/11/24/us/politics/state-department-tillerson.html.

4. The Lowry Institute Global Democracy Index, "2019 Country Comparison," accessed October 17, 2021, https://globaldiplomacyindex.lowyinstitute.org/country_comparison.html.

5. Joseph Biden, "Remarks by President Biden on America's Place in the World" (speech, Washington, DC, February 4, 2021), https://www.whitehouse.gov/briefing-room/speeches-remarks/2021/02/04/remarks-by-president-biden-on-americas-place-in-the-world/.

6. For example, see "China Calls for Strengthening IAEA Safeguards," *Global Security Newswire*, May 1, 2012, http://www.nti.org/gsn/article/china-urges-global-cooperation-combat-nuclear-proliferation.

7. "Emerging Nuclear Energy Countries," World Nuclear Association, September 2021, https://www.world-nuclear.org/information-library/country-profiles/others/emerging-nuclear-energy-countries.aspx.

8. "The World Relies on Russia to Build Its Nuclear Power Plants," *The Economist*, August 2, 2018, https://www.economist.com/europe/2018/08/02/the-world-relies-on-russia-to-build-its-nuclear-power-plants.

9. Jeffrey W. Knopf explores these arguments in "Nuclear Disarmament and Nonproliferation: Examining the Linkage Argument," *International Security* 37, no. 3 (2012–2013): 92–132, https://www.jstor.org/stable/41804175.

10. Author interview with former US official, Washington, DC, June 18, 2015.

11. Daryl G. Kimball, "2010 NPT Review Conference Approaches the Finish Line," (presentation for Hudson Institute-Partnership for a Secure America Event, Washington DC, March 24, 2020), https://www.armscontrol.org/events/2010-05/2010-npt-review-conference-approaches-finish-line.

12. Author interview with former US official, Arlington, VA, April 14, 2015.

13. Benoît Pelopidas, "The birth of nuclear eternity," in *Futures*, ed. Sandra Kemp and Jenny Andersson (Oxford: Oxford University Press, 2017), 484–500.

14. Laura Ford Savarese and John Fabian Witt, "Strategy and Entailments: The Enduring Role of Law in the U.S. Armed Forces," *Daedalus* 146, no. 1 (2017): 11–23, https://doi.org/10.1162/DAED_a_00419.

15. The full treaty text is available here: UN General Assembly, "Treaty on the Prohibition of Nuclear Weapons," New York, July 7, 2017, https://undocs.org/A/CONF.229/2017/8.

16. Kjolv Egeland, "The Road to Prohibition: Nuclear Hierarchy and Disarmament, 1968–2017" (PhD diss. University of Oxford, 2017).

17. Rebecca Davis Gibbons, "The Humanitarian Turn in Nuclear Disarmament and the Treaty on the Prohibition of Nuclear Weapons," *Nonproliferation Review* 25, nos. 1–2 (2018): 11–36, https://doi.org/10.1080/10736700.2018.1486960.

18. See, for example, Rebecca Davis Gibbons, "Addressing the Nuclear Ban Treaty," *Washington Quarterly* 41, no. 1 (2019): 27–40, https://doi.org/10.1080/0163660X.2019.1590080; and Stephen Herzog, Jonathon Baron, and Rebecca Davis Gibbons, "Antinormative Messaging, Group Cues, and the Nuclear Ban Treaty," *The Journal of Politics* 84, no. 1 (2021), https://doi.org/10.1086/714924.

19. See, for example, Bill Chappell, "U.N. Treaty Banning Nuclear Weapons Takes Effect, without the U.S. and Other Powers" *NPR*, January 22, 2021, https://www.npr.org/2021/01/22/959583731/u-n-treaty-banning-nuclear-weapons-takes-effect-without-the-u-s-and-others.

Index

Notes and tables are indicated by *n* and *t* following the page number.
Surnames starting with "al-" or "el-" are alphabetized by remaining portion of name.

CPSIA information can be obtained
at www.ICGtesting.com
Printed in the USA
LVHW111955240622
721975LV00034B/356/J